OCE-1   OCCUPATIONAL COMPETENCY EXAM SERIES

This is your
PASSBOOK for...

Air Conditioning and Refrigeration

Test Preparation Study Guide
Questions & Answers

COPYRIGHT NOTICE

This book is SOLELY intended for, is sold ONLY to, and its use is RESTRICTED to individual, bona fide applicants or candidates who qualify by virtue of having seriously filed applications for appropriate license, certificate, professional and/or promotional advancement, higher school matriculation, scholarship, or other legitimate requirements of education and/or governmental authorities.

This book is NOT intended for use, class instruction, tutoring, training, duplication, copying, reprinting, excerption, or adaptation, etc., by:

1) Other publishers
2) Proprietors and/or Instructors of "Coaching" and/or Preparatory Courses
3) Personnel and/or Training Divisions of commercial, industrial, and governmental organizations
4) Schools, colleges, or universities and/or their departments and staffs, including teachers and other personnel
5) Testing Agencies or Bureaus
6) Study groups which seek by the purchase of a single volume to copy and/or duplicate and/or adapt this material for use by the group as a whole without having purchased individual volumes for each of the members of the group
7) Et al.

Such persons would be in violation of appropriate Federal and State statutes.

PROVISION OF LICENSING AGREEMENTS – Recognized educational, commercial, industrial, and governmental institutions and organizations, and others legitimately engaged in educational pursuits, including training, testing, and measurement activities, may address request for a licensing agreement to the copyright owners, who will determine whether, and under what conditions, including fees and charges, the materials in this book may be used them. In other words, a licensing facility exists for the legitimate use of the material in this book on other than an individual basis. However, it is asseverated and affirmed here that the material in this book CANNOT be used without the receipt of the express permission of such a licensing agreement from the Publishers. Inquiries re licensing should be addressed to the company, attention rights and permissions department.

All rights reserved, including the right of reproduction in whole or in part, in any form or by any means, electronic or mechanical, including photocopying, recording, or by any information storage and retrieval system, without permission in writing from the Publisher.

Copyright © 2025 by
National Learning Corporation

212 Michael Drive, Syosset, NY 11791
(516) 921-8888 • www.passbooks.com
E-mail: info@passbooks.com

PASSBOOK® SERIES

THE *PASSBOOK® SERIES* has been created to prepare applicants and candidates for the ultimate academic battlefield – the examination room.

At some time in our lives, each and every one of us may be required to take an examination – for validation, matriculation, admission, qualification, registration, certification, or licensure.

Based on the assumption that every applicant or candidate has met the basic formal educational standards, has taken the required number of courses, and read the necessary texts, the *PASSBOOK® SERIES* furnishes the one special preparation which may assure passing with confidence, instead of failing with insecurity. Examination questions – together with answers – are furnished as the basic vehicle for study so that the mysteries of the examination and its compounding difficulties may be eliminated or diminished by a sure method.

This book is meant to help you pass your examination provided that you qualify and are serious in your objective.

The entire field is reviewed through the huge store of content information which is succinctly presented through a provocative and challenging approach – the question-and-answer method.

A climate of success is established by furnishing the correct answers at the end of each test.

You soon learn to recognize types of questions, forms of questions, and patterns of questioning. You may even begin to anticipate expected outcomes.

You perceive that many questions are repeated or adapted so that you can gain acute insights, which may enable you to score many sure points.

You learn how to confront new questions, or types of questions, and to attack them confidently and work out the correct answers.

You note objectives and emphases, and recognize pitfalls and dangers, so that you may make positive educational adjustments.

Moreover, you are kept fully informed in relation to new concepts, methods, practices, and directions in the field.

You discover that you are actually taking the examination all the time: you are preparing for the examination by "taking" an examination, not by reading extraneous and/or supererogatory textbooks.

In short, this PASSBOOK®, used directedly, should be an important factor in helping you to pass your test.

OCCUPATIONAL COMPETENCY EXAMINATIONS (OCE)

GENERAL

The Occupational Competency Examinations are intended for those individuals experienced in skilled trades or occupations who need to present objective evidence of their competency to become vocational teachers, to obtain academic credit from a higher institution, or to secure teacher certification.

In addition to meeting university admission requirements for fully matriculated students -- and for teacher certification -successful completion of the exam provides opportunity to earn up to 36 semester hours of collegiate credit for applied occupational skills and technical knowledge. The credit may be used toward advanced study and degrees in occupational education in several states.

NATURE OF THE EXAMINATION

The examination consists of two parts -- Written and Performance. The written test covers factual knowledge, technical information, understanding of principles and problem solving abilities related to the occupation. The performance test is designed to sample the manipulative skills required by an occupation. Thus it enables the candidate to demonstrate that he possesses the knowledge and skills that a competent craftsman employs in his daily work.

ADVANTAGES

The Prospective Teacher - Tradesmen and other technically competent persons who wish to enter industrial education training programs.

Industrial Teacher Educators - The OCE Tests provide the industrial teacher educator with an objective and dependable means for assessing the trade competency of applicants for admission to their programs.

Certifying Agencies - The OCE Tests provide an objective method for assessing occupational competence in qualifying for certification.

Directors of Vocational Education Programs - The OCE Tests provide a recruitment and selection procedure that is reliable, objective and fair to all recipients

Candidates for Academic Degrees - The OCE Tests are accepted by many colleges and universities for granting of credit or advanced standing for occupational experience.

PLACE OF EXAMINATION

A network of 36 Area Test Centers has been established throughout the United States in the States listed below. Tests are generally conducted twice a year at these centers, as well as other locations, depending on need.

Alabama	Kentucky	Oregon
Arkansas	Massachusetts	Pennsylvania
California	Michigan	South Dakota
Colorado	Missouri	Tennessee
Connecticut	Montana	Texas
Florida	Nebraska	Utah
Georgia	New Jersey	Vermont
Hawaii	New York	Virginia
Idaho	North Dakota	Washington
Illinois	Ohio	West Virginia
Iowa	Oklahoma	Wisconsin

OCE TESTS OFFERED

Interested candidates are alerted to the occupations listed below as scheduled for examination. Individuals should notify the NOCTI if they wish to be examined in an occupation not listed.

- Air Conditioning and Refrigeration
- Airframe or Power plant Mechanics
- Appliance Repair
- Architectural Drafting
- Auto Body Repair
- Automatic Heating
- Auto Mechanics
- Building Maintenance
- Cabinetmaking and Millwork
- Carpentry
- Commercial and Advertising Art
- Commercial Photography
- Cosmetology
- Data Processing
- Dental Assisting
- Diesel Engine Repair
- Dressmaking
- Electrical Installation
- Electronics Communication
- General Printing Industrial Electronics
- Machine Trades
- Masonry
- Machine Drafting
- Mechanical Technology
- Medical Assisting Offset Lithography
- Ornamental Horticulture
- Plumbing
- Quantity Food Preparation
- Sheet Metal Fabrication
- Small Engine Repair
- Welding

HOW TO REGISTER

For registration information contact Educational Testing Service of Princeton, New Jersey.

AIR CONDITIONING AND REFRIGERATION

AC/Refrigeration Mechanic – Under general supervision, incumbent is responsible for the full range of service, maintenance and repair (including installation, troubleshooting and calibrating) on complex refrigeration and associated HVAC systems, equipment, instruments and controls using electrical, electronic, pneumatic or digitally controlled systems. Incumbent oils, cleans, adjusts, and repairs motors, condensers, compressors, oil and vacuum pumps and similar equipment. Performs major overhauls, and uses a wide variety of test equipment and instruments to diagnose malfunctions and analyze the efficiency of refrigeration and air conditioning systems.

Objectives – Properly installed, repaired and maintained air conditioning and refrigeration equipment and systems.

Expectations – Properly operating plant equipment and a safe and clean working environment; thorough and accurate accounting of time and materials. Completion of routine work assignments and performance of additional duties as assigned. Consistent meeting of university needs in a timely and professional manner with increasingly improved skill; Follow-up on every project or task to insure that all items are completed to the satisfaction of the supervisor/manager and a responsible attendance record, punctuality and consistent meeting of deadlines; performance of work in a manner that supports and facilitates the work of others; a positive and cooperative working relationship with members of department and community.

Responsibilities

Maintenance and repair work - Operates and performs minor maintenance on centrifugal and absorption chillers, heat pumps, reciprocating units, package air conditioning units, window units, cooling towers, supply and return ventilation air handlers, pumps, pressure reducing stations, heat exchangers, refrigeration air dryers, computer room air conditioning units, and electro/pneumatic control systems. Performs on-site chemical testing and water treatment; repairs/replaces chill water coils, valves, piping, and pumps, condenser water pumping and piping systems. Maintains chemical treatment and chiller operation logs. Maintains all mechanical equipment spaces designated as support systems for AC operations; maintains all steam/condensate underground utility manholes, piping and pumping systems. May provide instruction and direction to unskilled and semi-skilled assistants.

Emergency AC/refrigeration work – Responds to trouble calls and minor work requests; troubleshoots and repairs or adjusts air flow, temperature, humidity balances (for buildings, building areas and individual rooms); repairs leaks in distribution systems; makes related urgent minor repairs; uses building automation system to diagnose and troubleshoot problems in HVAC and refrigeration systems.

Renovation and improvement work - Assists in design and installation of equipment, piping and all associated instruments vital to the function of refrigeration and air conditioning systems; makes recommendations and implements strategies/equipment adjustments to optimize energy usage.

Preventive maintenance work – Maintains, troubleshoots and tests AC installations; performs PM tasks.

Documentation, Work Coordination and accountability - interprets plans and drawings; prepares working sketches; calculates shop estimates, estimates material costs; obtains phone quotations and prepares requisitions for ordering material, takes inventory of bench stock material and re-orders when necessary. Maintains records and retrieves data related to work performed using manual/computerized record-keeping systems; prepares standard reports; consults and works with other trades workers.

Maintenance/Operation of Shop and General Support – Maintains and services tools and equipment used in the performance of duties; performs shop clean-up and maintains a safe and clean work area. Assists custodial services, grounds, trades and mechanical services staff in the accomplishment of their work (projects, events, on-going programs), and performs other tasks as assigned by the manager in support of facilities services.

Knowledge, Skills & Abilities

The ideal candidate will possess the following:

Knowledge – Thorough knowledge of the theory and operation of major types of refrigeration and air conditioning equipment and of the materials, equipment and techniques used in the repair and maintenance of such equipment; must have working knowledge of electrical voltage, plumbing, refrigeration, electrical and plumbing codes, thermodynamics and automated energy/environmental management systems.

Ability – Ability to install, operate and repair HVAC equipment and systems; demonstrate a high degree of mechanical skill equivalent to journey-level in one or more related trades; read, interpret, and work from blueprints, plans, drawings and specifications; make rough sketches; estimate cost, time and materials of mechanical work; maintain records and retrieve data related to work performed using manual and/or computerized record-keeping systems; prepare standard reports; provide instruction to skilled and semi-skilled assistants; analyze and respond appropriately to emergency situations; read and write at a level appropriate to the position.

Ability to use judgment and discretion in determining the methods and priorities of work orders; perform skilled electrical and plumbing work; diagnose and repair major malfunctions in the complex multi-zone air conditioning systems; devise and control air distribution efficiently with maximum comfort; and diagnose and repair the full range of refrigeration equipment including centrifugal and absorber equipment and/or screw, scroll and reciprocating refrigeration equipment.

Experience and Education

Journey-level skill equivalent to that acquired through the completion of a refrigeration or air conditioning mechanic's apprenticeship program and progressively responsible experience in the installation, adjustment, maintenance and repair of commercial and domestic refrigeration and air conditioning systems involving modulatory and safety controls, thermostats, humidifiers and duct stats. One year of experience in the installation and repair of central multi-zone air conditioning systems.

Specialized Requirements

• Must have ability to analyze and respond appropriately to emergency situations and to recognize, secure and report unsafe conditions immediately.

• Must have knowledge of safe working techniques and safety equipment and must be aware of the typical hazards of the work place as well as the special hazards that maybe encountered (biohazards, chemicals, asbestos/lead containing materials).
• Universal EPA Refrigeration Certificate for the use and disposal of compressed refrigerants.

Preferred Qualifications
• Ability to perform skilled work on HVAC equipment and system, make rough sketches of HVAC installations, estimate materials and labor cost of standard HVAC maintenance and repair work, and use/track refrigerant through use of refrigerant management software. Ability to work unsupervised on a variety of job tasks from simple to complex; perform strenuous physical work; utilize mechanical aptitude and motor coordination; read and write at a level appropriate to the position; must be able to follow simple written and oral instructions; ability to work independently or as a member of a team; consult and work with other trades workers; develop and maintain effective working relationships; ability to analyze situations, procedures and work methods and exercise appropriate judgment in resolving problems and establishing priorities and work methods; ability to be flexible and respond to changes in demands for service and priorities.

HOW TO TAKE A TEST

I. YOU MUST PASS AN EXAMINATION

A. WHAT EVERY CANDIDATE SHOULD KNOW

Examination applicants often ask us for help in preparing for the written test. What can I study in advance? What kinds of questions will be asked? How will the test be given? How will the papers be graded?

As an applicant for a civil service examination, you may be wondering about some of these things. Our purpose here is to suggest effective methods of advance study and to describe civil service examinations.

Your chances for success on this examination can be increased if you know how to prepare. Those "pre-examination jitters" can be reduced if you know what to expect. You can even experience an adventure in good citizenship if you know why civil service exams are given.

B. WHY ARE CIVIL SERVICE EXAMINATIONS GIVEN?

Civil service examinations are important to you in two ways. As a citizen, you want public jobs filled by employees who know how to do their work. As a job seeker, you want a fair chance to compete for that job on an equal footing with other candidates. The best-known means of accomplishing this two-fold goal is the competitive examination.

Exams are widely publicized throughout the nation. They may be administered for jobs in federal, state, city, municipal, town or village governments or agencies.

Any citizen may apply, with some limitations, such as the age or residence of applicants. Your experience and education may be reviewed to see whether you meet the requirements for the particular examination. When these requirements exist, they are reasonable and applied consistently to all applicants. Thus, a competitive examination may cause you some uneasiness now, but it is your privilege and safeguard.

C. HOW ARE CIVIL SERVICE EXAMS DEVELOPED?

Examinations are carefully written by trained technicians who are specialists in the field known as "psychological measurement," in consultation with recognized authorities in the field of work that the test will cover. These experts recommend the subject matter areas or skills to be tested; only those knowledges or skills important to your success on the job are included. The most reliable books and source materials available are used as references. Together, the experts and technicians judge the difficulty level of the questions.

Test technicians know how to phrase questions so that the problem is clearly stated. Their ethics do not permit "trick" or "catch" questions. Questions may have been tried out on sample groups, or subjected to statistical analysis, to determine their usefulness.

Written tests are often used in combination with performance tests, ratings of training and experience, and oral interviews. All of these measures combine to form the best-known means of finding the right person for the right job.

II. HOW TO PASS THE WRITTEN TEST

A. NATURE OF THE EXAMINATION

To prepare intelligently for civil service examinations, you should know how they differ from school examinations you have taken. In school you were assigned certain definite pages to read or subjects to cover. The examination questions were quite detailed and usually emphasized memory. Civil service exams, on the other hand, try to discover your present ability to perform the duties of a position, plus your potentiality to learn these duties. In other words, a civil service exam attempts to predict how successful you will be. Questions cover such a broad area that they cannot be as minute and detailed as school exam questions.

In the public service similar kinds of work, or positions, are grouped together in one "class." This process is known as *position-classification*. All the positions in a class are paid according to the salary range for that class. One class title covers all of these positions, and they are all tested by the same examination.

B. FOUR BASIC STEPS

1) Study the announcement

How, then, can you know what subjects to study? Our best answer is: "Learn as much as possible about the class of positions for which you've applied." The exam will test the knowledge, skills and abilities needed to do the work.

Your most valuable source of information about the position you want is the official exam announcement. This announcement lists the training and experience qualifications. Check these standards and apply only if you come reasonably close to meeting them.

The brief description of the position in the examination announcement offers some clues to the subjects which will be tested. Think about the job itself. Review the duties in your mind. Can you perform them, or are there some in which you are rusty? Fill in the blank spots in your preparation.

Many jurisdictions preview the written test in the exam announcement by including a section called "Knowledge and Abilities Required," "Scope of the Examination," or some similar heading. Here you will find out specifically what fields will be tested.

2) Review your own background

Once you learn in general what the position is all about, and what you need to know to do the work, ask yourself which subjects you already know fairly well and which need improvement. You may wonder whether to concentrate on improving your strong areas or on building some background in your fields of weakness. When the announcement has specified "some knowledge" or "considerable knowledge," or has used adjectives like "beginning principles of..." or "advanced ... methods," you can get a clue as to the number and difficulty of questions to be asked in any given field. More questions, and hence broader coverage, would be included for those subjects which are more important in the work. Now weigh your strengths and weaknesses against the job requirements and prepare accordingly.

3) Determine the level of the position

Another way to tell how intensively you should prepare is to understand the level of the job for which you are applying. Is it the entering level? In other words, is this the position in which beginners in a field of work are hired? Or is it an intermediate or advanced level? Sometimes this is indicated by such words as "Junior" or "Senior" in the class title. Other jurisdictions use Roman numerals to designate the level – Clerk I, Clerk II, for example. The word "Supervisor" sometimes appears in the title. If the level is not indicated by the title, check the description of duties. Will you be working under very close supervision, or will you have responsibility for independent decisions in this work?

4) Choose appropriate study materials

Now that you know the subjects to be examined and the relative amount of each subject to be covered, you can choose suitable study materials. For beginning level jobs, or even advanced ones, if you have a pronounced weakness in some aspect of your training, read a modern, standard textbook in that field. Be sure it is up to date and has general coverage. Such books are normally available at your library, and the librarian will be glad to help you locate one. For entry-level positions, questions of appropriate difficulty are chosen – neither highly advanced questions, nor those too simple. Such questions require careful thought but not advanced training.

If the position for which you are applying is technical or advanced, you will read more advanced, specialized material. If you are already familiar with the basic principles of your field, elementary textbooks would waste your time. Concentrate on advanced textbooks and technical periodicals. Think through the concepts and review difficult problems in your field.

These are all general sources. You can get more ideas on your own initiative, following these leads. For example, training manuals and publications of the government agency which employs workers in your field can be useful, particularly for technical and professional positions. A letter or visit to the government department involved may result in more specific study suggestions, and certainly will provide you with a more definite idea of the exact nature of the position you are seeking.

III. KINDS OF TESTS

Tests are used for purposes other than measuring knowledge and ability to perform specified duties. For some positions, it is equally important to test ability to make adjustments to new situations or to profit from training. In others, basic mental abilities not dependent on information are essential. Questions which test these things may not appear as pertinent to the duties of the position as those which test for knowledge and information. Yet they are often highly important parts of a fair examination. For very general questions, it is almost impossible to help you direct your study efforts. What we can do is to point out some of the more common of these general abilities needed in public service positions and describe some typical questions.

1) General information

Broad, general information has been found useful for predicting job success in some kinds of work. This is tested in a variety of ways, from vocabulary lists to questions about current events. Basic background in some field of work, such as sociology or economics, may be sampled in a group of questions. Often these are principles which have become familiar to most persons through exposure rather than through formal training. It is difficult to advise you how to study for these questions; being alert to the world around you is our best suggestion.

2) Verbal ability

An example of an ability needed in many positions is verbal or language ability. Verbal ability is, in brief, the ability to use and understand words. Vocabulary and grammar tests are typical measures of this ability. Reading comprehension or paragraph interpretation questions are common in many kinds of civil service tests. You are given a paragraph of written material and asked to find its central meaning.

3) Numerical ability

Number skills can be tested by the familiar arithmetic problem, by checking paired lists of numbers to see which are alike and which are different, or by interpreting charts and graphs. In the latter test, a graph may be printed in the test booklet which you are asked to use as the basis for answering questions.

4) Observation

A popular test for law-enforcement positions is the observation test. A picture is shown to you for several minutes, then taken away. Questions about the picture test your ability to observe both details and larger elements.

5) Following directions

In many positions in the public service, the employee must be able to carry out written instructions dependably and accurately. You may be given a chart with several columns, each column listing a variety of information. The questions require you to carry out directions involving the information given in the chart.

6) Skills and aptitudes

Performance tests effectively measure some manual skills and aptitudes. When the skill is one in which you are trained, such as typing or shorthand, you can practice. These tests are often very much like those given in business school or high school courses. For many of the other skills and aptitudes, however, no short-time preparation can be made. Skills and abilities natural to you or that you have developed throughout your lifetime are being tested.

Many of the general questions just described provide all the data needed to answer the questions and ask you to use your reasoning ability to find the answers. Your best preparation for these tests, as well as for tests of facts and ideas, is to be at your physical and mental best. You, no doubt, have your own methods of getting into an exam-taking mood and keeping "in shape." The next section lists some ideas on this subject.

IV. KINDS OF QUESTIONS

Only rarely is the "essay" question, which you answer in narrative form, used in civil service tests. Civil service tests are usually of the short-answer type. Full instructions for answering these questions will be given to you at the examination. But in case this is your first experience with short-answer questions and separate answer sheets, here is what you need to know:

1) Multiple-choice Questions

Most popular of the short-answer questions is the "multiple choice" or "best answer" question. It can be used, for example, to test for factual knowledge, ability to solve problems or judgment in meeting situations found at work.

A multiple-choice question is normally one of three types—
- It can begin with an incomplete statement followed by several possible endings. You are to find the one ending which *best* completes the statement, although some of the others may not be entirely wrong.
- It can also be a complete statement in the form of a question which is answered by choosing one of the statements listed.

- It can be in the form of a problem – again you select the best answer.

Here is an example of a multiple-choice question with a discussion which should give you some clues as to the method for choosing the right answer:

When an employee has a complaint about his assignment, the action which will *best* help him overcome his difficulty is to
    A. discuss his difficulty with his coworkers
    B. take the problem to the head of the organization
    C. take the problem to the person who gave him the assignment
    D. say nothing to anyone about his complaint

In answering this question, you should study each of the choices to find which is best. Consider choice "A" – Certainly an employee may discuss his complaint with fellow employees, but no change or improvement can result, and the complaint remains unresolved. Choice "B" is a poor choice since the head of the organization probably does not know what assignment you have been given, and taking your problem to him is known as "going over the head" of the supervisor. The supervisor, or person who made the assignment, is the person who can clarify it or correct any injustice. Choice "C" is, therefore, correct. To say nothing, as in choice "D," is unwise. Supervisors have and interest in knowing the problems employees are facing, and the employee is seeking a solution to his problem.

2) True/False Questions

The "true/false" or "right/wrong" form of question is sometimes used. Here a complete statement is given. Your job is to decide whether the statement is right or wrong.

SAMPLE: A roaming cell-phone call to a nearby city costs less than a non-roaming call to a distant city.

This statement is wrong, or false, since roaming calls are more expensive.

This is not a complete list of all possible question forms, although most of the others are variations of these common types. You will always get complete directions for answering questions. Be sure you understand *how* to mark your answers – ask questions until you do.

V. RECORDING YOUR ANSWERS

Computer terminals are used more and more today for many different kinds of exams.

For an examination with very few applicants, you may be told to record your answers in the test booklet itself. Separate answer sheets are much more common. If this separate answer sheet is to be scored by machine – and this is often the case – it is highly important that you mark your answers correctly in order to get credit.

An electronic scoring machine is often used in civil service offices because of the speed with which papers can be scored. Machine-scored answer sheets must be marked with a pencil, which will be given to you. This pencil has a high graphite content which responds to the electronic scoring machine. As a matter of fact, stray dots may register as answers, so do not let your pencil rest on the answer sheet while you are pondering the correct answer. Also, if your pencil lead breaks or is otherwise defective, ask for another.

Since the answer sheet will be dropped in a slot in the scoring machine, be careful not to bend the corners or get the paper crumpled.

The answer sheet normally has five vertical columns of numbers, with 30 numbers to a column. These numbers correspond to the question numbers in your test booklet. After each number, going across the page are four or five pairs of dotted lines. These short dotted lines have small letters or numbers above them. The first two pairs may also have a "T" or "F" above the letters. This indicates that the first two pairs only are to be used if the questions are of the true-false type. If the questions are multiple choice, disregard the "T" and "F" and pay attention only to the small letters or numbers.

Answer your questions in the manner of the sample that follows:

32. The largest city in the United States is
   A. Washington, D.C.
   B. New York City
   C. Chicago
   D. Detroit
   E. San Francisco

1) Choose the answer you think is best. (New York City is the largest, so "B" is correct.)
2) Find the row of dotted lines numbered the same as the question you are answering. (Find row number 32)
3) Find the pair of dotted lines corresponding to the answer. (Find the pair of lines under the mark "B.")
4) Make a solid black mark between the dotted lines.

VI. BEFORE THE TEST

Common sense will help you find procedures to follow to get ready for an examination. Too many of us, however, overlook these sensible measures. Indeed, nervousness and fatigue have been found to be the most serious reasons why applicants fail to do their best on civil service tests. Here is a list of reminders:

- Begin your preparation early – Don't wait until the last minute to go scurrying around for books and materials or to find out what the position is all about.
- Prepare continuously – An hour a night for a week is better than an all-night cram session. This has been definitely established. What is more, a night a week for a month will return better dividends than crowding your study into a shorter period of time.
- Locate the place of the exam – You have been sent a notice telling you when and where to report for the examination. If the location is in a different town or otherwise unfamiliar to you, it would be well to inquire the best route and learn something about the building.
- Relax the night before the test – Allow your mind to rest. Do not study at all that night. Plan some mild recreation or diversion; then go to bed early and get a good night's sleep.
- Get up early enough to make a leisurely trip to the place for the test – This way unforeseen events, traffic snarls, unfamiliar buildings, etc. will not upset you.
- Dress comfortably – A written test is not a fashion show. You will be known by number and not by name, so wear something comfortable.

- Leave excess paraphernalia at home – Shopping bags and odd bundles will get in your way. You need bring only the items mentioned in the official notice you received; usually everything you need is provided. Do not bring reference books to the exam. They will only confuse those last minutes and be taken away from you when in the test room.
- Arrive somewhat ahead of time – If because of transportation schedules you must get there very early, bring a newspaper or magazine to take your mind off yourself while waiting.
- Locate the examination room – When you have found the proper room, you will be directed to the seat or part of the room where you will sit. Sometimes you are given a sheet of instructions to read while you are waiting. Do not fill out any forms until you are told to do so; just read them and be prepared.
- Relax and prepare to listen to the instructions
- If you have any physical problem that may keep you from doing your best, be sure to tell the test administrator. If you are sick or in poor health, you really cannot do your best on the exam. You can come back and take the test some other time.

VII. AT THE TEST

The day of the test is here and you have the test booklet in your hand. The temptation to get going is very strong. Caution! There is more to success than knowing the right answers. You must know how to identify your papers and understand variations in the type of short-answer question used in this particular examination. Follow these suggestions for maximum results from your efforts:

1) Cooperate with the monitor

The test administrator has a duty to create a situation in which you can be as much at ease as possible. He will give instructions, tell you when to begin, check to see that you are marking your answer sheet correctly, and so on. He is not there to guard you, although he will see that your competitors do not take unfair advantage. He wants to help you do your best.

2) Listen to all instructions

Don't jump the gun! Wait until you understand all directions. In most civil service tests you get more time than you need to answer the questions. So don't be in a hurry. Read each word of instructions until you clearly understand the meaning. Study the examples, listen to all announcements and follow directions. Ask questions if you do not understand what to do.

3) Identify your papers

Civil service exams are usually identified by number only. You will be assigned a number; you must not put your name on your test papers. Be sure to copy your number correctly. Since more than one exam may be given, copy your exact examination title.

4) Plan your time

Unless you are told that a test is a "speed" or "rate of work" test, speed itself is usually not important. Time enough to answer all the questions will be provided, but this does not mean that you have all day. An overall time limit has been set. Divide the total time (in minutes) by the number of questions to determine the approximate time you have for each question.

5) Do not linger over difficult questions

If you come across a difficult question, mark it with a paper clip (useful to have along) and come back to it when you have been through the booklet. One caution if you do this – be sure to skip a number on your answer sheet as well. Check often to be sure that you have not lost your place and that you are marking in the row numbered the same as the question you are answering.

6) Read the questions

Be sure you know what the question asks! Many capable people are unsuccessful because they failed to *read* the questions correctly.

7) Answer all questions

Unless you have been instructed that a penalty will be deducted for incorrect answers, it is better to guess than to omit a question.

8) Speed tests

It is often better NOT to guess on speed tests. It has been found that on timed tests people are tempted to spend the last few seconds before time is called in marking answers at random – without even reading them – in the hope of picking up a few extra points. To discourage this practice, the instructions may warn you that your score will be "corrected" for guessing. That is, a penalty will be applied. The incorrect answers will be deducted from the correct ones, or some other penalty formula will be used.

9) Review your answers

If you finish before time is called, go back to the questions you guessed or omitted to give them further thought. Review other answers if you have time.

10) Return your test materials

If you are ready to leave before others have finished or time is called, take ALL your materials to the monitor and leave quietly. Never take any test material with you. The monitor can discover whose papers are not complete, and taking a test booklet may be grounds for disqualification.

VIII. EXAMINATION TECHNIQUES

1) Read the general instructions carefully. These are usually printed on the first page of the exam booklet. As a rule, these instructions refer to the timing of the examination; the fact that you should not start work until the signal and must stop work at a signal, etc. If there are any *special* instructions, such as a choice of questions to be answered, make sure that you note this instruction carefully.

2) When you are ready to start work on the examination, that is as soon as the signal has been given, read the instructions to each question booklet, underline any key words or phrases, such as *least, best, outline, describe* and the like. In this way you will tend to answer as requested rather than discover on reviewing your paper that you *listed without describing*, that you selected the *worst* choice rather than the *best* choice, etc.

3) If the examination is of the objective or multiple-choice type – that is, each question will also give a series of possible answers: A, B, C or D, and you are called upon to select the best answer and write the letter next to that answer on your answer paper – it is advisable to start answering each question in turn. There may be anywhere from 50 to 100 such questions in the three or four hours allotted and you can see how much time would be taken if you read through all the questions before beginning to answer any. Furthermore, if you come across a question or group of questions which you know would be difficult to answer, it would undoubtedly affect your handling of all the other questions.

4) If the examination is of the essay type and contains but a few questions, it is a moot point as to whether you should read all the questions before starting to answer any one. Of course, if you are given a choice – say five out of seven and the like – then it is essential to read all the questions so you can eliminate the two that are most difficult. If, however, you are asked to answer all the questions, there may be danger in trying to answer the easiest one first because you may find that you will spend too much time on it. The best technique is to answer the first question, then proceed to the second, etc.

5) Time your answers. Before the exam begins, write down the time it started, then add the time allowed for the examination and write down the time it must be completed, then divide the time available somewhat as follows:
   - If 3-1/2 hours are allowed, that would be 210 minutes. If you have 80 objective-type questions, that would be an average of 2-1/2 minutes per question. Allow yourself no more than 2 minutes per question, or a total of 160 minutes, which will permit about 50 minutes to review.
   - If for the time allotment of 210 minutes there are 7 essay questions to answer, that would average about 30 minutes a question. Give yourself only 25 minutes per question so that you have about 35 minutes to review.

6) The most important instruction is to *read each question* and make sure you know what is wanted. The second most important instruction is to *time yourself properly* so that you answer every question. The third most important instruction is to *answer every question*. Guess if you have to but include something for each question. Remember that you will receive no credit for a blank and will probably receive some credit if you write something in answer to an essay question. If you guess a letter – say "B" for a multiple-choice question – you may have guessed right. If you leave a blank as an answer to a multiple-choice question, the examiners may respect your feelings but it will not add a point to your score. Some exams may penalize you for wrong answers, so in such cases *only*, you may not want to guess unless you have some basis for your answer.

7) Suggestions
   a. Objective-type questions
      1. Examine the question booklet for proper sequence of pages and questions
      2. Read all instructions carefully
      3. Skip any question which seems too difficult; return to it after all other questions have been answered
      4. Apportion your time properly; do not spend too much time on any single question or group of questions

5. Note and underline key words – *all, most, fewest, least, best, worst, same, opposite,* etc.
6. Pay particular attention to negatives
7. Note unusual option, e.g., unduly long, short, complex, different or similar in content to the body of the question
8. Observe the use of "hedging" words – *probably, may, most likely,* etc.
9. Make sure that your answer is put next to the same number as the question
10. Do not second-guess unless you have good reason to believe the second answer is definitely more correct
11. Cross out original answer if you decide another answer is more accurate; do not erase until you are ready to hand your paper in
12. Answer all questions; guess unless instructed otherwise
13. Leave time for review

  b. Essay questions
   1. Read each question carefully
   2. Determine exactly what is wanted. Underline key words or phrases.
   3. Decide on outline or paragraph answer
   4. Include many different points and elements unless asked to develop any one or two points or elements
   5. Show impartiality by giving pros and cons unless directed to select one side only
   6. Make and write down any assumptions you find necessary to answer the questions
   7. Watch your English, grammar, punctuation and choice of words
   8. Time your answers; don't crowd material

8) Answering the essay question

Most essay questions can be answered by framing the specific response around several key words or ideas. Here are a few such key words or ideas:

M's: manpower, materials, methods, money, management
P's: purpose, program, policy, plan, procedure, practice, problems, pitfalls, personnel, public relations

  a. Six basic steps in handling problems:
   1. Preliminary plan and background development
   2. Collect information, data and facts
   3. Analyze and interpret information, data and facts
   4. Analyze and develop solutions as well as make recommendations
   5. Prepare report and sell recommendations
   6. Install recommendations and follow up effectiveness

  b. Pitfalls to avoid
   1. *Taking things for granted* – A statement of the situation does not necessarily imply that each of the elements is necessarily true; for example, a complaint may be invalid and biased so that all that can be taken for granted is that a complaint has been registered

2. *Considering only one side of a situation* – Wherever possible, indicate several alternatives and then point out the reasons you selected the best one
3. *Failing to indicate follow up* – Whenever your answer indicates action on your part, make certain that you will take proper follow-up action to see how successful your recommendations, procedures or actions turn out to be
4. *Taking too long in answering any single question* – Remember to time your answers properly

IX. AFTER THE TEST

Scoring procedures differ in detail among civil service jurisdictions although the general principles are the same. Whether the papers are hand-scored or graded by machine we have described, they are nearly always graded by number. That is, the person who marks the paper knows only the number – never the name – of the applicant. Not until all the papers have been graded will they be matched with names. If other tests, such as training and experience or oral interview ratings have been given, scores will be combined. Different parts of the examination usually have different weights. For example, the written test might count 60 percent of the final grade, and a rating of training and experience 40 percent. In many jurisdictions, veterans will have a certain number of points added to their grades.

After the final grade has been determined, the names are placed in grade order and an eligible list is established. There are various methods for resolving ties between those who get the same final grade – probably the most common is to place first the name of the person whose application was received first. Job offers are made from the eligible list in the order the names appear on it. You will be notified of your grade and your rank as soon as all these computations have been made. This will be done as rapidly as possible.

People who are found to meet the requirements in the announcement are called "eligibles." Their names are put on a list of eligible candidates. An eligible's chances of getting a job depend on how high he stands on this list and how fast agencies are filling jobs from the list.

When a job is to be filled from a list of eligibles, the agency asks for the names of people on the list of eligibles for that job. When the civil service commission receives this request, it sends to the agency the names of the three people highest on this list. Or, if the job to be filled has specialized requirements, the office sends the agency the names of the top three persons who meet these requirements from the general list.

The appointing officer makes a choice from among the three people whose names were sent to him. If the selected person accepts the appointment, the names of the others are put back on the list to be considered for future openings.

That is the rule in hiring from all kinds of eligible lists, whether they are for typist, carpenter, chemist, or something else. For every vacancy, the appointing officer has his choice of any one of the top three eligibles on the list. This explains why the person whose name is on top of the list sometimes does not get an appointment when some of the persons lower on the list do. If the appointing officer chooses the second or third eligible, the No. 1 eligible does not get a job at once, but stays on the list until he is appointed or the list is terminated.

X. HOW TO PASS THE INTERVIEW TEST

The examination for which you applied requires an oral interview test. You have already taken the written test and you are now being called for the interview test – the final part of the formal examination.

You may think that it is not possible to prepare for an interview test and that there are no procedures to follow during an interview. Our purpose is to point out some things you can do in advance that will help you and some good rules to follow and pitfalls to avoid while you are being interviewed.

What is an interview supposed to test?

The written examination is designed to test the technical knowledge and competence of the candidate; the oral is designed to evaluate intangible qualities, not readily measured otherwise, and to establish a list showing the relative fitness of each candidate – as measured against his competitors – for the position sought. Scoring is not on the basis of "right" and "wrong," but on a sliding scale of values ranging from "not passable" to "outstanding." As a matter of fact, it is possible to achieve a relatively low score without a single "incorrect" answer because of evident weakness in the qualities being measured.

Occasionally, an examination may consist entirely of an oral test – either an individual or a group oral. In such cases, information is sought concerning the technical knowledges and abilities of the candidate, since there has been no written examination for this purpose. More commonly, however, an oral test is used to supplement a written examination.

Who conducts interviews?

The composition of oral boards varies among different jurisdictions. In nearly all, a representative of the personnel department serves as chairman. One of the members of the board may be a representative of the department in which the candidate would work. In some cases, "outside experts" are used, and, frequently, a businessman or some other representative of the general public is asked to serve. Labor and management or other special groups may be represented. The aim is to secure the services of experts in the appropriate field.

However the board is composed, it is a good idea (and not at all improper or unethical) to ascertain in advance of the interview who the members are and what groups they represent. When you are introduced to them, you will have some idea of their backgrounds and interests, and at least you will not stutter and stammer over their names.

What should be done before the interview?

While knowledge about the board members is useful and takes some of the surprise element out of the interview, there is other preparation which is more substantive. It *is* possible to prepare for an oral interview – in several ways:

1) Keep a copy of your application and review it carefully before the interview

This may be the only document before the oral board, and the starting point of the interview. Know what education and experience you have listed there, and the sequence and dates of all of it. Sometimes the board will ask you to review the highlights of your experience for them; you should not have to hem and haw doing it.

2) Study the class specification and the examination announcement

Usually, the oral board has one or both of these to guide them. The qualities, characteristics or knowledges required by the position sought are stated in these documents. They offer valuable clues as to the nature of the oral interview. For example, if the job involves supervisory responsibilities, the announcement will usually indicate that knowledge of modern supervisory methods and the qualifications of the candidate as a supervisor will be tested. If so, you can expect such questions, frequently in the form of a hypothetical situation which you are expected to solve. NEVER go into an oral without knowledge of the duties and responsibilities of the job you seek.

3) Think through each qualification required

Try to visualize the kind of questions you would ask if you were a board member. How well could you answer them? Try especially to appraise your own knowledge and background in each area, *measured against the job sought*, and identify any areas in which you are weak. Be critical and realistic – do not flatter yourself.

4) Do some general reading in areas in which you feel you may be weak

For example, if the job involves supervision and your past experience has NOT, some general reading in supervisory methods and practices, particularly in the field of human relations, might be useful. Do NOT study agency procedures or detailed manuals. The oral board will be testing your understanding and capacity, not your memory.

5) Get a good night's sleep and watch your general health and mental attitude

You will want a clear head at the interview. Take care of a cold or any other minor ailment, and of course, no hangovers.

What should be done on the day of the interview?

Now comes the day of the interview itself. Give yourself plenty of time to get there. Plan to arrive somewhat ahead of the scheduled time, particularly if your appointment is in the fore part of the day. If a previous candidate fails to appear, the board might be ready for you a bit early. By early afternoon an oral board is almost invariably behind schedule if there are many candidates, and you may have to wait. Take along a book or magazine to read, or your application to review, but leave any extraneous material in the waiting room when you go in for your interview. In any event, relax and compose yourself.

The matter of dress is important. The board is forming impressions about you – from your experience, your manners, your attitude, and your appearance. Give your personal appearance careful attention. Dress your best, but not your flashiest. Choose conservative, appropriate clothing, and be sure it is immaculate. This is a business interview, and your appearance should indicate that you regard it as such. Besides, being well groomed and properly dressed will help boost your confidence.

Sooner or later, someone will call your name and escort you into the interview room. *This is it.* From here on you are on your own. It is too late for any more preparation. But remember, you asked for this opportunity to prove your fitness, and you are here because your request was granted.

What happens when you go in?

The usual sequence of events will be as follows: The clerk (who is often the board stenographer) will introduce you to the chairman of the oral board, who will introduce you to the other members of the board. Acknowledge the introductions before you sit down. Do not be surprised if you find a microphone facing you or a stenotypist sitting by. Oral interviews are usually recorded in the event of an appeal or other review.

Usually the chairman of the board will open the interview by reviewing the highlights of your education and work experience from your application – primarily for the benefit of the other members of the board, as well as to get the material into the record. Do not interrupt or comment unless there is an error or significant misinterpretation; if that is the case, do not hesitate. But do not quibble about insignificant matters. Also, he will usually ask you some question about your education, experience or your present job – partly to get you to start talking and to establish the interviewing "rapport." He may start the actual questioning, or turn it over to one of the other members. Frequently, each member undertakes the questioning on a particular area, one in which he is perhaps most competent, so you can expect each member to participate in the examination. Because time is limited, you may also expect some rather abrupt switches in the direction the questioning takes, so do not be upset by it. Normally, a board member will not pursue a single line of questioning unless he discovers a particular strength or weakness.

After each member has participated, the chairman will usually ask whether any member has any further questions, then will ask you if you have anything you wish to add. Unless you are expecting this question, it may floor you. Worse, it may start you off on an extended, extemporaneous speech. The board is not usually seeking more information. The question is principally to offer you a last opportunity to present further qualifications or to indicate that you have nothing to add. So, if you feel that a significant qualification or characteristic has been overlooked, it is proper to point it out in a sentence or so. Do not compliment the board on the thoroughness of their examination – they have been sketchy, and you know it. If you wish, merely say, "No thank you, I have nothing further to add." This is a point where you can "talk yourself out" of a good impression or fail to present an important bit of information. Remember, *you close the interview yourself.*

The chairman will then say, "That is all, Mr. _____, thank you." Do not be startled; the interview is over, and quicker than you think. Thank him, gather your belongings and take your leave. Save your sigh of relief for the other side of the door.

How to put your best foot forward

Throughout this entire process, you may feel that the board individually and collectively is trying to pierce your defenses, seek out your hidden weaknesses and embarrass and confuse you. Actually, this is not true. They are obliged to make an appraisal of your qualifications for the job you are seeking, and they want to see you in your best light. Remember, they must interview all candidates and a non-cooperative candidate may become a failure in spite of their best efforts to bring out his qualifications. Here are 15 suggestions that will help you:

1) Be natural – Keep your attitude confident, not cocky

If you are not confident that you can do the job, do not expect the board to be. Do not apologize for your weaknesses, try to bring out your strong points. The board is interested in a positive, not negative, presentation. Cockiness will antagonize any board member and make him wonder if you are covering up a weakness by a false show of strength.

2) Get comfortable, but don't lounge or sprawl

Sit erectly but not stiffly. A careless posture may lead the board to conclude that you are careless in other things, or at least that you are not impressed by the importance of the occasion. Either conclusion is natural, even if incorrect. Do not fuss with your clothing, a pencil or an ashtray. Your hands may occasionally be useful to emphasize a point; do not let them become a point of distraction.

3) Do not wisecrack or make small talk

This is a serious situation, and your attitude should show that you consider it as such. Further, the time of the board is limited – they do not want to waste it, and neither should you.

4) Do not exaggerate your experience or abilities

In the first place, from information in the application or other interviews and sources, the board may know more about you than you think. Secondly, you probably will not get away with it. An experienced board is rather adept at spotting such a situation, so do not take the chance.

5) If you know a board member, do not make a point of it, yet do not hide it

Certainly you are not fooling him, and probably not the other members of the board. Do not try to take advantage of your acquaintanceship – it will probably do you little good.

6) Do not dominate the interview

Let the board do that. They will give you the clues – do not assume that you have to do all the talking. Realize that the board has a number of questions to ask you, and do not try to take up all the interview time by showing off your extensive knowledge of the answer to the first one.

7) Be attentive

You only have 20 minutes or so, and you should keep your attention at its sharpest throughout. When a member is addressing a problem or question to you, give him your undivided attention. Address your reply principally to him, but do not exclude the other board members.

8) Do not interrupt

A board member may be stating a problem for you to analyze. He will ask you a question when the time comes. Let him state the problem, and wait for the question.

9) Make sure you understand the question

Do not try to answer until you are sure what the question is. If it is not clear, restate it in your own words or ask the board member to clarify it for you. However, do not haggle about minor elements.

10) Reply promptly but not hastily

A common entry on oral board rating sheets is "candidate responded readily," or "candidate hesitated in replies." Respond as promptly and quickly as you can, but do not jump to a hasty, ill-considered answer.

11) Do not be peremptory in your answers

A brief answer is proper – but do not fire your answer back. That is a losing game from your point of view. The board member can probably ask questions much faster than you can answer them.

12) Do not try to create the answer you think the board member wants

He is interested in what kind of mind you have and how it works – not in playing games. Furthermore, he can usually spot this practice and will actually grade you down on it.

13) Do not switch sides in your reply merely to agree with a board member

Frequently, a member will take a contrary position merely to draw you out and to see if you are willing and able to defend your point of view. Do not start a debate, yet do not surrender a good position. If a position is worth taking, it is worth defending.

14) Do not be afraid to admit an error in judgment if you are shown to be wrong
   The board knows that you are forced to reply without any opportunity for careful consideration. Your answer may be demonstrably wrong. If so, admit it and get on with the interview.

15) Do not dwell at length on your present job
   The opening question may relate to your present assignment. Answer the question but do not go into an extended discussion. You are being examined for a *new* job, not your present one. As a matter of fact, try to phrase ALL your answers in terms of the job for which you are being examined.

Basis of Rating
   Probably you will forget most of these "do's" and "don'ts" when you walk into the oral interview room. Even remembering them all will not ensure you a passing grade. Perhaps you did not have the qualifications in the first place. But remembering them will help you to put your best foot forward, without treading on the toes of the board members.
   Rumor and popular opinion to the contrary notwithstanding, an oral board wants you to make the best appearance possible. They know you are under pressure – but they also want to see how you respond to it as a guide to what your reaction would be under the pressures of the job you seek. They will be influenced by the degree of poise you display, the personal traits you show and the manner in which you respond.

ABOUT THIS BOOK

   This book contains tests divided into Examination Sections. Go through each test, answering every question in the margin. We have also attached a sample answer sheet at the back of the book that can be removed and used. At the end of each test look at the answer key and check your answers. On the ones you got wrong, look at the right answer choice and learn. Do not fill in the answers first. Do not memorize the questions and answers, but understand the answer and principles involved. On your test, the questions will likely be different from the samples. Questions are changed and new ones added. If you understand these past questions you should have success with any changes that arise. Tests may consist of several types of questions. We have additional books on each subject should more study be advisable or necessary for you. Finally, the more you study, the better prepared you will be. This book is intended to be the last thing you study before you walk into the examination room. Prior study of relevant texts is also recommended. NLC publishes some of these in our Fundamental Series. Knowledge and good sense are important factors in passing your exam. Good luck also helps. So now study this Passbook, absorb the material contained within and take that knowledge into the examination. Then do your best to pass that exam.

EXAMINATION SECTION

EXAMINATION SECTION
TEST 1

DIRECTIONS: Each question or incomplete statement is followed by several suggested answers or completions. Select the one that BEST answers the question or completes the statement. *PRINT THE LETTER OF THE CORRECT ANSWER IN THE SPACE AT THE RIGHT.*

1. In modern ice making, using ammonia equipment, the freezing tank coils should be maintained with the

    A. highest possible pressure consistent with the required brine temperature
    B. lowest possible pressure consistent with the required brine temperature
    C. pressure at a minimum of 10 psig.
    D. pressure at a minimum of 30 psig.

2. In ammonia plants, it is IMPORTANT to keep the coils free of oil accumulation by drawing oil out of the coils AT LEAST

    A. weekly   B. monthly   C. quarterly   D. yearly

3. A suction line to a compressor that is too SMALL will cause

    A. reduction in the compressor capacity
    B. pressure loss in the line between the suction outlet of the coil and the suction inlet to the compressor
    C. reduction in the overall capacity of the plant
    D. all of the above

4. The term *volumetric efficiency* is used in discussing

    A. condenser capacity
    B. evaporator capacity
    C. compressor capacity
    D. all of the above

5. Non-condensible gases in a refrigerating system

    A. causes a decrease in condensing pressure
    B. is minute and has no way of entering a system under pressure
    C. contributes to high power cost and a reduction in capacity
    D. all of the above

6. The capacity of an evaporative condenser depends on

    A. fan volume
    B. the temperature of the entering air
    C. entering air wet bulb
    D. all of the above

7. The determining factor in the selection of the method of removing and storing system refrigerant is USUALLY

    A. system size
    B. nature of refrigerant
    C. system value
    D. all of the above

8. When removing reusable refrigerant from a system, the line to the refrigerant storage drum MUST

   A. contain a sweat fitting
   B. be flexible
   C. be of copper
   D. be of ample size

9. The common methods of determining proper oil charge are

   A. dip stick, paper method, and compressor sight glass
   B. weight measurement, dip stick, liquid line sight glass, and paper method
   C. weight measurement, dip stick, pressure method, and paper method
   D. all of the above

10. When charging or removing oil, the MAIN precautions to be taken are to

    A. use clean oil, watch the crankcase pressure, and slightly overcharge
    B. use clean oil and do not overcharge
    C. watch the crankcase pressure and use dry oil
    D. none of the above

11. The four BASIC methods of determining whether the proper amount of refrigerant is being introduced into the system are

    A. sight glass, weight, pressure, and frost line
    B. bulls eye, weight, pressure, and frost line
    C. sight glass, weight, pressure, and dip stick
    D. all of the above

12. The thermostatic expansion valve has three operating pressures.
    They are

    A. evaporator, spring, suction
    B. evaporator, bulk, condensing
    C. evaporator, spring, bulb
    D. all of the above

13. The touching surfaces between a thermostatic expansion valve bulb and the suction line MUST be

    A. clean and tight
    B. downstream of the equalizing line
    C. above the coil
    D. all of the above

14. There are three major areas in which care must be taken in designing the multiple refrigeration cycle system.
    They are

    A. oil return, compressor protection, and electrical overload
    B. oil return, compressor protection, and off-cycle protection
    C. compressor protection, off-cycle protection, and electrical overload
    D. all of the above

15. Pilot operated valves are FREQUENTLY used because

    A. solenoids are more positive acting
    B. the control point need not be at the valve
    C. they protect against freeze-up
    D. all of the above

16. The oil safety switch is operated by

    A. oil pressure
    B. the sum of oil pressure and crankcase pressure
    C. the difference between crankcase pressure and oil pressure
    D. all of the above

17. A refrigeration accessory is an article or device that

    A. adds to the convenience of a system
    B. is not essential in a refrigeration system
    C. adds to the effectiveness of a system
    D. none of the above

18. The material within a strainer drier is known as a

    A. designate   B. desecrate
    C. desiccant   D. all of the above

19. Before deciding on the capacity of a cooling tower to be installed, it is FIRST necessary to determine the

    A. temperature of the water which will enter the tower
    B. amount of heat that is to be taken up by the condensing water and the amount of water to be circulated
    C. average wind velocity
    D. all of the above

20. The estimated heat gain of a building is 480,000 Btu per hour.
    What size compressor, in tons, will be required by the air conditioning machine to cool the building?

    A. 100   B. 80   C. 60   D. 40

21. The function of the expansion valve in a refrigerating system is to

    A. control or meter the liquid flow to the expansion coils or evaporator
    B. regulate the gas flow to the expansion coils or evaporator
    C. control the temperature in the expansion coils or evaporator
    D. all of the above

22. The capacity of a compressor is determined by the

    A. weight of the refrigerant pumped
    B. temperature and pressure of the evaporator and condenser
    C. volumetric efficiency of the compressor
    D. all of the above

23. Which type of condenser requires the MOST cooling surface?

    A. Shell and tube   B. Submerged
    C. Atmospheric or surface   D. All of the above

24. How does the presence of a non-condensable gas in the condenser affect the transmission of heat between the water and refrigerant?
    The non-condensable gas

    A. displaces the refrigerant
    B. acts as an insulation and reduces the heat transfer
    C. reduces the capacity of the condenser
    D. all of the above

25. Frost on cooling coils affects suction pressure by

    A. raising the boiling point of the refrigerant
    B. forcing the suction pressure down
    C. raising the suction pressure up
    D. none of the above

26. Human comfort is MOST closely associated with

    A. temperature and relative humidity of the air
    B. carbon dioxide content of the air
    C. temperature and specific humidity of the air
    D. heat content and dew point of the air

27. An air conditioning cooling coil is actually the _____ of a refrigeration system.

    A. evaporator   B. condenser
    C. expansion valve   D. liquid received

28. In a typical commercial refrigeration system such as would be associated with a cold storage warehouse or a walk-in freezer locker, the thermostat in the cooled spaces controls the action of the

    A. compressor motor starter switch
    B. high pressure cut-out switch
    C. solenoid value in the liquid refrigerant line
    D. all of the above

29. What danger comes from using a low flash point oil in air compressors?

    A. The oil will not lubricate the cylinder walls
    B. Excessive moisture is formed
    C. Possible explosion in the air compressor, receiver, or piping
    D. All of the above

30. You would know that there is sufficient water going to the cylinder jackets by the temperature of the

    A. air leaving the compressor
    B. jacket water leaving the compressor
    C. air leaving the intercooler
    D. all of the above

31. What unit of measure is COMMONLY used to indicate the quantity of heat? 31.____

    A. Degrees Fahrenheit   B. Degrees centigrade
    C. B.t.u.   D. All of the above

32. Humidity is IMPORTANT in cold storage rooms to 32.____

    A. prevent shrinkage and drying
    B. lower the temperature
    C. increase formation of frost
    D. all of the above

33. For MAXIMUM capacity and efficiency, the 33.____

    A. condenser pressure and the suction pressure should be as near together as possible
    B. suction pressure should be as high as practicable
    C. discharge pressure should be as low as practicable
    D. all of the above

34. A receiver in an air compression system is used to 34.____

    A. avoid cooling air before using
    B. reduce the work needed during compression
    C. collect water and grease suspended in the air
    D. increase the air discharge p'ressure

35. The speed of a centrifugal compressor is changed from 1,000 to 3,000 rpm. 35.____
    If the compressor originally delivered 2,000 cfm, the new delivery will be _____ cfm.

    A. 6,000   B. 16,000   C. 22,000   D. 36,000

KEY (CORRECT ANSWERS)

1.	B	16.	C
2.	A	17.	B
3.	D	18.	C
4.	C	19.	B
5.	C	20.	D
6.	D	21.	D
7.	B	22.	C
8.	D	23.	C
9.	A	24.	D
10.	B	25.	D
11.	A	26.	A
12.	C	27.	A
13.	A	28.	C
14.	B	29.	C
15.	B	30.	D

31. C
32. A
33. D
34. C
35. A

EXAMINATION SECTION
TEST 1

DIRECTIONS: Each question or incomplete statement is followed by several suggested answers or completions. Select the one that BEST answers the question or completes the statement. *PRINT THE LETTER OF THE CORRECT ANSWER IN THE SPACE AT THE RIGHT.*

1. In refrigerating work, the term *automatic* expansion valve refers to a

    A. thermostatic expansion valve
    B. high side float valve
    C. capillary tube used to produce a pressure drop
    D. constant pressure expansion valve

2. In a given refrigerating system, the ratio of the heat absorbed in the evaporator to the heat equivalent of the energy supplied by the compressor is 4.5.
    The theoretical horsepower per ton of refrigeration is MOST NEARLY

    A. 0.69   B. 0.87   C. 1.04   D. 1.73

3. In an air-water vapor mixture, the temperature which is the measure of the total heat of the mixture is the

    A. dewpoint
    B. dry bulb
    C. sum of dry bulb and wet bulb
    D. wet bulb

4. In a refrigerating system, the

    A. refrigerating capacity of the machine is equal to the ice-making capacity of the plant
    B. standard ton is the abstraction of 12,000 Btu per hour
    C. rectifier of the absorption system is on the low pressure side
    D. cooling water temperature for a CO_2 system should be as high as possible

5. In a two-stage double-acting air compressor, the

    A. unloaders operate on head and crank end of both cylinders simultaneously
    B. intercooler pressure is the arithmetic average of inlet and discharge pressures
    C. unloaders act on the inlet valves
    D. unloaders commonly unload the high pressure cylinder first

6. Air passing through a spray chamber in which the spray water is recirculated but not heated or cooled will

    A. be humidified at approximately constant wet bulb temperature
    B. always leave in a saturated condition
    C. be de-humidified
    D. leave the spray chamber at the same water vapor pressure

2 (#1)

7. When the solid absorbent silica-gel is used in an air conditioning system, the air passing over it

   A. will be humidified
   B. has its dry bulb temperature increased
   C. will have its wet bulb temperature decreased
   D. will reach a higher water vapor pressure

8. In the process of heating atmospheric air in an air conditioning apparatus, the

   A. absolute or specific humidity increases
   B. relative humidity remains constant
   C. absolute or specific humidity does not change
   D. water vapor pressure decreases

9. 100 pounds per minute of outside air at 90° F. dry bulb and 200 pounds per minute of recirculated air at 72° F. dry bulb are mixed in an air conditioning system.
   The resulting dry bulb temperature will be, in °F., MOST NEARLY

   A. 84   B. 78   C. 88   D. 81

10. In a compression refrigerating system, the principal useful refrigerating effect is obtained in the

    A. condenser   B. evaporator
    C. expansion valve   D. compressor

11. Recirculation of conditioned air in an air conditioned building is done MAINLY to

    A. reduce refrigeration tonnage required
    B. increase room entropy
    C. increase air specific humidity
    D. reduce room temperature below the dewpoint

12. *Sweating* of cold water pipes in a room is due to the

    A. surface of the pipe being below the wet bulb temperature of the room air
    B. surface of the pipe being below the dew point temperature of the room air
    C. air in the room exceeding 100% relative humidity
    D. specific humidity exceeding the relative humidity

13. In a two-stage air compressor, the intercooler is placed between the

    A. compressor and air receiver
    B. compressor and intake pipe
    C. after cooler and air receiver
    D. intake of the second stage and the discharge of the first stage

14. The quantity of heat required to change the stage (e.g., liquid to vapor, or solid to liquid) of a body within a change in temperature is USUALLY called

    A. specific heat   B. enthalpy
    C. latent heat   D. entropy

15. When a refrigeration machine is in operation under normal load, the refrigerant leaving the compressor is in a state of

    A. low pressure vapor
    B. hot liquid
    C. high pressure vapor
    D. cold liquid

16. In a commercial ammonia refrigerating system, the ammonia that has just passed through the expansion valve

    A. is partially vaporized
    B. has become highly superheated
    C. has a greater enthalpy than it had before entering the expansion valve
    D. is all in a liquid state

17. An ice making machine freezes 50 lbs. of water at 45° F. to ice at 25° F. (under atmospheric conditions) in one hour.
    The cooling load, in tons, of refrigeration is MOST NEARLY

    A. 0.7   B. 1.4   C. 6.8   D. 13.6

18. The pressure drop through a ventilating duct is 3.8 inches of water when the air velocity is 32 feet per second.
    The pressure drop, in inches of water, when the air velocity is reduced to 24 feet per second will be MOST NEARLY

    A. 6.8   B. 3.8   C. 3.0   D. 2.1

19. The three methods in common use in the design and sizing of air duct systems are known as

    A. abrupt enlargement, dynamic loss, maximum velocity
    B. turbulent loss, equal friction, static regain
    C. velocity reduction, equal friction, static regain
    D. velocity reduction, maximum velocity, dynamic loss

20. The actual amount of water vapor which atmospheric air can hold is governed by the

    A. pressure
    B. temperature
    C. relative humidity
    D. specific volume

21. A pitot tube inserted in a ventilating duct is USUALLY used to determine the _____ in the duct.

    A. velocity pressure
    B. total pressure
    C. barometric pressure
    D. static pressure in p.s.i. absolute

22. Wetness forming inside frame building walls is often due to water vapor migration into the wall. The vapor movement is usually from the warm air side to the cool air side.
    The vapor USUALLY moves in this direction because the

    A. relative humidity of cool air is lower than the relative humidity of warm air
    B. partial pressure of the vapor is lower on the cool side than on the warm air side of the wall

C. warm air has a lower dewpoint temperature
D. specific humidity or humidity ratio is so much lower for the warm air than for the cool air

23. Of the following, the dividing point between the high pressure and low pressure side of a refrigeration system is the

   A. evaporator
   B. receiver
   C. condenser
   D. expansion valve

24. In operating a closed water circulating system, it is good practice to

   A. treat the water chemically for corrosion control
   B. drain and flush the system regularly to control corrosion
   C. leave the system undisturbed because it is sealed and needs no maintenance
   D. replace the pump shaft seals every three months

25. The function of an unloader on an electric motor-driven air compressor is to

   A. release the pressure in the cylinders in order to reduce the starting load
   B. reduce the speed of the motor when the maximum pressure is reached
   C. prevent excess pressure in the receiver
   D. drain the condensate from the cylinder head

26. The MOST highly toxic of the following refrigerants is

   A. sulphur dioxide
   B. ammonia
   C. methyl chloride
   D. freon 12

27. Of the following piping materials, the one which is NOT generally used for pneumatic temperature control systems is

   A. copper
   B. plastic
   C. steel
   D. galvanized iron

28. In accordance with recommended maintenance practice, thermostats used in a pneumatic temperature control system should be checked

   A. weekly
   B. bi-monthly
   C. monthly
   D. once a year

29. Of the following, the BEST method to use to determine the moisture level in a refrigeration system is to

   A. weigh the drier after it has been in the system for a period of time
   B. visually check the sight glass for particles of corrosion
   C. use a moisture indicator
   D. test a sample of lubricating oil with phosphorus pentoxide

30. A full-flow drier is USUALLY recommended to be used in a hermetic refrigeration compressor system to keep the system dry and to

   A. prevent the products of decomposition from getting into the evaporator in the event of a motor burn-out
   B. condense out liquid refrigerant during compressor off cycles and compressor start-up

C. prevent the compressor unit from decreasing in capacity
D. prevent the liquid from dumping into the compressor crankcase

31. The rating of a unit ventilator is USUALLY determined by a(n)

    A. anemometer
    B. hydrometer
    C. psychrometer
    D. ammeter

32. The STANDARD capacity rating conditions for any refrigeration compressor is _____ for the suction and _____ for the discharge.

    A. 5° F., 19.6 psig; 86° F., 154.5 psig
    B. 5° F., 9.6 psig; 96° F., 154.5 psig
    C. 10° F., 9.6 psig; 96° F., 144.5 psig
    D. 10° F., 19.6 psig; 96° F., 134.5 psig

33. Of the following, the MAIN purpose of a subcooler in a refrigerant piping system for a two-stage system is to

    A. reduce the total power requirements and total heat rejection to the second stage
    B. reduce total power requirements and return oil to the compressor
    C. improve the flow of evaporator gas per ton and increase the temperature
    D. increase the heat rejection per ton and avoid system shutdown

34. In large refrigeration systems, the USUAL location for charging the refrigeration system is into the

    A. suction line
    B. liquid line between the receiver shut-off valve and the expansion valve
    C. line between the condenser and the compressor
    D. line between the high pressure cut-off switch and the expansion valve

35. Assume that one of your assistants was near the Freon 11 refrigeration system when a liquid Freon line ruptured. Some of the liquid Freon 11 has gotten into your assis-tant's right eye.
    Of the following actions, the one which you should NOT take is to

    A. immediately call for an eye specialist (medical doctor)
    B. gently and quickly rub the Freon 11 out of the eye
    C. use a boric-acid solution to clean out the Freon 11 from his eye
    D. wash the eye by gently blowing the Freon 11 out of his eye with air

KEY (CORRECT ANSWERS)

1.	D	16.	A
2.	C	17.	A
3.	D	18.	D
4.	B	19.	C
5.	C	20.	B
6.	A	21.	A
7.	B	22.	B
8.	C	23.	D
9.	B	24.	A
10.	B	25.	A
11.	A	26.	A
12.	B	27.	C
13.	D	28.	D
14.	C	29.	C
15.	C	30.	A

31. A
32. A
33. A
34. B
35. B

EXAMINATION SECTION
TEST 1

DIRECTIONS: Each question or incomplete statement is followed by several suggested answers or completions. Select the one that BEST answers the question or completes the statement. *PRINT THE LETTER OF THE CORRECT ANSWER IN THE SPACE AT THE RIGHT.*

1. *Separates from the lubricating oil in operating with oil floating on top of the liquid refrigerant..*
   To which refrigerant does this statement apply?
   A. Freon-12
   B. Freon-22
   C. Ammonia
   D. Carbon dioxide

   1.____

2. Refrigerants withdrawn from refrigerating systems shall be

   A. placed in Interstate Commerce Commission containers only
   B. discharged to the sewer
   C. slowly discharged into the atmosphere
   D. placed in containers meeting the requirements of Local Law 373 only

   2.____

3. If an operator carelessly used a paraffin oil in an ammonia refrigeration system, the probability is that the

   A. compressor discharge valves would foul
   B. expansion valve would freeze
   C. evaporator would foul up with wax
   D. oil would flash at compressor discharge temperature

   3.____

4. In order for an electric induction motor to operate satisfactorily and deliver its full horsepower, the motor should operate MOST NEARLY at

   A. no more than 10% variation above its rated voltage and no greater than 20% variation below its rated frequency
   B. its rated voltage and at least 20% slip
   C. its rated voltage and a 20% frequency variation
   D. its rated frequency and at not more than 10% above or below its rated voltage

   4.____

5. In a comparison of the absorption system with the vapor compression system, the one of the following statements which is INCORRECT is that the

   A. expansion valves of both systems are similar
   B. absorption system requires heat and power and the compression system only requires power
   C. absorption system alone requires an analyzer
   D. compressors of both systems are similar

   5.____

6. A system using silica gel that has picked up moisture may be reactivated by heating it for a period of four hours or more at a temperature of APPROXIMATELY _____ °F.

   A. 200
   B. 450
   C. 700
   D. 850

   6.____

7. A two stage compression system is often used when it is desired to

   A. conserve lubricating oil
   B. use ammonia rather than Freon
   C. work evaporator at very low temperature
   D. get more work from a single stage compressor

8. The force exerted on a cylinder 6" in diameter at 100 psig is

   A. 3600#   B. 2800#   C. 1600#   D. 600#

9. The boiling temperature of Freon 22, compared with Freon 12, is

   A. 20° lower   B. 10° lower
   C. 25° higher   D. 15° higher

10. In the absorption system, the absorber absorbs

    A. any foreign matter in the system
    B. the heat directly from the brine coil or direct coil
    C. the suction gas into the weak liquid
    D. the weak liquid into the brine

11. Freon 12 systems shall have parts that will not cause corrosion of materials. PROHIBITED materials include _____ alloys.

    A. brass   B. copper
    C. extra heavy steel D. magnesium

12. A spray type of dehumidifier is to be used to air condition and give the best results to a set dew point of 54° F. The temperature of the return chilled water would be _____ ° F.

    A. 35.5   B. 48.0   C. 52.0   D. 46.5

13. With reference to a synchronous motor, it is NOT correct that

    A. it is a constant speed motor
    B. it can be run using 220, 440, or 2300 volts
    C. these motors are excited by direct current
    D. these motors are usually run with a lagging field current

14. In a calcium chloride brine tank of 1000 cubic feet, how many pounds of dichromate would you use in the INITIAL charge?

    A. 20   B. 40   C. 100   D. 200

15. In a refrigeration plant that is equipped with an automatic condenser water regulating valve, the line for actuating this valve should be tapped into the

    A. condenser water supply ahead of the valve
    B. condenser water waste line from the condenser
    C. refrigerant high pressure side of the system
    D. refrigerant low pressure side of the system

16. How many water boxes are on a shell and tube, vertical condenser?

    A. One on top
    B. Two on top
    C. One on top and bottom
    D. Two on bottom

17. If Nessler's solution is added to a sample of salt brine, in the event of there being a trace of ammonia present in the brine, the color of the solution will turn

    A. blue   B. red   C. pink   D. yellow

18. The refrigerant enters the condenser as a _____ and leaves as a _____.

    A. high pressure gas; low pressure liquid
    B. superheated gas; low pressure liquid
    C. high pressure liquid; low pressure liquid
    D. superheated gas; superheated gas

19. To remove water from an industrial ammonia system, you would

    A. use a regenerator
    B. drain from the low suction
    C. drain from the high side
    D. drain the entire system

20. Which of the following is an indication that the reciprocating type of compression system is short of refrigerant?

    A. High head pressure and low suction pressure
    B. Low suction pressure and low head pressure
    C. High suction and low discharge pressure
    D. Both pressures are always normal

21. In a refrigerating unit having a high side float, if the float is punctured and sinks, the result will be that the

    A. compressor will overload
    B. high side will fluctuate
    C. low side will go down
    D. expansion valve will frost

22. A sign on the wall of a motor room contains various pertinent information. Which of the following can be omitted?

    A. Number of condensers
    B. Pounds of refrigerant
    C. Name of installers
    D. Horsepower of prime mover

23. When withdrawing refrigerant from a system into containers, they cannot, in any case, be filled more than _____%.

    A. 70   B. 75   C. 80   D. 85

24. If a system contains 400 pounds of Group 2 refrigerant, the number of breathing service masks required is

    A. one   B. two   C. three   D. none

25. Where would you place an accumulator in the system?
    A. On the suction side of the compressor
    B. Just before the condenser on the discharge side of the system
    C. On the high side of the liquid line
    D. Before the king valve

KEY (CORRECT ANSWERS)

1.	D	11.	C
2.	A	12.	C
3.	C	13.	B
4.	D	14.	C
5.	D	15.	C
6.	B	16.	A
7.	C	17.	D
8.	B	18.	B
9.	A	19.	A
10.	C	20.	A

21. C
22. A
23. B
24. A
25. A

TEST 2

DIRECTIONS: Each question or incomplete statement is followed by several suggested answers or completions. Select the one that BEST answers the question or completes the statement. *PRINT THE LETTER OF THE CORRECT ANSWER IN THE SPACE AT THE RIGHT.*

1. The quantity of water flowing through an automatically controlled condenser will INCREASE as the

    A. head pressure decreases
    B. suction pressure decreases
    C. load increases
    D. head pressure increases

2. An indication that the refrigeration system is in need of purging of foul gases is _____ head pressure with _____.

    A. high; high suction pressure
    B. high; a little water on the condenser
    C. high; plenty of water on the condenser
    D. low; a hot receiver

3. In testing condenser water for carbon dioxide leaks, you would use

    A. Nessler's reagent in a sample of brine
    B. brom-thymol-blue in a sample of water
    C. a halide torch on a brine sample
    D. litmus paper in a sample of brine

4. The number of baffles in a three pass shell and tube brine cooler is

    A. one   B. two   C. three   D. four

5. In testing for ammonia leaks in a plant, red litmus paper was used. If ammonia was present, the paper would turn

    A. green   B. dark red
    C. blue   D. none of the above

6. A substance that CANNOT be used to make a brine solution that is to be used at -25° F is

    A. calcium chloride   B. ethylene glycol
    C. sodium chloride   D. anti-freeze

7. In a spray pond similar to a condenser to kill algae in the water, you would use

    A. silica gel   B. chromite
    C. potassium permanganate   D. potash

8. The accumulator on a single stage double-acting ammonia compressor

    A. acts like an analyzer in the absorption system
    B. is tied in on high side
    C. removes liquid entrained in the suction line
    D. is tied in on low side

9. If a system contains 400 pounds of Group 2 refrigerant, the number of breathing service masks required is

   A. one B. two C. three D. none

10. In a compression system with a low side float, the ball in the float is punctured and sinks. What would MOST likely happen?
    The

    A. low side would be falling with compressor running
    B. compressor would stop and head pressure would rise
    C. head pressure would fall
    D. low side would be rising with compressor running

11. The capacity of a water cooled condenser is LEAST affected by

    A. water temperature
    B. amount of water
    C. refrigerant temperature
    D. ambient temperature

12. The brine in a shell and tube cooler

    A. is in the shell
    B. is in the tube
    C. alternates between the tube and shell
    D. is in the refrigerant in tubes

13. The suction gas pressure in a system is 15" Hg.
    If this is converted to absolute pressure, it will be MOST NEARLY

    A. 0 B. 15 C. 7 D. 23

14. Sulphur dioxide may be discharged into

    A. carbonated brine
    B. absorptive brine
    C. calcium chloride
    D. water

15. A vertical compressor has trunk type pistons and is single-acting. If the oil rings leaked very badly, it would cause

    A. pounding upon starting
    B. a decreased capacity
    C. a slow start which speeds up
    D. scored and scratched cylinder walls

16. Which one of the following has items that are NOT part of a belt driven compressor?

    A. Piston, cylinder, frame, and crankcase
    B. Stuffing box, suction valve, and frame
    C. Crankcase, discharge valve, and stuffing box
    D. Frame, crankcase, suction valve, valve rod, and piston

17. The LOWEST operating temperature you would recommend for sodium chloride is _____ °F.

    A. 0 B. 5 C. 10 D. 20

18. What is the LOWEST operating temperature you would recommend for calcium chloride?

    A. -45° F   B. -60° F   C. -20° F   D. 0° F

19. The one of the following dessicants that would change physically and/or chemically under the absorption process of water is

    A. silica gel   B. activated alumina
    C. calcium chloride   D. activated bauxite

20. Which of the following refrigerants sublimates?

    A. CO_2 B. NH_3 C. R-12   D. R-502

21. Carbon dioxide has a critical point of 87° F.
    This means that, regardless of how high the pressure is raised, it will NOT

    A. evaporate   B. condense
    C. become saturated   D. gain sensible heat

22. You would NOT use muntz metal with

    A. carbon dioxide   B. Freon 12
    C. ammonia   D. methyl chloride

23. One ton of refrigeration is equal to _____ BTU per _____.

    A. 144; minute   B. 200; hour
    C. 288,000; hour   D. 12,000; hour

24. There are several test cocks on a Freon receiver-condenser, one at the end about one quarter of the way up from the bottom.
    This test cock is used for

    A. purging non-condensable gases or air from the system
    B. testing the liquid level in the receiver
    C. an auxiliary charging connection
    D. pumping down purposes

25. A 200 ton air conditioning plant is set up with Freon compressors.
    Assuming that neither of the compressors is equipped with bypass solenoids, in order to be able to get AT LEAST four steps of capacity with these two machines, they should be driven by _____ motors.

    A. synchronous   B. repulsion and induction
    C. capacitor type   D. wound rotor induction

KEY (CORRECT ANSWERS)

1.	D	11.	D
2.	C	12.	D
3.	B	13.	C
4.	B	14.	B
5.	A	15.	D
6.	C	16.	D
7.	C	17.	A
8.	C	18.	A
9.	A	19.	C
10.	D	20.	A

21. B
22. C
23. D
24. B
25. D

TEST 3

DIRECTIONS: Each question or incomplete statement is followed by several suggested answers or completions. Select the one that BEST answers the question or completes the statement. *PRINT THE LETTER OF THE CORRECT ANSWER IN THE SPACE AT THE RIGHT.*

1. In order to determine the actual operating capacity of a chilled water cooler, it is essential that an operator know the specific heat of the water as well as the poundage of water flow per unit of time. With respect to the specific heat of water, in the normal liquid temperature range, it can be properly said that the specific heat of water is 1.____

    A. the same at all temperatures from 32° F to 212° F
    B. high at low temperatures and low at high temperatures
    C. high at low temperatures and high at high temperatures
    D. low at low temperatures and high at high temperatures

2. A Freon refrigerating plant is being used in an air conditioning system to remove sensible heat from the air in a two stage after cooler to a silica gel air dehydrating unit. If the outside surface of the coils in the after cooler operate wet, the probability is that the 2.____

    A. suction pressure is too high
    B. refrigerant is wet
    C. coils in the after cooler are not properly vented
    D. none of the above

3. The use of screwed joints in refrigeration systems for refrigerant pressures above 250 psi is permitted, provided that the nominal size of the pipe is NOT more than _____ inches. 3.____

    A. 1 1/4   B. 1 3/4   C. 2 1/4   D. 3

4. Refrigerant 718 is 4.____

    A. propane   B. ammonia   C. water   D. air

5. Thirty gallons of water per minute are to be reduced from 80° F to 40° F. How many tons of refrigeration are required to do this? 5.____

    A. 10   B. 30   C. 50   D. 70

6. A plant refrigerating unit has 600 pounds of refrigerant in it. The CFM from the blower should be 6.____

    A. 1275   B. 1450   C. 1100   D. 600

7. If an absorption system was to be placed in operation and the low and high sides were to be 16# and 150# of steam, _____ # would be required per ton of refrigeration. 7.____

    A. 70   B. 20   C. 200   D. 10

8. It is NOT correct that a synchronous motor 8.____

    A. is a constant speed motor
    B. can be run using 220, 440, or 2300 volts
    C. is usually run with a lagging field current
    D. is excited by direct current

2 (#3)

9. The concentration of a brine which is used in an indirect system is determined by

   A. an Orsat meter
   B. Nessler's reagent
   C. a manometer
   D. a hydrometer

10. In the ammonia and Freon compression systems, the working pressure

    A. is the same for both ammonia and Freon
    B. is not comparable
    C. of Freon is higher
    D. of ammonia is higher

11. If the high pressure side of a compression system was reading considerably *higher* than normal, you would

    A. reduce compressor speed
    B. open the expansion valve
    C. increase the oil pressure
    D. send more water to the condenser

12. In the manufacturing of ice, air is piped into water cans to

    A. make clear ice
    B. speed up freezing time
    C. prevent ice from becoming brittle
    D. increase the brine velocity

13. How much liquid ammonia passes the expansion valve for 100 tons?

    A. 100#   B. 20#   C. 200#   D. 50#

14. One of the DISADVANTAGES of using carbon dioxide is that it has a lower critical point than usual, close to _____ °F.

    A. 67   B. 144   C. 39   D. 87

15. Upon noticing the discharge pressure gauge of a system that reads 980#, you would assume that the refrigerant was

    A. methyl chloride
    B. carbon dioxide
    C. ammonia
    D. Freon

16. The MAXIMUM permissible number of pounds of a Group 2 refrigerant for an indirect system in a commercial building having a Class T machinery room is

    A. 300   B. 500   C. 1000   D. unlimited

17. Upon increasing the supply of water to the condenser, the head pressure still remains the same.
    The NEXT thing you should do is

    A. speed up the compressor
    B. purge the receiver of refrigerant
    C. purge the system of non-condensable gases
    D. purge the system of gummy oil

18. With reference to specific minimum requirements for refrigerant pipe and tubing, the one of the following that is MOST NEARLY correct is:

    A. Standard soft annealed copper tubing used for refrigerant piping shall not be used in sizes larger than a half inch
    B. Joints in copper tubing systems containing Group 2 refrigerant should be soldered
    C. Standard I.P.S. copper and brass pipe and tubing shall not be less than 80% copper
    D. Standard wall steel or wrought iron pipe may be used for refrigeration liquid lines for one and a quarter inches or smaller

19. _____ gallons of water can fit in a pipe 14" in diameter and 110' long.

    A. 360 B. 880 C. 1090 D. 1276.4

20. The color of the lubricating oil in a CO_2 refrigerating plant manufacturing dry ice is

    A. lemon yellow
    B. pale lemon
    C. lily or water white
    D. pale orange

21. In a compression cycle, a multi-cylinder, single-acting compressor operates automatically on room temperature (the *on and off cycle*). Upon starting, it pounds for a while. The MOST likely reason for this would be

    A. a worn wrist-pin bushing
    B. oil pumping due to overcharge of oil
    C. piston slap
    D. worn crankcase bearing

22. What design of valve would you use for an expansion valve? A _____ valve.

    A. globe
    B. needle
    C. gate
    D. V-notched globe

23. Synchronous motors that are used for industrial refrigeration have

    A. AC and DC supplied to them
    B. constant speed
    C. ability to correct the power factor
    D. all of the above

24. An absorption system uses 100 pounds of steam per day. This is a _____ ton plant.

    A. five B. one C. ten D. fifty

25. The characteristics of ammonia include

    A. colorless gas
    B. sharp odor
    C. lighter than air
    D. all of the above

KEY (CORRECT ANSWERS)

1. A
2. C
3. D
4. C
5. C

6. B
7. B
8. B
9. D
10. D

11. D
12. A
13. D
14. D
15. B

16. A
17. C
18. C
19. B
20. C

21. B
22. B
23. D
24. A
25. D

TEST 4

DIRECTIONS: Each question or incomplete statement is followed by several suggested answers or completions. Select the one that BEST answers the question or completes the statement. *PRINT THE LETTER OF THE CORRECT ANSWER IN THE SPACE AT THE RIGHT.*

1. The use of screwed joints in piping systems for refrigerant pressures of 250 psi or less is permitted provided that the nominal size of the pipe is NOT more than _____ inches. 1.____

   A. 3   B. 4   C. 4 1/2   D. 2

2. The strong liquor in the absorption system is formed in the   2.____

   A. generator   B. evaporator
   C. condenser   D. absorber

3. An indicator card was taken on a horizontal double-acting single cylinder compressor, and the compression stroke was considerably left of its normal position. This would indicate that   3.____

   A. there was liquid in the cylinder
   B. the discharge valve was not seated properly
   C. the suction valve was not seated properly
   D. the suction gas was superheated

4. Assuming that all other factors remain the same,   4.____

   A. as the load on the evaporator decreases, the low side pressure decreases
   B. if the suction pressure increases, the capacity decreases
   C. if the head pressure increases, the capacity increases
   D. in refrigeration the coefficient of ammonia is lower than that of Freon 12

5. In a spray pond similar to a condenser, to kill algae in the water you would use   5.____

   A. silica gel   B. chromite
   C. potassium permanganate   D. potash

6. Regarding centrifugal compressors, it is TRUE that   6.____

   A. refrigerant leaks into the coiling system are common
   B. only the main bearing and thrust need to be oiled
   C. they have no auxiliary oil pump
   D. the auxiliary oil pump is hand-operated

7. Sweat joints in copper tubing for Group 1 refrigerant shall be   7.____

   A. threaded with 75% pitch
   B. brazed
   C. brazed or soldered
   D. gas free and using 50% glycerine and 50% litharge

8. The result of a Freon compressor not having properly seated magnetic bypass valves is   8.____

   A. reduced capacity   B. loss of oil
   C. loss of refrigerant   D. increased capacity

25

2 (#4)

9. The area of a piston 16" in diameter is _____ square inches.

   A. 148.9   B. 200   C. 154   D. 162

10. With a broken sight glass, what devices are used for safety and loss of refrigerant on a receiver?

    A. Automatic safety valves, piped to outside
    B. Metal guards about glass
    C. Manual hand valves
    D. Automatic shut-off valves and metal guards about glass

11. The strong liquor in the absorber will become WEAKER when the

    A. expansion valve is closed
    B. evaporator load increases
    C. evaporator load decreases
    D. condenser pressure decreases

12. If the liquid line becomes partly clogged between the receiver and the expansion valve, the line

    A. between restriction and receiver will become hot
    B. between restriction and receiver will have 2" of frost
    C. above restriction will become hot
    D. above restriction will become frosted

13. When withdrawing refrigerant from a system into containers, the containers CANNOT be filled more than _____%.

    A. 20   B. 50   C. 75   D. 85

14. The oil pressure in a reciprocating compressor should be _____ # above the _____ pressure.

    A. 40 to 60; suction   B. 40 to 60; discharge
    C. 10 to 30; suction   D. 10 to 30; discharge

15. The one of the following Freons that has the MOST refrigeration effect per pound is F-

    A. 11   B. 12   C. 113   D. 114

16. What effect will moisture have on a Freon system?

    A. Frozen king valve   B. Frozen compressor
    C. No effect   D. Frozen expansion valve

17. An absorption system is to be placed into operation under standard ton conditions, a suction of 19.5#, and discharge of 156#. The steam gauge reads 5 psig. What is the consumption of steam per ton hour of refrigerant?

    A. 20   B. 41   C. 51   D. 61

18. The balance in an absorption system is maintained by the

    A. governor on the ammonia pump
    B. steam pressure to the generator

C. liquid regulator valve in weak liquid line to absorber
D. temperature on the exchanger

19. Methyl chloride refrigerant is classified in group

    A. 4 B. 3 C. 2 D. 1

20. The term *viscosity* in a refrigeration oil means

    A. ability to mix
    B. corrosive action
    C. internal friction
    D. cold

21. A refrigerant that will break down into phosgene and other compounds when exposed to a hot gas flame such as cooking gas is

    A. ammonia anhydrous
    B. carbon dioxide
    C. aqua ammonia
    D. Freon 11

22. In some NH_3 plants, a unit is used which cools the gases being purged before they are passed over to the water bottle.
    This cooling is done in order to

    A. increase the rate of purging
    B. cool the gases before passing to the water bottle
    C. save the operator from manually purging the system
    D. recover ammonia which is still with the gas

23. *Carron oil* is used for ammonia burns and is made up of equal parts of linseed oil and

    A. nitric acid
    B. lime water
    C. water
    D. vinegar

24. The refrigerant that usually operates with a condenser pressure above 1050# is

    A. ammonia
    B. sulphur dioxide
    C. carbon dioxide
    D. F-114

25. The FIRST indication that a shipping drum of refrigerant used to charge a refrigeration system is EMPTYING is

    A. the appearance of frost on the drum
    B. a gurgling noise
    C. the appearance of a fog in the vicinity of the drum
    D. a hissing noise

KEY (CORRECT ANSWERS)

1. A
2. B
3. D
4. A
5. C

6. B
7. C
8. A
9. B
10. D

11. C
12. D
13. C
14. C
15. A

16. D
17. A
18. C
19. C
20. C

21. D
22. D
23. B
24. C
25. A

EXAMINATION SECTION
TEST 1

DIRECTIONS: Each question or incomplete statement is followed by several suggested answers or completions. Select the one that BEST answers the question or completes the statement. *PRINT THE LETTER OF THE CORRECT ANSWER IN THE SPACE AT THE RIGHT.*

1. What type of condenser would you install to conserve water? 1.____

   A. Shell and tube   B. Evaporative
   C. Atmospheric   D. Double pipe

2. The engine room first aid kit should contain _____ acid. 2.____

   A. hydrochloric   B. nitric
   C. sulphuric   D. picric

3. The steam jet refrigeration system is used for 3.____

   A. deep freezing work   B. air conditioning work
   C. cold storage   D. the noon whistle

4. A flooded evaporator USUALLY has a(n) _____ metering device. 4.____

   A. high side float
   B. low side float
   C. automatic expansion valve
   D. thermostatic expansion valve

5. Refrigerant enters the condenser as a _____ and leaves as a _____. 5.____

   A. high pressure gas; high pressure liquid
   B. high pressure gas; low pressure liquid
   C. high pressure liquid; low pressure liquid
   D. superheated gas; superheated gas

6. When a high side float is punctured and sinks, it results in 6.____

   A. starved evaporator   B. flooded evaporator
   C. frozen valve   D. high head pressure

7. A compound gauge registers 7.____

   A. inches of pressure present
   B. pounds of pressure below atmospheric pressure
   C. inches of water above atmosphere and inches of air below
   D. pounds of pressure above atmosphere and inches of vacuum below

8. An air conditioning Freon compressor is equipped with a unit shell and coil condenser-receiver slung under the base of the compressor. 8.____
   If the system is overcharged with refrigerant, the PROBABILITY is that

   A. only head pressure would go up
   B. both head pressure and suction pressure would go up
   C. capacity of the compressor would go up
   D. system would continue to operate without change

9. In relation to compressors, which statement is MOST correct?

   A. Valve lift for low speed reciprocating compressors is less.
   B. The HP per ton decreases as the suction decreases.
   C. The refrigerating effect per pound of refrigerant decreases as the suction pressure increases.
   D. The valve lift for high speed reciprocating compressors should be less than required for low speed compressors.

10. What type of constant speed motor is generally used in large refrigerating plants?

    A. Slip ring
    B. Synchronous
    C. Squirrel gauge
    D. Double wound squirrel gauge

11. The capacity of an evaporative condenser will INCREASE if the

    A. wet bulb reading is high
    B. wet bulb reading is low
    C. capacity does not change
    D. amount of water used is less

12. One ton of refrigeration is equal to how many BTUs?

    A. 1,200 per minute
    B. 200 per hour
    C. 12,000 per hour
    D. 288,000 per hour

13. A(n) _____ condenser could be used in winter without water.

    A. submerged
    B. shell and tube
    C. shell and coil
    D. atmospheric with drip

14. The evaporative coils in a cooler are along the ceiling, and one of these coils has insulating baffles.
    The baffles are there to

    A. catch the dripping when the coils are defrosting
    B. supply gravity air to circulate in the cooler
    C. see that gravity air circulates over the coils
    D. none of the above

15. In methyl chloride systems, a dryer would PROBABLY be placed in the _____ near the _____.

    A. discharge; compressor
    B. liquid line; expansion valve
    C. suction line; compressor
    D. suction line; evaporator

16. A Freon 12 compressor used in an air conditioning system has a magnetic bypass to   16._____

    A. equalize pressure in the cylinder
    B. relieve pressure when it becomes high
    C. regulate compressor capacity
    D. relieve oil from the cylinder to the crankcase

17. The formula $C = 0.8P_1D^2$ is used for determining the capacity of a   17._____

    A. fusible plug   B. stop valve
    C. safety valve   D. venturi

18. A scale trap is placed in the suction line of a compression system to remove foreign matter. It would be MOST effective when the plant is   18._____

    A. new
    B. shut down for a long time
    C. old
    D. none of the above

19. In a small ammonia plant using brine as a cooling agent, due to a leak, the brine became saturated with ammonia. After fixing the leak, you, as an operator, would   19._____

    A. dump the brine and make up a new batch
    B. recirculate the brine through the system; if no leaks, reuse it
    C. treat the brine with Nessler's solution and reuse it
    D. treat the brine with sulphur and reuse it

20. When starting a large air conditioning system of the reciprocating type on a day when the latent heat load is high, one of the FIRST things an engineer should do is   20._____

    A. open the bypass valve to lighten the load
    B. set the thermostat a few degrees higher
    C. install larger fuses to take the starting load
    D. turn on the cooling water and start the air blower

21. Which of the following statements is CORRECT?   21._____
    A(n)

    A. enclosed cooling tower has a forced draft effect
    B. spray pond works exactly like an evaporative condenser
    C. evaporative condenser depends upon the evaporation of some water for its economical operation
    D. evaporative condenser has no refrigerant coil in it

22. The symbol for refrigeration shown at the right represents   22._____

    A. high side float   B. low side float
    C. water valve   D. oil trap

23. The one of the following types of condensers in which eliminator plates are USUALLY found is the _____ type   23._____

    A. shell and coil   B. shell and tube
    C. evaporative   D. double tube

24. There are several test cocks on a Freon receiver condenser. The one at the end, about one quarter of the way up from the bottom. This test cock is used for

    A. purging non-condensable gases or air from the system
    B. testing the liquid level in the receiver
    C. an auxiliary charging connection
    D. pumping down purposes

24.____

25. The FASTEST way to remove the frost from direct expansion coils in a cold storage room is to

    A. spray water over them
    B. shut the coils off and let the frost melt off
    C. chop or scrape the frost off
    D. run a hot gas line to the coils

25.____

KEY (CORRECT ANSWERS)

1.	B		11.	B
2.	D		12.	C
3.	B		13.	D
4.	B		14.	C
5.	A		15.	B
6.	A		16.	C
7.	D		17.	A
8.	B		18.	A
9.	D		19.	A
10.	B		20.	D

    21. C
    22. A
    23. C
    24. B
    25. D

TEST 2

DIRECTIONS: Each question or incomplete statement is followed by several suggested answers or completions. Select the one that BEST answers the question or completes the statement. *PRINT THE LETTER OF THE CORRECT ANSWER IN THE SPACE AT THE RIGHT.*

1. In a shell and tube brine cooler with an electric float valve, if the gas equalizer line is clogged,   1.____

    A. it operates normally
    B. liquid in the tank goes up and down
    C. liquid in the tank does not correspond with the level in the float
    D. there is no change

2. The weak liquor heat exchanger or an ammonia absorption system is used to pre-   2.____

    A. heat weak liquor   B. heat strong liquor
    C. cool strong liquor   D. cool suction gas

3. The subcooling of liquid refrigerant, immediately before the liquid passes through the expansion valve, would MOST likely result in an increase   3.____

    A. of 50% in the horsepower per ton factor
    B. in head pressure
    C. in compressor speed
    D. in the net available refrigerating effect

4. A Freon compressor was V-belt driven when installed, but the belts were too tight. After the unit has been running for a while, this will   4.____

    A. increase the speed of the compressor
    B. decrease the speed of the motor and the compressor
    C. increase the speed of the motor
    D. cause the motor to run hot

5. In a room, there is a cylinder half-filled with ammonia at 50° F. The pressure inside the tank will be _____ pounds.   5.____

    A. 40   B. 125   C. 75   D. 250

6. What percentage of oil travels with refrigerant in a system?   6.____

    A. 10%   B. 125%   C. 30%   D. 50%

7. When attempting to read the high side pressure gauge on an operating ammonia compressor, it is noted that the pointer *hunts,* or has a wide and relatively slow back and forth movement. This would MOST likely indicate that the compressor   7.____

    A. is overloaded   B. valve action is sluggish
    C. suction valves are stuck   D. is operating normally

8. One DISADVANTAGE of using carbon dioxide is that it has a lower critical point than usual, close to _____ ° F.   8.____

    A. 67   B. 144   C. 39.4   D. 87

9. If a Freon 12 single-acting compressor had oil foaming in the crankcase, this would be caused by

   A. addition of liquid Freon
   B. sudden drop in oil temperature
   C. addition of oil to the crankcase
   D. sudden drop in crankcase pressure

10. The refrigerant that separates from the lubricating oil in an operating evaporator with oil floating on top of the liquid refrigerant is

    A. Freon 12
    B. Freon 22
    C. ammonia
    D. carbon dioxide

11. In a system using a silica gel drier that has picked up moisture, it may be reactivated by heating it for a period of four hours or more, at a temperature of APPROXIMATELY _____ °F.

    A. 200   B. 700   C. 450   D. 850

12. In a large plant, there are several squirrel gauge motors and three or four synchronous motors.
    One purpose of the synchronous motor is

    A. to correct the power factor
    B. to correct the plant power demand
    C. to allow for more than one speed
    D. its high speed

13. Of the different types of solenoid valves used in refrigeration, the one which, when energized, tends to close the port is the _____ type.

    A. closed
    B. normally open
    C. fluctuating
    D. partially closed

14. A Freon 12 compressor used for air conditioning has a low temperature cooling coil of 45° (no superheat).
    The low temperature gas coming back to the compressor would be

    A. 20#   B. 40#   C. 60#   D. 80#

15. In a given temperature of air, the ratio of vapor pressure to humidity is called

    A. absolute humidity
    B. relative humidity
    C. pressure
    D. partial pressure

16. A compressor that has two compression strokes and two suction strokes per cylinder per revolution of the crankshaft is a

    A. single-acting compressor
    B. double-acting compressor
    C. two stage compressor
    D. compressor in duplex

17. In the lubrication of a Freon refrigeration compressor, 17.____

    A. vegetable oil is preferred for best results
    B. Freon has the same degree of miscibility with oils as does ammonia
    C. a chemical action between the Freon and lubricating oil occurs
    D. the refrigerant mixes with the lubricating oil

18. The refrigerant stored in a machinery room shall NOT be more than _____% of the normal charge or more than _____ pounds of refrigerant in addition to the charge in the system. 18.____

    A. 20; 300   B. 30; 300   C. 35; 350   D. 25; 325

19. A motor has a protection device to prevent burning out or damage called a 19.____

    A. fusetron   B. dual fuse
    C. circuit breaker   D. thermal protector

20. For a pressure testing of newly installed R-12 systems, it is BEST to use 20.____

    A. dry carbon dioxide with a trace of R-12 in it
    B. water in a hydrostatic test
    C. dry hydrogen with a trace of R-12 in it
    D. anhydrous ammonia

21. A dehydrator should be used in a(n) _____ system. 21.____

    A. sulphur dioxide   B. Freon 12
    C. ammonia   D. carbon dioxide

22. In the absorption system, the flow of ammonia gas in relation to the strong liquor in the analyzer is _____ flow. 22.____

    A. cross   B. counter   C. parallel   D. diagonal

23. A volume of water of 10,000 cubic inches weighs _____ pounds. 23.____

    A. 144   B. 970   C. 361   D. 231

24. The refrigerant known as *Refrigerant 40* is 24.____

    A. propane   B. sulphur dioxide
    C. methyl chloride   D. ammonia

25. What design of valve would you use for an expansion valve? 25.____
    A _____ valve.

    A. globe   B. needle
    C. gate   D. V-notched globe

KEY (CORRECT ANSWERS)

1.	C	11.	C
2.	B	12.	A
3.	D	13.	B
4.	D	14.	B
5.	C	15.	B
6.	A	16.	B
7.	B	17.	D
8.	D	18.	A
9.	D	19.	D
10.	D	20.	A

21. B
22. B
23. C
24. C
25. B

TEST 3

DIRECTIONS: Each question or incomplete statement is followed by several suggested answers or completions. Select the one that BEST answers the question or completes the statement. *PRINT THE LETTER OF THE CORRECT ANSWER IN THE SPACE AT THE RIGHT.*

1. In comparing the absorption system with the compression system, the steam coil in the generator is equivalent to the   1.____

    A. hot discharge refrigerant vapor
    B. electric motor
    C. hot discharge valve assembly
    D. compressor

2. On a horizontal compressor having a gravity feed oil system from a tank above the compressor, the pressure inside the tank is   2.____

    A. zero psig
    B. 14.7 gauge
    C. 20 pounds
    D. 10 pounds above suction

3. Which of the following would cause frost to form on the outer surface of an evaporator coil?   3.____

    A. Water in the refrigerant
    B. Water in the liquid line
    C. Moisture in the refrigerant
    D. Moisture in the air within the cooler

4. The material used for the packing of an ammonia stuffing box would MOST likely be   4.____

    A. steel
    B. solid lead
    C. bellows and spring arrangement
    D. graphite, hemp, and lead

5. It is CORRECT to state that   5.____

    A. copper cannot be used with R-12
    B. aluminum cannot be used with methyl chloride
    C. black iron cannot be used with R-22
    D. magnesium can be used with Freon

6. What color does blue litmus paper turn when ammonia is present?   6.____

    A. Red
    B. White
    C. Green
    D. None of the above

7. In the absorption system, the condenser, receiver, expansion valve, and the evaporator can be designed   7.____

    A. similar to the compression equipment
    B. as an open type design

C. the same as the compression equipment, only zinc coated
D. of copper only

8. You would NOT use muntz metal with

   A. carbon dioxide B. Freon 12
   C. ammonia D. methyl chloride

9. A ten-ton refrigeration unit has the capacity of _____ BTU per minute.

   A. 2,000 B. 20,000 C. 12,000 D. 288,000

10. The oil gauge pressure on an ammonia vertical compressor should be

    A. zero pounds when the suction pressure is zero per inch
    B. forty pounds
    C. 30 psig when the suction pressure is 10 psig
    D. 50 pounds fluctuating with the discharge pressure

11. The MINIMUM required rated discharge capacity of a pressure relief device or fusible plug for a refrigerant-containing vessel, shall be determined by the formula C = Fdl. C is equal to

    A. feet per second B. feet per hour
    C. refrigerant per ton D. air in # per minute

12. What percentage of oil is mixed with the refrigerant in the compression cycle?

    A. 10% B. 20% C. 30% D. 40%

13. If the liquid line were *warmer* than usual, it would indicate

    A. excessive refrigerant B. shortage of refrigerant
    C. receiver full of liquid D. high head pressure

14. A spare rupture member can be substituted for a relief valve in a(n) _____ system.

    A. aqua ammonia B. sulphur dioxide
    C. carbon dioxide D. ammonia

15. What kind of piping would you NOT choose for anhydrous ammonia or aqua ammonia?

    A. Black steel B. Stainless steel
    C. Galvanized steel D. Wrought iron

16. In an absorption system, if the heat exchanger were removed, the result would be to

    A. more steam added to the generator to get results
    B. stop the liquid pump from the absorber
    C. stop the weak liquor pump from the generator
    D. pipe the cold gas from the evaporator directly to the generator

17. What produces the LOWER reading of the wet bulb?

    A. The thermometer is calibrated that way
    B. Cooling by evaporation
    C. The cloth and water form a cooling solution
    D. It does not read lower

18. The color of the lubricating oil in a carbon dioxide refrigerating plant manufacturing dry ice is

    A. lemon yellow
    B. pale lemon
    C. lily or water white
    D. pale orange

19. In a packaged air conditioning unit, the refrigeration unit was overcharged.
    The result would be

    A. increased head pressure and suction pressure
    B. decreased head pressure
    C. low suction pressure
    D. low head and low suction pressure

20. The GREATEST operating capacity can be maintained by a MAXIMUM

    A. suction and discharge superheat
    B. discharge pressure
    C. suction pressure
    D. constant water flow to the system

21. An ammonia type compression system uses sea water as found in the New York Harbor for condensing service.
    In order to test for the presence of ammonia in this water, one should use _____ solution.

    A. Carrene
    B. sulphur
    C. Nessler's
    D. halide

22. A vertical single-acting compressor has pistons with suction valves. In this arrangement, only the top of the cylinder is water jacketed.
    The BEST reason for this is

    A. lower cost of the casting
    B. less water is used
    C. the lower part of the cylinder would be cooler than the jacket water
    D. only the discharge valves need cooling

23. In order to prevent rust or corrosion in a salt brine used to manufacture ice, an operator would add

    A. sodium dichromate
    B. aluminum sulphate
    C. Nessler's solution
    D. universal indicator solution

24. The brine in an icemaking plant will PROBABLY be between

    A. 0° and 11° C
    B. 0° and 11° F
    C. 25° and 29° C
    D. 14° and 22° F

4 (#3)

25. In a reciprocating compressor, the pistons are of double trunk type. The ADVANTAGE of this is   25.____

    A. oil will not mix with refrigerant
    B. lighter piston
    C. more piston rings can be used
    D. shorter connecting rods

KEY (CORRECT ANSWERS)

1. D
2. A
3. D
4. D
5. B

6. D
7. A
8. C
9. A
10. C

11. D
12. A
13. B
14. C
15. C

16. A
17. B
18. C
19. A
20. C

21. C
22. C
23. A
24. B
25. A

EXAMINATION SECTION
TEST 1

DIRECTIONS: Each question or incomplete statement is followed by several suggested answers or completions. Select the one that BEST answers the question or completes the statement. *PRINT THE LETTER OF THE CORRECT ANSWER IN THE SPACE AT THE RIGHT.*

1. A plant refrigerating unit has 600 pounds of refrigerant in it. The CFM from the exhaust blower should be

    A. 1275   B. 1450   C. 1100   D. 600

2. A rupture member can be substituted for a relief valve in a(n) _____ system.

    A. aqua ammonia
    B. sulphur dioxide
    C. carbon dioxide
    D. ammonia

3. Which of the following groups of refrigerants is in Group 3?

    A. CO_2
       F-12
       F-22
       Propane

    B. F-11
       F-113
       Ammonia
       Butane

    C. Ethane
       Butane
       F-12
       Carbon dioxide

    D. Butane
       Ethane
       Propane
       Ethylene

4. When withdrawing refrigerant from a system into containers, they cannot be filled more than _____ %.

    A. 70   B. 75   C. 80   D. 85

5. When field testing Refrigerant 12, the high and low sides should be tested to _____ #.

    A. 300-150   B. 235-140   C. 95-50   D. 1500-1000

6. In a refrigerating system with a gauge where the dial points to 100 psi, under normal operating conditions, the LAST number of the gauge should read

    A. 105   B. 110   C. 115   D. 120

7. The MAXIMUM pounds in a direct system, per 1,000 cubic feet of occupied space, for Refrigerant 12 is

    A. 31   B. 41   C. 51   D. 61

8. The metallic mixtures of alloys used to make a gas tight soldered joint should melt at _____ °F.

    A. 600
    B. 800° F and above 300
    C. 935
    D. 1000° F and above 400

9. A specification calls for the installation of a unit air conditioning system in the lobby of a building. This is to contain 30# Freon 12.
   In keeping with the rules, this system may

   A. be installed
   B. be installed, if the system is reduced to 20#
   C. not be installed; no unit can be placed in the lobby
   D. not be installed, as it contains a group 2 refrigerant

10. The minimum required rated discharge capacity of the pressure relief device or fusible plug for a refrigerant containing vessel shall be determined by the formula C = Fdl. What is C equal to?

    A. Feet per hour
    B. Refrigerant per minute
    C. Air in pounds per minute
    D. Amount of second

11. To pack tongue and groove, flanges on ammonia lines should be made of

    A. rubber
    B. asbestos sheet
    C. tin
    D. sheet lead

12. How many kinds of lubricants are used in a horizontal double-acting compressor?

    A. One   B. Two   C. Three   D. Four

13. Flash gas would be found in the

    A. receiver
    B. condenser
    C. king valve
    D. evaporator

14. The accepted method to test oil for moisture content is the dielectric test. This test imposes high voltage electric pressure on electrodes immersed in an oil sample. If any current flows, there is moisture present.
    The electrodes are spaced _____ inch(es), _____ volts.

    A. 1/2 to 1; 40,000
    B. 1 to 2; 25,000
    C. 2 to 3; 22,000
    D. 1 1/2 to 4; 33,000

15. Heat transfer takes place by
    I. evaporation
    II. convection
    III. conduction
    IV. radiation
    The CORRECT answer is:

    A. I, II
    B. II, III, IV
    C. I, II, III
    D. III, IV

16. A pan of an evaporative condenser 8 feet long, 4 feet wide, and 9 inches deep contains _____ gallons of water.

    A. 120   B. 180   C. 280   D. 204.5

17. A hermetically sealed unit is a unit with the

   A. motor and compressor, *both* enclosed in a sealed casing
   B. motor *only* sealed in a casing
   C. compressor *only* sealed in a casing
   D. carrier absorption system

17.____

18. Regarding centrifugal compressors, it is TRUE that

   A. only the main bearing and thrust need to be oiled
   B. refrigerant leaks into the oiling system are common
   C. they have no auxiliary oil pump
   D. the auxiliary oil pump is hand-operated

18.____

19. There are dummy tubes or a *Tell Tale* welded to the shell of a large accumulator in an industrial ammonia plant. The pipe extends through the insulation.
Its purpose is to

   A. increase the capacity of the system
   B. facilitate taking ammonia samples
   C. check and mark the refrigerant level in the vessel
   D. make the accumulator physically stronger

19.____

20. Synchronous motors that are used for industrial refrigeration have

   A. AC and DC supplied to them
   B. constant speed
   C. ability to correct the power factor
   D. all of the above

20.____

21. An absorption system uses 100 pounds of steam per day.
This is a _____ -ton plant.

   A. five   B. one   C. ten   D. fifty

21.____

22. The characteristics of ammonia include

   A. colorless gas   B. sharp odor
   C. lighter than air   D. all of the above

22.____

23. Where would you place an accumulator in the system?

   A. On the suction side of the compressor
   B. Just before the condenser on the discharge side of the system
   C. On the high side of the liquid line
   D. Before the king valve

23.____

24. Methyl chloride refrigerant is classified in Group

   A. 4   B. 3   C. 2   D. 1

24.____

25. A rotary booster compressor has _____ bearing(s).

   A. one   B. two   C. three   D. four

25.____

KEY (CORRECT ANSWERS)

1.	B	11.	D
2.	C	12.	B
3.	D	13.	D
4.	B	14.	B
5.	B	15.	B
6.	D	16.	A
7.	A	17.	A
8.	D	18.	A
9.	A	19.	C
10.	C	20.	D

21. A
22. D
23. A
24. C
25. B

TEST 2

DIRECTIONS: Each question or incomplete statement is followed by several suggested answers or completions. Select the one that BEST answers the question or completes the statement. *PRINT THE LETTER OF THE CORRECT ANSWER IN THE SPACE AT THE RIGHT.*

1. How many BTU's are removed to cool 2,000 bars of butter from 70° F to 36° F if the specific heat of butter is .87 and each bar weighs 1.5 pounds?

    A. 74,130   B. 51,000   C. 88,500   D. 104,731

    1._____

2. A system with one compressor is using two evaporators of different temperatures, one with 35° F and the other with 20° F.
    The back pressure valve would be located on the

    A. common suction line
    B. common liquid line
    C. suction line nearer to the lower temperature cooler
    D. suction line of the high temperature cooler

    2._____

3. There are several refrigerants in the Freon group that are in common use. In connection with Freon 11, it can be stated that this refrigerant is widely used in air conditioning systems that have a _____ compressor.

    A. small reciprocating   B. large reciprocating
    C. rotary   D. large centrifugal

    3._____

4. With the same compressor displacement, the refrigerant that will give the MOST refrigerating effect per pound circulated is

    A. Freon 12   B. ammonia   C. butane   D. Freon 11

    4._____

5. The term *anhydrous* is used with a refrigerant to indicate the

    A. presence of ammonia   B. presence of water
    C. absence of Freon   D. absence of water

    5._____

6. A *swirl* is a device used in a(n) _____ condenser.

    A. shell and coil   B. closed shell and tube
    C. open shell and tube   D. atmospheric

    6._____

7. Carbon dioxide is in refrigerant Group

    A. 1   B. 2   C. 3   D. 6

    7._____

8. In many direct refrigerant systems, thermal expansion valves with equalizer lines may be installed.
    If the equalizer line became plugged, the effect on the cooling coil with a full load would be

    A. a starved coil   B. a flooded coil
    C. 4% superheat   D. 7% superheat

    8._____

45

9. In a Freon 12 air conditioning system, the finned evaporator coil is wet. It can be CORRECTLY stated that

   A. the system is not operating efficiently
   B. there is a shortage of refrigerant
   C. there is an oversized expansion valve
   D. the system is operating efficiently

10. In absorption systems, the ammonia pump transfers _____ from the _____.

    A. strong liquor; absorber to the generator
    B. ammonia gas; generator to the condenser
    C. weak liquor; generator to the absorber
    D. liquid ammonia; condenser to the receiver

11. In an automatic Freon 12 system for air conditioning, you, as the original installer, have to make a tight pipe joint.
    You would use a

    A. serrated flange without a leak gasket
    B. threaded *streamline fitting* and white lead
    C. combination of solder, litharge, glycerine, and white lead
    D. *streamline fitting* and solder to copper piping

12. The chemical in a dehydrator for a Freon or methyl chloride system is

    A. sawdust   B. silica gel
    C. aluminum   D. dichromate

13. A brine cooler in a refrigeration cycle is between the

    A. evaporator and the compressor
    B. compressor and the receiver
    C. compressor and the condenser
    D. expansion valve and the compressor

14. A piston design for a compressor without a cross-head is

    A. box   B. balanced   C. trunk   D. telescopic

15. In an automatic Freon unit with a low pressure control (off and on type), upon starting, there is a pounding condition.
    This is due to

    A. a worn piston pin
    B. a slapping piston pin
    C. excessive oil in the compressor
    D. a worn crank bearing

16. When the crosshead is properly aligned, the piston rod of a horizontal ammonia compressor is MOST likely to wear

    A. at the crosshead end   B. at the piston end
    C. at the middle of the rod   D. on the side

17. In a carbon dioxide system, the condenser cooling water rises to 87° F. Could some of the refrigeration be used to cool the cooling water so that the gas could condense at a savings?
The BEST response is:

   A. It is impractical because the water would freeze
   B. In general, it would be a very economical set-up
   C. Refrigeration loss would be greater, but the total would gain
   D. The cooling refrigeration gains, but the plant total would lose

   17._____

18. Upon testing for ammonia leaks with red litmus paper, if ammonia is present, the color changes to

   A. green   B. blue   C. red   D. yellow

   18._____

19. A horizontal shell and tube cooler is equipped with eliminators. The PRIMARY function of the eliminators is to

   A. prevent the carry-over of liquid refrigerant
   B. protect the tubes in the event of a freeze-up
   C. absorb noises and vibration impulses
   D. prevent oil from being carried into the cooler

   19._____

20. A large cooler is equipped with ceiling-hung brine cooling coils. The insulated baffles are properly arranged along one side and underneath the cooling coils. These baffles are PRIMARILY used

   A. as drip pans when defrosting
   B. to get proper gravity circulation of air through the coils
   C. to help support the weight of the coils when they frost up
   D. to collect the brine in case of a leak in the coils

   20._____

21. Anhydrous ammonia is MOST like water in

   A. odor
   B. color
   C. saturates at atmospheric pressure
   D. sublimes like water at 212° F and 14.69 pounds absolute

   21._____

22. Carron oil (a liniment used for ammonia burns) is made up of equal parts of

   A. linseed oil and lime water
   B. vaseline and picric acid
   C. lanolin and vinegar
   D. sulphur dioxide and water

   22._____

23. In an absorption type refrigerating plant, the weak liquor is very often used to

   A. precool the condenser water   B. precool the liquid ammonia
   C. preheat the strong liquor   D. preheat the steam

   23._____

24. The degree of solubility in reference to a refrigerating oil is usually the LOWEST when using

    A. genetron 141
    B. methyl chloride
    C. Freon 12
    D. carbon dioxide

24._____

25. In a large plant, there is a synchronous motor. It could be said that

    A. the speed will vary
    B. in a weak field, current will be leading
    C. a strong field will make up for the lagging
    D. excitation will cause current to lag

25._____

KEY (CORRECT ANSWERS)

1.	B	11.	D
2.	D	12.	B
3.	D	13.	D
4.	B	14.	C
5.	D	15.	C
6.	C	16.	C
7.	A	17.	D
8.	B	18.	B
9.	D	19.	A
10.	A	20.	B

21. B
22. A
23. C
24. D
25. B

TEST 3

DIRECTIONS: Each question or incomplete statement is followed by several suggested answers or completions. Select the one that BEST answers the question or completes the statement. *PRINT THE LETTER OF THE CORRECT ANSWER IN THE SPACE AT THE RIGHT.*

1. In a given temperature of air, the ratio of vapor pressure to humidity is called   1.____

    A. absolute humidity
    B. relative humidity
    C. pressure
    D. partial pressure

2. A compressor that has two compression strokes and two suction strokes per cylinder per revolution of the crankshaft is a   2.____

    A. single-acting compressor
    B. double-acting compressor
    C. two stage compressor
    D. compressor in duplex

3. In the lubrication of a Freon refrigeration compressor,   3.____

    A. vegetable oil is preferred for best results
    B. Freon has the same degree of miscibility with oils as does ammonia
    C. a chemical action between the Freon and lubricating oil occurs
    D. the refrigerant mixes with the lubricating oil

4. A Freon refrigeration plant is being used in an air conditioning system to remove the sensible heat from the air in a two stage after cooler to a silica gel air dehydrating unit. If the outside surface of the coils in the after cooler were to operate wet, the probability is that the   4.____

    A. suction pressure is too high
    B. refrigerant is wet
    C. coils of the after cooler are not properly vented
    D. none of the above

5. The speed, in revolutions per minute, of a six pole synchronous motor rated at 80 HP, 400 volts, and 60 cycles is   5.____

    A. 480   B. 900   C. 1200   D. 1800

6. The capacity of an evaporative condenser INCREASES as _____ bulb temperature _____.   6.____

    A. wet; decreases
    B. wet; increases
    C. wet and dry; increases
    D. dry; increases

7. For a pressure testing of newly installed R-12 systems, it is BEST to use   7.____

    A. dry carbon dioxide with a trace of R-12 in it
    B. water in a hydrostatic test
    C. dry hydrogen with a trace of R-12 in it
    D. anhydrous ammonia

8. A dehydrator should be used in a(n) _____ system.

   A. sulphur dioxide
   B. Freon 12
   C. ammonia
   D. carbon dioxide

9. In the absorption system, the flow of ammonia gas in relation to the strong liquor in the analyzer is called _____ flow.

   A. cross   B. parallel   C. counter   D. diagonal

10. In an ice plant, the agitation air is precooled because it

    A. lessens the load on the ice field
    B. increases air pressure capacity
    C. prevents freezing of air lines
    D. decreases air pressure capacity

11. The one of the following that can be used to make up a threaded joint (NH_3) is

    A. red lead and shellac
    B. Red Indian shellac
    C. white lead
    D. litharge and glycerine

12. If Nessler's solution is added to a sample of brine, in the event of ammonia being present, the color of the solution in the brine will turn

    A. blue   B. red   C. yellow   D. pink

13. An ammonia system was working with 8" vacuum on the return line. The absolute pressure would be CLOSE to _____#.

    A. 7   B. 22   C. 25   D. 10

14. A thermostatic expansion valve in a refrigeration system regulates the

    A. pressure of the evaporator
    B. pressure of the compressor
    C. flow of refrigerant to the precooler
    D. flow of refrigerant to the evaporator

15. In testing condenser water for carbon dioxide leaks, you would use

    A. Nessler's solution
    B. bromthymol blue
    C. a halide torch
    D. litmus paper

16. The purpose of the halide torch is

    A. to heat copper fitting for soldering
    B. a safety light
    C. to find carbon dioxide leaks
    D. to find Freon leaks

17. An oil lantern is used in the stuffing box

    A. to hold the seat tight and rigid
    B. as a guiding light
    C. as a seal
    D. as a space to hold oil

18. One of the effects of the presence of non-condensable gases in a refrigerating system is _____ pressure.

    A. high condensing
    B. low suction
    C. high suction
    D. low condensing

19. It is true that the greater the temperature differential between the water and the refrigerant gas, the more effective the condenser is.
    An operator, keeping this in mind, would

    A. raise the condenser pressure
    B. cut back on the inlet water
    C. raise the temperature of the incoming water
    D. reduce the power to the compressor (unit)

20. At a cost of .04 cents per KWH, what would be the cost per hour for a 100 HP motor running at 80% efficiency?

    A. $3.20   B. $3.70   C. $4.20   D. $4.90

21. In an air conditioning system having ducts, the evaporator coil has moisture on it during most days of the summer.
    This is due to

    A. not enough liquid refrigerant
    B. excessive liquid refrigerant
    C. the feeler bulb which requires movement to make frost
    D. generally a condition that is normal

22. Ammonia operates at higher pressures than Freon 12, but the higher temperatures and pressures required are offset by _____ volumetric displacement per ton.

    A. better
    B. worse
    C. the same
    D. none of the above

23. An oil interceptor placed in an ammonia plant of 300 tons is found

    A. so that it returns oil to the pump
    B. on the discharge line between the compressor and condenser
    C. lower than the compressor base
    D. before the pump and is used as an oil strainer

24. One ton of refrigeration equals

    A. 12,000 BTU per minute
    B. 1,200 BTU for 6 minutes
    C. 288,000 BTU per hour
    D. 144 BTU per minute

25. How many tons of ice would a 15 ton refrigeration unit make per day?

    A. 30   B. 15   C. 8   D. 5

KEY (CORRECT ANSWERS)

1.	B	11.	D
2.	B	12.	C
3.	D	13.	D
4.	C	14.	D
5.	B	15.	B
6.	D	16.	D
7.	A	17.	D
8.	B	18.	A
9.	C	19.	B
10.	B	20.	B

21. D
22. A
23. B
24. B
25. C

TEST 4

DIRECTIONS: Each question or incomplete statement is followed by several suggested answers or completions. Select the one that BEST answers the question or completes the statement. *PRINT THE LETTER OF THE CORRECT ANSWER IN THE SPACE AT THE RIGHT.*

1. In the absorption system, the weak liquid cooler is sometimes used to cool the   1.____

    A. liquid ammonia going to the evaporator
    B. strong liquid before it goes to the analyzer
    C. aqua ammonia before it goes to the condenser
    D. weak liquid before it goes to the absorber

2. In an ammonia flooded coil system, it is noticed that the evaporator tubes are dry and warm at the bottom and the upper coils are frosted. The reason for this is   2.____

    A. the evaporator is overloaded
    B. the evaporator is oil-logged
    C. the evaporator is underloaded
    D. this is normal operation for such a system

3. A thermostatic expansion valve has an external equalizer line. If the line became clogged while the system was operating, the evaporator would   3.____

    A. become flooded
    B. operate at 9 of superheat
    C. operate at full capacity
    D. starve

4. If the specific gravity of water is 1, then for a brine, it would be   4.____

    A. the same   B. greater   C. less   D. 1.44

5. In a large ammonia plant, the power factor reading on the panel board reads 90% or 90. This indicates that the power factor is   5.____

    A. good   B. bad   C. constant   D. irregular

6. _____ CANNOT be used with ammonia.   6.____

    A. Lead   B. Copper   C. Steel   D. Iron

7. A means to detect a carbon dioxide leak is a _____ test.   7.____

    A. white litmus paper   B. red litmus paper
    C. blue litmus paper   D. soapy water

8. The BEST evaporator to overcome flash gas is   8.____

    A. a direct expansion with a thermal expansion valve
    B. a coil with a bypass valve
    C. the flooded evaporator type
    D. one with a constant pressure valve

9. The _____ pump is the only moving part in the absorption system.

   A. steam
   B. water
   C. aqua ammonia
   D. compressed air

10. A system having less than 50# of refrigerant in it is usually stopped before purging of non-condensable gases. The reason for this is that

    A. it prevents the loss of large amounts of refrigerant
    B. the operator is present
    C. it saves time in the long run
    D. it is better because it takes longer

11. In a cold storage plant of 21 rooms with expansion coils in each, EVERY coil should have

    A. a strainer
    B. a common header
    C. an oil accumulator
    D. its own expansion valve

12. In a low temperature Freon 12 system, you would expect to find the booster compressor

    A. on the low pressure side of the system
    B. on the high side of the plant
    C. in a special room
    D. separate

13. With the same compressor displacement and the same suction pressure, which will give the MOST effective refrigeration per pound pumped?

    A. Freon 12
    B. Carrene
    C. Ammonia
    D. Carbon dioxide

14. If the liquid line becomes partly clogged between the receiver and the expansion valve, the result may be that the line

    A. between restriction and receiver will become hot
    B. between restriction and receiver will have 2" of frost
    C. above restriction will become hot
    D. above restriction will become frosted

15. Methyl chloride belongs to refrigerant group

    A. 1   B. 2   C. 3   D. 4

16. Assuming that all other conditions in a refrigeration system remain constant, the horsepower per ton of refrigeration will MOST likely _____ as the _____.

    A. increase; suction pressure increases
    B. increase; head pressure decreases
    C. increase; head pressure increases
    D. decrease; suction pressure decreases

17. The pump in the absorption system should PREFERABLY handle

    A. 50% gas and 50% liquid
    B. 100% liquid
    C. 100% gas
    D. none of the above

18. An employee received an ammonia burn near his eyes. You should apply _____ solution.

    A. 10% sulphuric acid
    B. 1% hydrochloric
    C. 2% boric acid
    D. 6% muriatic

19. To test for a leak in a CO_2 plant,

    A. pump NH_3 into the system and use Nessler's solution
    B. pump methyl chloride in and use litmus paper
    C. leave the CO_2 plant in operation and use a soapy water solution
    D. pump Freon into the system and use litmus paper

20. The CORRECT sequence of flow of refrigerant in the NH_3 compression system is

    A. compressor, scale trap, condenser, expansion valve, and evaporator
    B. compressor, oil trap, condenser, king valve, expansion valve, evaporator, and scale trap
    C. generator, condenser, expansion valve, evaporator, and absorber
    D. expansion valve, evaporator, condenser, oil trap, and condenser

21. Lithium bromide absorption systems, for use in air conditioning, have the LOWEST possible water temperature of _____ °F.

    A. 31   B. 33   C. 35   D. 38

22. The one of the following that could NOT be used in dehumidifying and cooling air in a modern air conditioning system is

    A. silica gel
    B. solution of calcium chloride
    C. zeolite method
    D. direct expansion refrigerating coil

23. To INCREASE the capacity of an absorption system, you would

    A. increase the steam pressure on the generator and pump
    B. increase the water in the condenser
    C. decrease the water in the absorber
    D. close the expansion valve

24. In changing a plant from Freon 12 to another refrigerant, which of the following would require the LEAST change in machinery?

    A. Ammonia
    B. Methyl chloride
    C. Carrene
    D. Carbon dioxide

25. In a calcium chloride brine tank of 1000 cubic feet, how many pounds of sodium dichromate would you use?

    A. 20   B. 40   C. 100   D. 200

KEY (CORRECT ANSWERS)

1. D
2. B
3. A
4. B
5. A

6. B
7. D
8. C
9. C
10. A

11. D
12. A
13. C
14. B
15. B

16. C
17. B
18. C
19. C
20. B

21. D
22. C
23. A
24. B
25. C

EXAMINATION SECTION
TEST 1

DIRECTIONS: Each question or incomplete statement is followed by several suggested answers or completions. Select the one that BEST answers the question or completes the statement. *PRINT THE LETTER OF THE CORRECT ANSWER IN THE SPACE AT THE RIGHT.*

1. A thermostatic expansion valve in a refrigeration system is used to regulate the   1.____

    A. pressure of the evaporator
    B. pressure of the compressor
    C. flow of the refrigerant to the precooler
    D. flow of refrigerant to the evaporator

2. The refrigerant is liquified in the compression system in the   2.____

    A. compressor   B. evaporator
    C. receiver   D. condenser

3. A compressor that has two compression strokes and two suction strokes per cylinder per revolution of the crank is a(n) _____ compressor.   3.____

    A. single-acting   B. double-acting
    C. two stage   D. in duplex

4. The MAIN bearings on the exciter in a large cold storage plant are   4.____

    A. ball bearings in a race
    B. barrel bearings in a race
    C. split babbitt bearings
    D. bronze sleeve bearings

5. Upon inspecting a rotary type booster system, you would expect to find the intercooler   5.____

    A. between the booster compressor and main compressor suction
    B. before the condenser of the main plant
    C. before the booster compressor on the suction line of the system
    D. between the booster compressor and the condenser

6. In a compression system driven by an induction motor, the compressor can USUALLY be run at _____ speed(s).   6.____

    A. one   B. two   C. three   D. four

7. How would you test for a carbon dioxide leak?   7.____

    A. Make a hydrostatic test
    B. Drain the system and use a trace of F-12
    C. Use a soapy water solution
    D. Pour hot water on the expansion coils

8. When a bypass valve is used, its object is for the purpose of   8.____

    A. starting the compressor   B. pumping down the compressor
    C. using a synchronous motor   D. increasing the compression

9. In the absorption system, the flow of ammonia gas in relation to the strong liquor in the analyzer is called _____ flow.

   A. A. cross
   B. counter
   C. parallel
   D. diagonal

10. A horizontal shell and tube cooler is equipped with eliminators. The PRIMARY function of the eliminators is to

    A. prevent the carry-over of liquid refrigerant
    B. protect the tubes in the event of a freeze-up
    C. absorb noises and vibration impulses
    D. prevent oil from being carried into the cooler

11. A Freon 12 system is operating with a discharge of 93.34 psi and a suction of 11.75 psig. Accordingly, the condenser is at 86F. What is the compression ratio?

    A. 8 to 1
    B. 5.6 to 1
    C. 4.1 to 1
    D. 2.5 to 1

12. A solenoid valve has a closed port when energized. This is normally referred to as a(n) _____ type valve.

    A. open
    B. closed
    C. dual
    D. multi

13. How many BTU's must be removed to cool twenty gallons of water from $80°$ F to $40°$ F?

    A. 2.000
    B. 6,666
    C. 5.550
    D. 7.777

14. A system using 80 lbs. of Group 1 refrigerant with two liquid receivers and two compressors requires _____ stop valves.

    A. 3
    B. 4
    C. 5
    D. 6

15. The adjustable bypass in a Freon vertical compressor is to

    A. increase refrigeration
    B. help the engineer on watch
    C. regulate capacity
    D. regulate the oil level

16. In reference to an ammonia compression system, the number of cubic feet pumped per minute per ton is

    A. 8
    B. 2
    C. 3.8
    D. 1.25

17. The LARGEST size *threaded* pipe allowed in an ammonia refrigeration system with a maximum of 250# pressure is _____ inches.

    A. 3
    B. 3 1/2
    C. 4
    D. 4 1/2

18. One of the thermal properties of a refrigerant that is NOT recommended is

    A. convenient evaporating and condensing pressures
    B. a low critical and high freezing point
    C. a high latent heat of evaporation
    D. low viscosity and high film heat conductivity

19. In a Freon 12 compressor type plant, the liquid is cooled by the suction gas before the liquid passes to the evaporator. The PRIMARY reason for doing this is to

   A. dry the suction gas
   B. boil off any oil which may be present in the suction gas
   C. take advantage of a simpler piping arrangement
   D. increase the refrigerating effect per pound of refrigerant pumped

19.____

20. The face air velocity going through a dry filter at 425 cubic feet per minute had a filter media of 1.0. If it increased to 0.50, the velocity of the air going through would

   A. decrease and remain steady
   B. increase and remain steady
   C. decrease and fluctuate
   D. remain the same

20.____

21. How would you install a cartridge type of dehydrator in an F-12, F-22, or F-500 system? _____ in the liquid line with the flange on the _____.

   A. Vertical; bottom
   B. Vertical; top
   C. Horizontal and vertical; top
   D. Horizontal or vertical; bottom

21.____

22. The term *anhydrous* used in connection with refrigerants indicates the

   A. presence of ammonia
   B. presence of water
   C. absence of Freon
   D. absence of water

22.____

23. The MAXIMUM amount of refrigerant that could be stored in a machinery room is _____ pounds.

   A. 600   B. 500   C. 400   D. 300

23.____

24. The purpose of using eliminators at the top of an evaporative condenser is to

   A. eliminate gas noises and vibration
   B. eliminate oil carry-over
   C. control the gas flow
   D. eliminate moisture carry-over

24.____

25. Unless approved by the proper authority, a flammable refrigerant shall NOT be used in a refrigerating system in excess of _____ lbs.

   A. 1000   B. 1200   C. 1400   D. 1500

25.____

KEY (CORRECT ANSWERS)

1. D
2. D
3. B
4. D
5. A

6. A
7. C
8. A
9. B
10. A

11. A
12. A
13. B
14. D
15. C

16. C
17. A
18. B
19. D
20. A

21. D
22. D
23. D
24. D
25. A

TEST 2

DIRECTIONS: Each question or incomplete statement is followed by several suggested answers or completions. Select the one that BEST answers the question or completes the statement. *PRINT THE LETTER OF THE CORRECT ANSWER IN THE SPACE AT THE RIGHT.*

1. When attempting to read the high side pressure gauge on an operating ammonia compressor, it is noted that the pointer *hunts,* or has a wide and relatively slow back and forth movement. This would MOST likely indicate that the compressor

    A. suction valves are stuck open
    B. is overloaded
    C. valve action is sluggish
    D. is operating normally

    1._____

2. In a two cylinder vertical single stage compressor equipped with a gear type oil pump for pressure lubrication, for good performance, the oil discharge pressure should range APPROXIMATELY from _____ psig above _____ pressure.

    A. 10 to 30; suction
    B. 10 to 30; head
    C. 50 to 90; suction
    D. 50 to 90; head

    2._____

3. An air conditioning system has mechanical refrigeration equipment which consists of 3 compressors, each of which may be operated at 50% or 100% capacity. The MAXIMUM number of capacities that this set can operate at is

    A. 3   B. 4   C. 6   D. 8

    3._____

4. What determines the MAXIMUM output of an electric motor?

    A. Engineers' rating
    B. Temperature of the motor
    C. Name plate rating
    D. Power supply

    4._____

5. The cylinder of an H.D.A. compressor is running hot and under decreased capacity. The reason for this is

    A. the suction is coming to compressor saturated
    B. a high plant demand
    C. broken oil and leaking piston rings
    D. suction coming back at 35 superheated

    5._____

6. There is (are) _____ baffle(s) in a three pass shell and tube condenser.

    A. one   B. two   C. three   D. four

    6._____

7. A 200 ton air conditioning plant is set up with 2 Freon compressors. Assuming that neither of the compressors is equipped with bypass solenoids, in order to be able to get AT LEAST four steps of capacity, these machines would be driven by _____ motors.

    A. synchronous
    B. capacitor
    C. induction repulsion
    D. wound rotor induction

    7._____

8. The term *viscosity* in refrigeration oil means

    A. internal friction
    B. corrosive action
    C. weight value
    D. ability to mix

    8._____

9. Muntz metal CANNOT be used with

   A. ammonia
   B. Freon 12
   C. carbon dioxide
   D. methyl chloride

10. What color does red litmus paper turn when ammonia is present?

    A. Red   B. White   C. Blue   D. No change

11. Good chemical structure of a refrigerant is determined by

    A. viscosity
    B. refrigerant stability
    C. flammability
    D. a low critical point

12. _____ does NOT increase the capacity of a water cooled condenser.

    A. Refrigerant gas
    B. Ambient temperature
    C. Water temperature
    D. Quantity of water

13. If an equalizer line is placed immediately on the discharge side of the thermostatic expansion valve, it is installed

    A. incorrectly
    B. very well
    C. well, but not practically
    D. according to manufacturer's specifications

14. In a refrigerating system with a gauge, the dial points to 100 psig. Under normal operating conditions, the LAST number of the gauge should read

    A. 105   B. 110   C. 115   D. 120

15. Many Freons are used for air conditioning. Regarding F-11, it can be said that a _____ type compressor is needed.

    A. large centrifugal
    B. large rotary
    C. small rotary
    D. large reciprocating

16. The thermal expansion valve is rated by

    A. tons of refrigeration
    B. pounds of pressure per hour
    C. pounds of pressure per minute
    D. cubic inches per minute

17. For a given application, a particular compressor is found to have a volumetric efficiency of 72% when operating at its design speed of 300 rpm. If the speed is increased to 500 rpm, it is MOST likely that the volumetric efficiency will

    A. decrease
    B. increase and remain higher as long as it is run at the higher speed
    C. remain constant at 72%
    D. increase for the first 24 hours of operation at the higher speed and then decrease

18. A finned evaporator coil is equipped with a thermal expansion valve. The bulb of this valve is properly clamped to the suction line at the coil. In normal operation, the suction gas will leave this coil MOST NEARLY in a state of

    A. 5° F to 9° F of superheat
    B. 20° F to 30° F of superheat
    C. saturation
    D. 1° F to 2° F of superheat

18.____

19. Of the following types of water-cooled condensers, the one which consists of one or more assemblies of two tubes, one within the other, in which the refrigerant vapor is condensed in the annular space or in the inner tube, is known as the _____ condenser.

    A. atmospheric   B. shell and coil
    C. shell and U-tube   D. double pipe

19.____

20. How many gallons of water can an irregular-shaped container having a volume of 8085 cubic inches hold?

    A. 25   B. 30   C. 35   D. 40

20.____

21. The use of screwed joints in refrigeration systems for refrigerant pressures above 250 psi is permitted, provided that the nominal size of the pipe is NOT more than _____ inches.

    A. 1 1/4   B. 1 3/4   C. 2 1/4   D. 3

21.____

22. The capacity of a water-cooled condenser will increase whenever the temperature difference between the refrigerant gas and the water is increased. To INCREASE the capacity of a water-cooled condenser, an operator would

    A. increase the quantity of water
    B. raise the temperature of the entering water
    C. raise the condensing pressure
    D. decrease the power input to the compressor

22.____

23. In a large air conditioning installation consisting of three direct expansion conditioners and a single Freon compressor, a thermostat is installed on each conditioner. The compressor would be under the control of

    A. condenser water   B. any two thermostats
    C. any one thermostat   D. a low pressurestat

23.____

24. The volume of a cylinder with a 10" bore and a 12" stroke is _____ cubic inches.

    A. 502   B. 621   C. 892   D. 942

24.____

25. In an F-12 compression system used for an air conditioning installation operating at a suction pressure of 45 psi, the evaporating temperature would be _____ F.

    A. 60   B. 50   C. 40   D. 30

25.____

KEY (CORRECT ANSWERS)

1.	C	11.	B
2.	A	12.	B
3.	C	13.	A
4.	B	14.	D
5.	B	15.	A
6.	B	16.	A
7.	D	17.	A
8.	A	18.	A
9.	A	19.	D
10.	C	20.	C

21. D
22. A
23. D
24. D
25. B

TEST 3

DIRECTIONS: Each question or incomplete statement is followed by several suggested answers or completions. Select the one that BEST answers the question or completes the statement. *PRINT THE LETTER OF THE CORRECT ANSWER IN THE SPACE AT THE RIGHT.*

1. The percentage of oil circulated with the refrigerant in a well-designed refrigeration system should NOT be more than _____ %. 1.____

   A. 10 B. 20 C. 25 D. 30

2. In an air conditioning plant equipped with an indirect low side using water as a brine, the sequence to follow for plant operation is to 2.____

   A. start the compressor
   B. test safety valves
   C. start fan and circulating pump first
   D. set expansion valve

3. The strong liquor in the absorber will become WEAKER when the 3.____

   A. expansion valve is closed
   B. evaporator load increases
   C. evaporator load decreases
   D. condenser pressure decreases

4. Copper and its alloys would NOT be used with 4.____

   A. ammonia   B. sulphur dioxide
   C. carbon dioxide   D. methyl chloride

5. To detect a Freon 12 leak, the halide torch flame would 5.____

   A. go out   B. change color
   C. stay the same   D. give off white smoke

6. A refrigerant unit used for air conditioning is pumped down and secured for the fall and winter. As an operator, you notice frost on the outlet side of the king valve. This would be caused by 6.____

   A. foul air or non-condensable gases in the receiver
   B. water in refrigerant
   C. valve seized in closed position
   D. leaky valve seat or plug

7. What type fittings are used on an ammonia compression system? 7.____

   A. Flanged   B. Tongue and groove
   C. Male and female face D. Serrated

8. A ten ton refrigeration unit has the capacity of _____ BTU per minute. 8.____

   A. 2,000 B. 20,000 C. 12,000 D. 288,000

9. A forced feed lubricator for a horizontal compressor uses refrigeration oil and has two lines leading to the

   A. cross head and seal
   B. stuffing box and crank pin
   C. wrist pin and cylinder
   D. stuffing box and cylinder

10. In the compression system with a low side float, the ball in the float is punctured and sinks. What would MOST likely happen? The

    A. low side would be falling with compressor running
    B. low side would be rising with compressor running
    C. head pressure would fall
    D. compressor would stop and head pressure would rise

11. In order to get long-term protection against rust action of brine in the ice field, you would use

    A. aluminum sulphate
    B. sodium dichromate
    C. Nessler's solution
    D. universal indicator solution

12. Of the following Freons, the one which has the HIGHEST refrigeration effect is F-

    A. 12   B. 114   C. 11   D. 113

13. Upon inspecting a TEV installation, you find that the thermal bulb is clamped to the pipe right after the expansion valve. The result is that

    A. the expansion valve would continually flood the coil
    B. the opening would continually freeze in a wide open position
    C. this is incorrect and would starve the cooling coil
    D. oil and moisture would be more likely to accumulate

14. The NEAREST boiling point for F-22 in degrees minus Fahrenheit is

    A. 40   B. 50   C. 30   D. 20

15. In a vertical single-acting compressor with an oil pump as part of the compressor, the suction pressure is 30#. The oil gauge should read APPROXIMATELY _____ pounds.

    A. 30   B. 20   C. 80   D. 50

16. A water-cooled condenser with a tube within a tube and the refrigerant in the outer tube is a(n) _____ condenser.

    A. shell and coil   B. double pipe
    C. shell and tube   D. atmospheric

17. In a carbon dioxide system, the oiling method is USUALLY

    A. splash system   B. low pressure oiling
    C. high pressure oiling   D. excess refrigerant receiver

18. When Freon 12 compressors are running in parallel, the reason for connecting the crankcases in parallel is to

   A. maintain steady suction pressure
   B. maintain the oil at the same level
   C. equalize the load
   D. obtain lower temperature

19. Refrigerant enters the condenser as a _____ gas and leaves as a _____.

   A. superheated; high temperature gas
   B. high pressure; low pressure liquid
   C. high pressure; high pressure liquid
   D. superheated; superheated gas

20. In a Freon air conditioning system that is used to cool the entire office, the ratio or horsepower in reference to tons of refrigeration is MOST NEARLY

   A. 1   B. 2   C. 2.50   D. 3.5

21. Of the following thermal properties of a refrigerant, the one that is NOT desirable is

   A. a convenient evaporator and condensing pressure
   B. high latent heat of evaporization and high vapor specific heat
   C. low critical and high freezing temperature
   D. low viscosity and high film heat conductivity

22. An accumulator is MOST commonly used with a

   A. condenser
   B. direct expansion evaporator
   C. flooded evaporator
   D. high pressure system

23. An absorption system is to be placed into operation under standard ton conditions, a suction of 19.5#, and discharge of 156#. The steam gauge reads 5 psig. What is the consumption of steam per ton hour of refrigeration?

   A. 10   B. 20   C. 50   D. 100

24. The MAXIMUM pounds in a direct system per 1,000 cubic foot of occupied space for Freon 12 is

   A. 31   B. 41   C. 51   D. 61

25. How many stop valves are required by the code in a system using 30# of Group 1 refrigerant and having two compressors and two receivers?

   A. Two   B. Four   C. Five   D. 'Six

KEY (CORRECT ANSWERS)

1. A
2. B
3. C
4. A
5. B

6. D
7. C
8. A
9. D
10. B

11. B
12. C
13. C
14. A
15. D

16. B
17. C
18. B
19. C
20. A

21. C
22. C
23. C
24. A
25. D

EXAMINATION SECTION
TEST 1

DIRECTIONS: Each question or incomplete statement is followed by several suggested answers or completions. Select the one that BEST answers the question or completes the statement. *PRINT THE LETTER OF THE CORRECT ANSWER IN THE SPACE AT THE RIGHT.*

1. When attempting to read the high side pressure gauge on an operating ammonia compressor, it is noted that the pointer *hunts,* or has a wide and relatively slow back and forth movement.
   This would MOST likely indicate that the compressor

   A. suction valves are stuck open
   B. is overloaded
   C. valve action is sluggish
   D. is operating normally

   1.____

2. Most of the modern refrigerating compressors operate on dry compression.
   A result of this method of operation is that the refrigerant leaves the compressor as a

   A. superheated gas
   B. mixture of superheated gas and liquid
   C. saturated gas
   D. saturated liquid with gas mixed in

   2.____

3. Change 65° Centigrade to a Fahrenheit reading.

   A. 157° F   B. 180° F   C. 135° F   D. 149° F

   3.____

4. In comparing a waterless air conditioning unit to a regular water-cooled type, under normal operating conditions, you would find the

   A. head pressure for the waterless to be lower
   B. head pressure for the waterless to be higher
   C. aqua pump is lower than the condenser
   D. suction pressure to be continually the same

   4.____

5. How many stop valves are required by code in a system using 80# of Group 1 refrigerant and having two compressors and two receivers?

   A. 2   B. 4   C. 5   D. 6

   5.____

6. Refrigerant 40 is

   A. ammonia   B. sulphur dioxide
   C. ethylene   D. methyl chloride

   6.____

7. In a calcium chloride brine tank of 1000 cubic feet, how many pounds of dichromate would you use in the initial batch?

   A. 20   B. 40   C. 100   D. 200

   7.____

8. In an automatic Freon 12 system for air conditioning, you, as the original installer, have to make a tight pipe joint.
   You would use a

   A. *streamline fitting* and solder to copper piping
   B. *threaded fitting* and white lead
   C. combination of solder, litharge, glycerine, and white lead
   D. serrated flange without a lead gasket

9. The LEAST effective way to remove gaseous odors from a plant is by

   A. ventilation
   B. water spray
   C. charcoal filter
   D. neutralization

10. Which of the following refrigerants is in Group 2?

    A. F-12
    B. Methyl chloride
    C. Isobutane
    D. Ethane

11. A motor has a protection device to prevent burning out or damage called a

    A. fusetron
    B. thermal protector
    C. circuit breaker
    D. dual fuse

12. What is the LOWEST operating temperature you would recommend for a calcium chloride brine at a specific gravity of 1.28?
    _____ °F.

    A. 40   B. 60   C. 20   D. 0

13. A brine solution having a pH value of 10, as compared to a similar brine solution with a pH value of 8, is said to be _____ as alkaline.

    A. twice
    B. 10 times
    C. 100 times
    D. 50 times

14. If it were decided to DECREASE the condenser exit water temperature from 12° to 9° with a fixed load, you would

    A. increase the condenser water 25%
    B. reduce the condenser water 25%
    C. reduce the charge
    D. increase the compressor 25%

15. The color of the lubricating oil that is USUALLY used in a carbon dioxide refrigeration system in the production of dry ice is

    A. pale orange
    B. lily or water white
    C. extra pale lemon
    D. pale lemon

16. A pipe 2" in diameter and 288' long weighs 1500 pounds when empty.
    How much would it weigh when full of water?

    A. 1700#   B. 1800#   C. 1900#   D. 2000#

17. A brine coil in a cooler is along the ceiling. 17.____
    The coil has insulating baffles that are used to

    A. catch the dripping when the coils are defrosting
    B. supply gravity air to circulate over the coil
    C. support the brine coil
    D. defrost the coil

18. Carron oil (a liniment used for ammonia burns) is made up of equal parts of 18.____

    A. vaseline and picric acid
    B. lanolin and vinegar
    C. linseed oil and lime water
    D. sulphur dioxide and water

19. The units of vacuum given on a compound pressure gauge is inches of 19.____

    A. water   B. mercury   C. ammonia   D. air

20. A large synchronous motor uses both AC and DC to run it and is at a constant speed. 20.____
    What current is used to start this motor?

    A. DC   B. AC and DC
    C. AC   D. Single phase

21. You would NOT use muntz metal with 21.____

    A. carbon dioxide   B. ammonia
    C. Freon 12   D. methyl chloride

22. A Freon compressor was V-belt driven when installed, but the belts were too tight. 22.____
    After the unit has been running for a while, this will

    A. increase the speed of the compressor
    B. decrease the speed of the motor and the compressor
    C. increase the speed of the motor
    D. cause the motor to run hot

23. In a room, there is a cylinder half-filled with ammonia at 50° F. 23.____
    The pressure inside the tank will be

    A. 40#   B. 125#   C. 75#   D. 250#

24. The percentage of oil that travels with refrigerant in a system is _____ %. 24.____

    A. 10   B. 125   C. 30   D. 50

25. A hermetically sealed unit is a unit with the 25.____

    A. motor and compressor both enclosed in a sealed casing
    B. motor only sealed in a casing
    C. compressor only sealed in a casing
    D. carrier absorption system

KEY (CORRECT ANSWERS)

1.	C	11.	B
2.	A	12.	A
3.	D	13.	C
4.	B	14.	A
5.	D	15.	B
6.	D	16.	C
7.	C	17.	B
8.	A	18.	C
9.	D	19.	B
10.	B	20.	C

21. C
22. D
23. C
24. A
25. A

TEST 2

DIRECTIONS: Each question or incomplete statement is followed by several suggested answers or completions. Select the one that BEST answers the question or completes the statement. *PRINT THE LETTER OF THE CORRECT ANSWER IN THE SPACE AT THE RIGHT.*

1. If the liquid line is warmer than usual, this indicates

    A. too much refrigerant
    B. shortage of refrigerant
    C. receiver is full of liquid
    D. high head pressure

2. If the line between the king valve and the expansion valve begins to sweat, the cause is MOST likely

    A. partially clogged liquid line
    B. air in the system
    C. completely clogged liquid line
    D. excessive oil in the system

3. There is a sight glass in the liquid line before the expansion valve. Upon inspection, bubbles are seen, which indicate

    A. non-condensable gases in the receiver
    B. the purger will rectify this
    C. air is going to the expansion valve
    D. there is a shortage of refrigerant

4. If you were to put a line vibration eliminator in a Freon 12 system to make the joints gas-tight, you would use

    A. garlock packing
    B. red indian shellac
    C. silver solder or braze the joints
    D. litharge and glycerine

5. The capacity of a water-cooled condenser is LEAST affected by the

    A. temperature of the water
    B. temperature of the refrigerant gas
    C. ambient air temperature
    D. quantity of water circulated

6. In relationship to brine, as the specific gravity INCREASES,

    A. freezing temperature is lowered
    B. freezing point will vary
    C. density is decreased
    D. freezing temperature goes up

7. If the float of a low pressure side float is punctured and sinks, the

   A. suction pressure is lowered
   B. head pressure is increased
   C. suction pressure is increased
   D. evaporator coils will frost

8. When withdrawing refrigerant from a system into containers, they CANNOT be filled more than _____ %.

   A. 70   B. 75   C. 80   D. 85

9. In the absorption system, the counterflow heat exchanger is located between the

   A. condenser and receiver
   B. generator and absorber
   C. generator and rectifier
   D. aqua pump and absorber

10. The concentration of a brine which is used in an indirect system is determined by

    A. an Orsat meter
    B. a pitot device
    C. Nessler's reagent
    D. a hydrometer

11. In a brine cooler system, the suction pressure dropped, and it was noticed at the same time that the brine temperature also dropped.
    To correct this,

    A. readjust the expansion valve and check the brine temperature of the indicator
    B. readjust the brine temperature indicator and watch the temperature of the brine
    C. throttle the suction valve and watch the brine indicator
    D. purge the system and watch the indicator

12. If you were operating a condenser on the roof surrounded by water in pans and were having trouble with a heavy formation of ice on the coils during the cold winter months, the BEST procedure would be to

    A. remove the heavy ice from the coils
    B. disregard the matter entirely
    C. bypass hot gas through the coils
    D. shut off the water and operate strictly atmospheric

13. In a reciprocating system, the *cubic feet pumped per minute per ton* for ammonia would be _____ cubic feet.

    A. 2   B. 4   C. 5.5   D. 6.25

14. Where does the steam condensate go when it leaves the rectifier?

    A. Absorber
    B. Generator
    C. Liquid cooler
    D. Evaporator

15. Gaskets used for ammonia flanges are made of

    A. rubber
    B. neoprene
    C. asbestos and copper
    D. sheet lead

16. How many pounds of refrigerant may be stored in a machinery room if the system has 150 pounds in it?

   A. 15 B. 30 C. 45 D. 60

17. A Fahrenheit thermometer that reads -10° F, if changed to Centigrade, would read -_____ °C.

   A. 18 B. 21 C. 23 D. 20.2

18. The scale trap is located between the

   A. compressor and condenser
   B. condenser and receiver
   C. evaporator and condenser
   D. evaporator and compressor

19. Regarding the centrifugal compressors, it is TRUE that

   A. only the main bearing and thrust need to be oiled
   B. refrigerant leaks into the oiling system are common
   C. they have no auxiliary oil pump
   D. the auxiliary oil pump is hand-operated

20. There are dummy tubes, or a *Tell Tale,* welded to the shell of a large accumulator in an industrial ammonia plant.
    The pipe extends through the insulation.
    Its purpose is to

   A. increase the capacity of the system
   B. facilitate taking ammonia samples
   C. check and mark the refrigerant level in the vessel
   D. make the accumulator physically stronger

21. In case of an accident with an absorption system, the

   A. ammonia pump should immediately be shut down
   B. water supply to the condenser should be increased
   C. steam should be shut off
   D. absorber pressure should be lowered or reduced by discharging it to the sewer

22. The formula $C = .8P_1D^2$ is used to compute the rated discharge of a rupture member. When P_1 is 30 and D is 2, C is

   A. 120 B. 96 C. 86 D. 60

23. A scale trap placed in the suction line of a compression system to remove foreign matter would be MOST effective when the plant is

   A. new
   B. shut down for a long time
   C. old
   D. only using modern compressors

24. When field testing refrigerant 12, the high and low side would be tested to

   A. 300# - 150#
   B. 235# - 110#
   C. 95# - 50#
   D. 1500# - 100#

25. If the sight glass on a receiver was to break, you would lose   25._____

    A. all the refrigerant in the system
    B. the refrigerant in the receiver
    C. gas refrigerant
    D. the refrigerant in the sight glass

KEY (CORRECT ANSWERS)

1.	D	11.	A
2.	A	12.	D
3.	D	13.	C
4.	C	14.	B
5.	C	15.	D
6.	A	16.	B
7.	C	17.	C
8.	B	18.	D
9.	B	19.	A
10.	D	20.	C

21. C
22. B
23. A
24. B
25. D

TEST 3

DIRECTIONS: Each question or incomplete statement is followed by several suggested answers or completions. Select the one that BEST answers the question or completes the statement. *PRINT THE LETTER OF THE CORRECT ANSWER IN THE SPACE AT THE RIGHT.*

1. Swirls in a condenser are for the purpose of directing water through the tubes. They are used in _____ condensers. 1._____

   A. double pipe
   B. horizontal
   C. multi-pass
   D. vertical shell and tube

2. How many kinds of lubricants are used in a horizontal double-acting compressor? 2._____

   A. One   B. Two   C. Three   D. Four

3. Flash gas would be found in the 3._____

   A. receiver
   B. condenser
   C. king valve
   D. evaporator

4. The accepted method to test oil for moisture content is the dielectric test. This test imposes high voltage electric pressure on electrodes immersed in an oil sample. If any current flows, there is moisture present. 4._____
   The electrodes are spaced _____ inch(es), _____ volts.

   A. 1/2 to 1; 40,000
   B. 1 to 2; 25,000
   C. 2 to 3; 22,000
   D. 1 1/2 to 4; 33,000

5. Heat transfer takes place by 5._____

   A. evaporation and convection
   B. radiation, conduction, and convection
   C. condensing, evaporation, and convection
   D. radiation, evaporation, and condensation

6. A pan of an evaporative condenser 8 feet long, 4 feet wide, and 9 inches deep can hold _____ gallons of water. 6._____

   A. 120   B. 180   C. 280   D. 204.5

7. A cartridge type dehydrator on a F-12, F-22, F-500 system should be installed vertical _____ with flange on _____. 7._____

   A. or horizontal in liquid line; bottom
   B. in liquid line; top
   C. and horizontal; top
   D. in liquid line; bottom

8. In testing condenser water for carbon dioxide leaks, you would use 8._____

   A. Nessler's solution
   B. bromthymol-blue
   C. a halide torch
   D. litmus paper

9. In a vertical shell and tube condenser, there are swirls at the top of the tubes. If a few of these swirls become blocked, then as a result the

   A. compressor would speed up
   B. suction pressure would drop
   C. plant capacity would decrease until suction pressure was constant
   D. flow of water would have to be increased to prevent head pressure from rising

10. A synchronous motor has 8 poles, 60 cycles, and 440 volts. The RPM of the motor is

    A. 900   B. 300   C. 3300   D. 4200

11. If the high pressure side of a compression system is reading considerably HIGHER than normal, you should

    A. slow compressor speed
    B. open the expansion valve
    C. increase the oil pressure
    D. send more water to the condenser

12. At standard ton conditions, the discharge of a system is 169.2 psia, and the suction pressure is 34.56 psia.
    The compression ratio is

    A. 2.5:1   B. 212:1   C. 4.98:1   D. 6.8:1

13. How many pounds of liquid ammonia pass the expansion valve for 100 tons?

    A. 100   B. 20   C. 200   D. 50

14. Assume that an engine indicator is in perfect condition; however, when testing a compressor, the gauge shows 20# lower than the card graph of the indicator.
    This occurs because

    A. the indicator is for carbon dioxide
    B. the pressure gauge is defective
    C. this is normal
    D. the gauge is improperly connected

15. A compression type plant is equipped with a receiver which is known to be gas-tight. This receiver has a gauge glass which also is gas-tight. With the plant in operation, the operator sees bubbles rising through the liquid in the receiver gauge glass.
    An ACCEPTABLE explanation of this condition is that the

    A. pressure in the receiver is lower than that corresponding to room air temperature
    B. system is in need of purging for non-condensable gases
    C. system was recently purged
    D. pressure in the receiver is higher than that corresponding to room air temperature

16. Of the following refrigerants, the LEAST toxic and LEAST flammable is

    A. propane   B. R-11
    C. ammonia   D. methyl chloride

17. The boiling point for ammonia at atmospheric pressure is _____ °F. 17.____

    A. -21   B. 32   C. -28   D. 0

18. A shell and tube vertical condenser has _____ water box(es) on the _____. 18.____

    A. one; top   B. one; bottom
    C. one; bottom   D. two; bottom

19. The volume of a cylinder, 10" bore and a 14" stroke, is _____ cubic inches. 19.____

    A. 502   B. 621   C. 892   D. 1010

20. The piston rod of a horizontal ammonia compressor, when the cross-head is properly aligned, is MOST likely to wear 20.____

    A. at the crosshead end   B. at the piston end
    C. at the middle of the rod   D. on the side

21. The number of baffles in a three pass shell and tube cooler is 21.____

    A. one   B. two   C. three   D. four

22. In testing for ammonia leaks in a plant, red litmus paper is used. If ammonia is present, the color would change to 22.____

    A. blue   B. red   C. yellow   D. pink

23. With the same compressor displacement and the same suction pressure, which of the following will give the MOST refrigeration effect per pound pumped? 23.____

    A. Freon 12   B. Carrene
    C. Ammonia   D. Carbon dioxide

24. If Nessler's solution is added to a sample brine, in the event of ammonia being present, the color of the sample brine will turn 24.____

    A. blue   B. red   C. yellow   D. pink

25. It is said that the engine indicator card is used to show 25.____

    A. control of the evaporator
    B. efficiency of the suction and discharge valves
    C. control of the main drive
    D. not used on ammonia machines

KEY (CORRECT ANSWERS)

1.	D	11.	D
2.	A	12.	C
3.	D	13.	D
4.	A	14.	B
5.	B	15.	A
6.	B	16.	B
7.	A	17.	C
8.	B	18.	A
9.	C	19.	D
10.	A	20.	C

21. B
22. A
23. C
24. C
25. B

TEST 4

DIRECTIONS: Each question or incomplete statement is followed by several suggested answers or completions. Select the one that BEST answers the question or completes the statement. *PRINT THE LETTER OF THE CORRECT ANSWER IN THE SPACE AT THE RIGHT.*

1. Upon entering an ice plant, you notice that the refrigeration is rated at 250 tons capacity. It will make NEARLY _____ tons of ice. 1.____

   A. 175   B. 250   C. 300   D. 150

2. In an ice plant, the agitation air is precooled because it 2.____

   A. lessens the load on the ice field
   B. increases air compressor capacity
   C. prevents freezing of air lines
   D. decreases air pressure resistance

3. The one of the following compressors that would have the LEAST amount of side thrust and consequently less bearing wear is a 3.____

   A. horizontal double-acting compressor with a cross-head
   B. V-type of compressor with poppet valves
   C. vertical compressor with a safety head
   D. vertical twin compressor

4. Which of the following is CLOSEST to the boiling point for F-22 in degrees minus? 4.____

   A. 50° F   B. 40° F   C. 30° F   D. 20° F

5. Find the number of gallons of brine in a tank 5' x 22' x 31'. 5.____

   A. 12,500   B. 22,575   C. 224,000   D. 25,575

6. A dry filter used in air conditioning work gives a face velocity of FPM with a pressure loss of 0.10. 6.____
   If the pressure loss rises to 0.50, the velocity will be

   A. unchanged and steady   B. decreased and steady
   C. increased and steady   D. decreased and fluctuating

7. The refrigerant is liquified in the compression system by the 7.____

   A. compressor   B. evaporator
   C. receiver   D. condenser

8. A double pipe condenser has _____ in the inner pipe, _____ in the outer pipe, and _____ flow. 8.____

   A. water; gas; parallel   B. water; gas; counter
   C. gas; water; counter   D. gas; water; parallel

9. Which of the following statements refers to a class T machine room?

   A. It must have a door opening into or under a fire escape.
   B. It must have a sealed room with no less than two hours of fireproof construction.
   C. All pipes must be sealed into the wall, ceiling, and floor.
   D. All pipes piercing the wall and ceiling should be tightly sealed in a room of no less than one hour of fire resistance.

10. In an absorption system, the auxiliary piece of equipment is the

    A. generator
    B. analyzer
    C. absorber
    D. evaporator

11. In a system with one compressor using two evaporators of different temperatures, one at 35° F and the other at 20° F, the back pressure valve would be located on the

    A. common suction line
    B. common liquid line
    C. suction line nearer to the lower temperature cooler
    D. suction line of the high temperature cooler

12. Which of the following dessicants CANNOT be used in a refrigeration system?

    A. Drierite
    B. Calcium oxide
    C. Activated alumina
    D. Soda lime

13. If a compressor has adjustable clearance pockets and the seats begin to leak, this will cause

    A. suction pressure to drop
    B. discharge to increase
    C. compressor capacity to drop
    D. compressor speed to drop

14. In a packaged air comfort cooler that uses Freon 12, the back pressure is 40 lbs. This should be CLOSE to _____ ° F.

    A. 55   B. 112   C. 72   D. 45

15. Cross-over lines on an ammonia compressor are to pump down the

    A. low side
    B. compressors
    C. high side
    D. brine tank

16. What causes bulging of ice cans?

    A. Distilled water is overheated.
    B. Temperature of the water is too warm when the cans are filled.
    C. Ice cans are filled to overflowing.
    D. Refreezing of partly thawed cans

17. If it was decided to decrease the condenser exit water temperature from 12° F to 9° F with a fixed load, it would be necessary to

   A. increase the condenser water by 25%
   B. reduce the charge by 25%
   C. reduce the condenser water by 25%
   D. increase the compressor speed by 25%

18. There are several refrigerants in the Freon group that are in common use. Freon 11 is widely used in air conditioning systems that have _____ compressors.

   A. large reciprocating   B. small reciprocating
   C. rotary   D. large centrifugal

19. What color does blue litmus paper turn when ammonia is present?

   A. Red   B. White   C. Blue   D. No change

20. When the specific gravity of a brine is 1.28 (calcium chloride), the NEAREST freezing point is - _____ ° F.

   A. 20   B. 30   C. 40   D. 59

21. In a given temperature of air, the ratio of vapor pressure to humidity is called

   A. absolute humidity   B. relative humidity
   C. pressure   D. partial pressure

22. In an R-12 refrigeration system with a correct-sized thermostatic expansion valve (on the basis of evaporator temperature and pressure drop), flash gas should be prevented. In order to do this, an operator would add to the system a(n)

   A. small rectifier
   B. liquid line heat exchanger
   C. after-cooler
   D. purifier of adequate size

23. A compressor that has two compression strokes and two suction strokes per cylinder per revolution of the crankshaft is a

   A. single-acting compressor
   B. double-acting compressor
   C. two-stage compressor
   D. compressor in duplex

24. The speed, in revolutions per minute, of a six pole, synchronous motor rated at 80 HP, 400 volts, and 60 cycles is

   A. 480   B. 900   C. 1200   D. 1800

25. The capacity of an evaporative condenser increases as _____ bulb temperature _____.

   A. wet; decreases   B. wet; increases
   C. wet and dry; increases   D. dry; increases

KEY (CORRECT ANSWERS)

1. D
2. C
3. A
4. B
5. D

6. B
7. D
8. B
9. D
10. B

11. D
12. D
13. C
14. D
15. C

16. D
17. A
18. D
19. D
20. C

21. B
22. B
23. B
24. C
25. D

EXAMINATION SECTION
TEST 1

DIRECTIONS: Each question or incomplete statement is followed by several suggested answers or completions. Select the one that BEST answers the question or completes the statement. *PRINT THE LETTER OF THE CORRECT ANSWER IN THE SPACE AT THE RIGHT.*

1. The number of pounds of liquid ammonia circulated per minute per ton is

   A. 1.2   B. 1.5   C. .45   D. .8

2. A brine solution having a pH value of 10, as compared to a similar brine solution with a pH value of 8, is said to be _____ as alkaline.

   A. twice   B. 10 times   C. 100 times   D. 50 times

3. An ammonia drum is half full of liquid ammonia at 50° F. This is NEAR _____ pounds.

   A. 75   B. 100   C. 50   D. 150

4. A dry compression refrigeration system typically

   A. has water cooler jackets
   B. injects refrigerant into cylinders
   C. does not use an oil separator
   D. vaporizes refrigerant directly into the evaporator

5. The recommended temperature and humidity for a bakery display case with no frozen food is _____ ° F and _____ % RH.

   A. 51-53; 55
   B. 46-50; 55
   C. 36-40; 60
   D. 42-55; 40

6. The LEAST effective way to remove gaseous odors from a plant is by

   A. ventilation   B. water spray
   C. charcoal filter   D. neutralization

7. In testing for a strong leak in Freon 12, the color of the flame turns

   A. pink   B. blue   C. green   D. orange

8. In a Freon 12 system, a shell and coil condenser was replaced by a properly designed evaporative condenser. The amount of water used with the NEW condenser in comparison with the old one would be

   A. decreased by 40 to 50%   B. increased by 80 to 90%
   C. decreased by 85 to 90%   D. increased by 40 to 50%

9. Upon installing an accumulator, where would you place it in the system?

   A. On the suction side of the compressor
   B. Just before the condenser on the discharge side of the system

C. On the high side of the liquid line
D. Before the king valve

10. In order to get long-term protection against rust action of brine in the ice field, you would use

    A. aluminum sulphate
    B. sodium dichromate
    C. Nessler's solution
    D. universal indicator solution

11. Frost that appears on the evaporator coils of a direct expansion system is BEST removed by

    A. a scraper
    B. passing hot vapor through the coils
    C. shutting down coils
    D. should not be removed

12. Regarding a centrifugal compressor, which one of the following is TRUE?

    A. Refrigerant leaks into the oiling system are common.
    B. Only the main bearings and thrust need to be oiled.
    C. There is no auxiliary oil pump.
    D. The auxiliary oil pump is hand-operated.

13. A bypass valve on a reciprocating compressor with two or more cylinders is to

    A. regulate the capacity
    B. regulate the oil level
    C. increase the refrigerating effect
    D. use when stopping unit

14. The gross volume of a cooler, in cubic feet, whose size is 5'0" in diameter and 25'0" long is MOST NEARLY

    A. 500   B. 650   C. 850   D. 950

15. An oil lantern as a packing gland is generally found in a _____ compressor.

    A. vertical multi-cylinder Freon
    B. horizontal double-acting ammonia
    C. vertical multi-cylinder sulphur dioxide
    D. carrene centrifugal

16. A cartridge type of dehydrator should be installed in an F-12, F-22, and F-500 system _____ with the flange on the _____ .

    A. vertical in the line; bottom
    B. horizontal or vertical in the liquid line; bottom
    C. vertical in the liquid line; top
    D. horizontal and vertical; top

17. The concentration of a brine, which is being used in an indirect cooling system, is MOST conveniently determined by

    A. Orsat analyzer
    B. hydrometer
    C. Nessler's reagent
    D. Pitot tube

18. An air conditioning Freon unit that uses the work developed by a 10 horsepower compressor motor drive would LIKELY have a capacity of nearly _____ tons.

    A. 14.0 B. 20.0 C. 30.0 D. 10

19. If the float of a low pressure side float is punctured and sinks, the

    A. suction pressure is lowered
    B. head pressure is increased
    C. suction pressure is increased
    D. evaporator coils will frost

20. How many stop valves are REQUIRED in a system using 80# of Group 1 refrigerant and having two compressors and two receivers?

    A. 2 B. 4 C. 5 D. 6

21. When withdrawing refrigerant from a system into containers, they CANNOT be filled more than _____ %.

    A. 70 B. 75 C. 80 D. 85

22. In the absorption system, the counterflow heat exchanger is located between the

    A. condenser and receiver
    B. generator and absorber
    C. generator and rectifier
    D. aqua pump and absorber

23. For a pressure testing of newly installed R-12 systems, it is BEST to use

    A. dry carbon dioxide with a trace of R-12 in it
    B. water in a hydrostatic test
    C. dry hydrogen with a trace of R-12 in it
    D. anhydrous ammonia

24. A dehydrator should be used in a(n) _____ system.

    A. sulphur dioxide
    B. Freon 12
    C. ammonia
    D. carbon dioxide

25. Anhydrous liquid ammonia is MOST like water in that it(s)

    A. saturates at atmospheric temperature
    B. color is the same
    C. sublimes at 212° and at 14.69# absolute
    D. odor is the same

KEY (CORRECT ANSWERS)

1. C
2. C
3. A
4. A
5. C

6. D
7. C
8. D
9. A
10. B

11. B
12. B
13. A
14. A
15. B

16. B
17. B
18. D
19. C
20. D

21. B
22. B
23. A
24. B
25. B

TEST 2

DIRECTIONS: Each question or incomplete statement is followed by several suggested answers or completions. Select the one that BEST answers the question or completes the statement. *PRINT THE LETTER OF THE CORRECT ANSWER IN THE SPACE AT THE RIGHT.*

1. The acceptable amount of superheat of the refrigerant leaving the evaporator coil is USUALLY

    A. 1-7°   B. 5-7°   C. 7-9°   D. 10-15°

    1._____

2. Refrigerating oils should NOT

    A. have a low pour point
    B. have a high flash point
    C. have a high flash viscosity
    D. be free from moisture

    2._____

3. If the Freon 12 air conditioning system was over-charged,

    A. it would operate normally
    B. suction pressure would decrease
    C. head pressure would increase
    D. the refrigeration effect would increase

    3._____

4. A standard for the barometric height at sea level is 29.92" of mercury. This would be equal to _____ mm.

    A. 760   B. 970   C. 1728   D. 144

    4._____

5. In an ammonia system using city harbor water, what would you use if you suspected a leak in the condenser water?

    A. Calcium chloride solution
    B. Alkaline solution
    C. Nessler's solution
    D. Halide torch

    5._____

6. The BEST explanation for a safety valve discharge is discharge to the

    A. low pressure side
    B. low pressure side and atmosphere
    C. atmosphere or low side, which in turn is protected by the mixer
    D. none of the above

    6._____

7. An agitator used in a large ice plant's brine system could be found in the

    A. receiver   B. ice tank
    C. ice room   D. accumulator

    7._____

8. If the head pressure of an ammonia absorption system went up, you would check the

    A. amount of water going to the condenser
    B. temperature of the water on the condenser

    8._____

C. steam pressure on the generator
D. all of the above

9. Admiralty brass is NOT used with

   A. Freon 22
   B. Freon 12
   C. ammonia
   D. carbon dioxide

10. Which of the following refrigerants is the LEAST toxic and LEAST flammable?

    A. F-11
    B. Propane
    C. Ammonia
    D. Methyl chloride

11. The CORRECT location for a gas charging connection in a refrigeration system is on the line between the

    A. compressor and condenser
    B. evaporator and compressor
    C. condenser and king valve
    D. condenser and receiver

12. In an air conditioning installation with three evaporators on one unit and each evaporator thermostatically controlled, the compressor is directly controlled by

    A. condenser water temperature
    B. any 2 or 3 thermostats
    C. any 1 thermostat
    D. pressurestat

13. In the compression system with a low side float, if the ball in the float is punctured and sinks, what would MOST likely happen?
    The

    A. low side would be falling with compressor running
    B. low side would be rising with compressor running
    C. head pressure would fall
    D. compressor would stop and head pressure would rise

14. In a well-designed system, _____ the refrigerant charge can be stored in the receiver.

    A. half
    B. a quarter of
    C. twice
    D. all of

15. How many pounds of refrigerant may be stored in a machine room if the system has 150 pounds in it?

    A. 15
    B. 30
    C. 45
    D. 60

16. In a brine tank of 1000 cubic feet, how many pounds of dichromate would you use for calcium chloride to inhibit the brine?

    A. 20
    B. 40
    C. 100
    D. 200

17. In the compression system, an oil separator is installed 17.____
    A. before the expansion valve
    B. in the line from the evaporator
    C. in the discharge line as far from the compressor as possible
    D. between the condenser and the receiver

18. The RPM of a 60 cycle, six pole synchronous motor is 18.____
    A. 2000   B. 1500   C. 1800   D. 1200

19. The capacity of an evaporative condenser will INCREASE 19.____
    A. if the wet bulb reading is high
    B. if the wet bulb reading is low
    C. never
    D. if less water is used

20. The cylinder of a horizontal double-acting compressor is running hot and at decreased capacity. 20.____
    This could occur because
    A. of broken piston rings and oil leaking
    B. gas to compressor is 35° F superheated
    C. gas to compressor is saturated
    D. of a high plant demand factor

21. From the following formula, compute the RPM of a single-acting compressor with a 6" stroke, piston travels 300 feet per minute. 21.____

    Speed in feet per minute = $\dfrac{2 \times S \times RPM}{12}$

    A. 100   B. 200   C. 300   D. 600

22. One gallon of dichromate brine is composed of _____ pounds of _____ . 22.____
    A. 2 1/2; sodium dichromate in brine
    B. 2 1/2; sodium dichromate per gallon of water
    C. 1 1/2; salt-free sodium chloride per gallon of water
    D. 1 1/2; sodium dichromate per gallon of water

23. In a room, there is a tank half-filled with ammonia at 50° F. 23.____
    The pressure inside the tank will be APPROXIMATELY _____ pounds.
    A. 40   B. 125   C. 75   D. 250

24. The _____ will prevent the liquid refrigerant from coming back to the compressor. 24.____
    A. oil trap   B. muffler
    C. accumulator   D. none of the above

25. Methyl chloride and Freon 12 are SIMILAR in 25.____
    A. cost   B. miscibility with oil
    C. vapor density   D. atomic structure

KEY (CORRECT ANSWERS)

1.	C	11.	B
2.	C	12.	D
3.	C	13.	B
4.	A	14.	D
5.	C	15.	B
6.	B	16.	C
7.	B	17.	C
8.	D	18.	D
9.	C	19.	B
10.	A	20.	A

21.	C
22.	B
23.	C
24.	C
25.	B

TEST 3

DIRECTIONS: Each question or incomplete statement is followed by several suggested answers or completions. Select the one that BEST answers the question or completes the statement. *PRINT THE LETTER OF THE CORRECT ANSWER IN THE SPACE AT THE RIGHT.*

1. A refrigeration plant has a single compressor which serves two evaporators, one of which operates at 40° F.
   For this condition, a back pressure or two temperature valve should be properly installed in the

   A. low pressure suction line
   B. high temperature suction line
   C. low pressure suction line
   D. liquid line to the high temperature coil

   1._____

2. In cold storage used for fresh meat for a retail market, it is good practice to keep the meat at _____ °F.

   A. 0   B. 10   C. 40   D. 65

   2._____

3. _____ determines the freezing point of a salt brine.

   A. Specific heat   B. Latent heat
   C. Specific gravity   D. Purity

   3._____

4. When a refrigerant passes through the expansion valve, the pressure and temperature drop.
   This is caused by

   A. some of the refrigerant evaporating as it passes through the expansion valve
   B. the rate of refrigerant flow through the system
   C. the temperature and pressure of the refrigerant before it passes through the expansion valve
   D. the superheat of the refrigerant

   4._____

5. To make an ammonia pipe gas-tight at a threaded joint, you would use

   A. white lead   B. litharge and glycerine
   C. graphite   D. red lead and oil

   5._____

6. The liquid seal in a compression refrigeration system is found in the

   A. compressor   B. evaporator
   C. condenser   D. receiver

   6._____

7. In detecting an ammonia leak with white litmus paper, the change in color would be from

   A. pink to red   B. gray to black
   C. yellow to orange   D. blue to black

   7._____

93

8. If the liquid seal in a receiver was lost, _____ would go to the _____.

    A. condenser hot vapor; liquid line and evaporate
    B. non-condensed hot vapor; liquid line
    C. condensed liquid refrigerant; compressor
    D. condensed liquid refrigerant; receiver

9. A large synchronous motor uses both AC and DC to run it, and it is at constant speed. What current is used to start this motor?

    A. AC and DC
    B. AC
    C. DC
    D. Single phase

10. Units of vacuum, as given on a compound pressure gauge, are in inches of

    A. water   B. ammonia   C. mercury   D. air

11. The frost that is formed on an evaporator coil operating at 35°F is caused by

    A. moisture in the refrigerant
    B. water in the refrigerant
    C. moisture in the area where the coil is located
    D. water in the liquid line

12. A vacuum gauge reads 11".
    This would be close to a pressure absolute of

    A. 14   B. 8   C. 30   D. 4

13. The BEST operating efficiency can be obtained by maintaining a maximum

    A. superheat
    B. suction pressure
    C. discharge pressure
    D. constant water flow

14. Which one of the following is a Group 2 refrigerant?

    A. Butane
    B. Methyl chloride
    C. Dichlorodifluoromethane
    D. Ethylene

15. A thermostat expansion valve is MOST likely set for which of the following superheats?

    A. 20° F   B. 5° F   C. 21° F   D. 10° F

16. With the same compressor displacement and the same suction pressure, which refrigerant will give the MOST effect per pound pumped?

    A. Freon   B. Carrene   C. Ammonia   D. CO_2

17. To test for ammonia leaks in a brine, you would use

    A. litmus paper
    B. a halide torch
    C. Nessier's solution
    D. carrene

18. A reciprocating compressor is operating with a matched set of five V belts. One of the belts is worn out.
    The operator would

    A. remove the worn belt and replace with a new one
    B. replace all of the five belts
    C. remove the worn belt and operate with four
    D. replace the worn belt plus two new belts

19. A compressor running for an extended period of time with the main suction valve closed and the main discharge valve open would

    A. increase capacity of the system
    B. blow head off the compressor
    C. draw in non-condensable gases
    D. warm liquid line or high suction pressure

20. An operator erroneously used an oil with a paraffin base.
    The result would be that(the)(it)

    A. expansion valve would freeze up and cause high suction
    B. would foul the low side and coat the inside of the evaporator with wax
    C. cylinder would foul and cut into the walls of the same
    D. compressor would seize because of stoppage

21. A shell and coil condenser has a pipe 1 inch in diameter, 144 feet long, and weighs 750 pounds when empty.
    How much does it weigh when FULL of water?

    A. 800#   B. 850#   C. 900#   D. 1000#

22. Upon entering an ice plant, you notice that the refrigeration capacity is rated at 250 tons. It can manufacture _____ tons of ice.

    A. 150   B. 200   C. 300   D. 250

23. Assume that you have a 100 ton plant and the following factors are true: harbor river water used for cooling; compressor is running full speed and the tonnage rate is 225 BTU per minute; compressor discharge gases are 120° F; inlet condenser water 85° F; discharge condenser water 90° F.
    What would be the GPM of water per ton of refrigeration required for the condenser?

    A. 3   B. 6   C. 12   D. 9

24. The color of the lubricating oil in a carbon dioxide refrigeration plant for the manufacture of dry ice is

    A. pale lemon   B. orange lemon
    C. lemon   D. lily white

25. In a modern Freon 12 installation, hard copper tubing and forged fittings are used. These connections are BEST made by

    A. threading   B. soldering or brazing
    C. flanging   D. flaring

KEY (CORRECT ANSWERS)

1. B
2. C
3. C
4. A
5. B

6. D
7. A
8. B
9. B
10. C

11. C
12. B
13. B
14. B
15. D

16. C
17. C
18. B
19. C
20. B

21. A
22. A
23. A
24. D
25. B

TEST 4

DIRECTIONS: Each question or incomplete statement is followed by several suggested answers or completions. Select the one that BEST answers the question or completes the statement. *PRINT THE LETTER OF THE CORRECT ANSWER IN THE SPACE AT THE RIGHT.*

1. The term *viscosity* in refrigeration oils means 1.____

   A. weight value
   B. corrosive action
   C. ability to mix
   D. internal friction

2. The ammonia gases are reclaimed from the foul gases by a purger. The foul gases are BEST let free to bubble through 2.____

   A. liquid air
   B. phennol
   C. water
   D. none of the above

3. The specific heat of a substance is generally defined as a ratio of the quantity of heat required to raise a given quantity of a substance through a given temperature range to the quantity of heat required to raise the same weight of water through the same temperature range.
   This statement is 3.____

   A. true
   B. false
   C. partly true
   D. none of the above

4. A shaft seal of the bellows type construction is found on the _____ type compressor. 4.____

   A. Freon 12
   B. ammonia
   C. carbon dioxide
   D. absorption

5. When charging a packaged air conditioning unit with Freon 12, it is BEST to connect the Freon cylinder 5.____

   A. directly to the crankcase
   B. to the high pressure side
   C. to the low pressure side
   D. to the receiver

6. The degree of solubility, in reference to a refrigeration oil, is usually the LOWEST when using 6.____

   A. genetron 141
   B. methyl chloride
   C. Freon 12
   D. carbon dioxide

7. A two cylinder vertical single-stage compressor is equipped with a gear type oil pump for pressure lubrication.
   For good performance of this equipment, the oil discharge pressure should range APPROXIMATELY from _____ psig above _____ pressure. 7.____

   A. 10 to 30; suction
   B. 50 to 90; suction
   C. 10 to 30; head
   D. 50 to 90; head

8. Muntz metal CANNOT be used with

   A. Freon 12
   B. ammonia
   C. carbon dioxide
   D. condenser and heat exchanger

9. In the absorption system, the analyzer is connected between the

   A. rectifier and receiver
   B. absorber and heat exchanger
   C. generator and condenser
   D. condenser and heat exchanger

10. With 30 psig suction on the condenser pressure, with an 80 HP synchronous motor, if the condenser pressure is increased to 160 psig, the HP consumed will

    A. become lower
    B. become greater
    C. remain the same
    D. require less oil

11. In reference to compressors, generally

    A. low speed compressors should have a valve life of 7/32"
    B. if the horsepower is increased, the suction pressure is increased
    C. if the horsepower per pound of refrigerant is increased, the suction pressure decreases
    D. high speed reciprocating compressors should have less value lift than low speed compressors

12. Two Freon compressors are running in parallel; the crank-cases are interconnected with pipes.
    The reason for this is

    A. the temperature of both will be balanced
    B. the operating oil level will be properly maintained
    C. the load will be the same
    D. both crankcases can be filled with oil at the same time

13. The pressure of R-12 with an evaporator temperature of 45° is _____ pounds.

    A. 30   B. 40   C. 60   D. 80

14. In testing for ammonia in a plant, red litmus paper is used.
    If ammonia is present, the color would change to

    A. blue   B. red   C. yellow   D. pink

15. A shell and tube evaporator has baffles or eliminators at the top of the cooler.
    There are to catch the

    A. oil from going into the suction line
    B. gas from going into the suction line
    C. moisture carry-over
    D. liquid from going into the suction line

16. The formula $C = 0.6 P_1 D^2$ is used to compute the discharge capacity of a   16._____

    A. fusible plug B. safety valve
    C. stop valve   D. venturi

17. To pack tongue and groove, flanges on ammonia lines should be made of   17._____

    A. rubber   B. asbestos sheet
    C. tin   D. sheet lead

18. There are several test cocks on a Freon receiver condenser. The one at the end, about one-quarter of the way up, is used for   18._____

    A. purging non-condensable gases or air from the system
    B. testing the liquid level in the receiver
    C. an auxiliary charging connection
    D. pumping down purposes

19. In general, in a refrigeration system, the compressor is run to keep a meat storage room at 30° F.   19._____
    The horsepower per ton is

    A. 7.5   B. 2.0   C. 3.0   D. .90

20. If Nessier's solution is added to a sample of salt brine, in the event of there being a trace of ammonia present, the color of the solution will turn   20._____

    A. blue   B. red   C. yellow   D. pink

21. The scale trap is located between the   21._____

    A. compressor and condenser
    B. condenser and receiver
    C. evaporator and condenser
    D. evaporator and compressor

22. Of the following refrigerants, the one which has the HIGHEST refrigeration effect is R-   22._____

    A. 12   B. 14   C. 11   D. 113

23. The percentage of oil circulated with the refrigerant in a well-designed refrigeration system should NOT be more than _____ %.   23._____

    A. 10   B. 20   C. 25   D. 30

24. Given a drum of ammonia with 150 pounds in it, you would know when you had charged 75 pounds into the system by   24._____

    A. the low pressure gauge
    B. the feeling when the drum was half-empty
    C. weighing the drum on a scale
    D. the pressure gauge

25. The system shown in the diagram at the right is BEST described as a
    A. two stage compression system
    B. cascade system
    C. compound system
    D. compound system with intercooler

25._____

KEY (CORRECT ANSWERS)

1.	D	11.	D
2.	C	12.	B
3.	A	13.	B
4.	A	14.	A
5.	C	15.	D
6.	D	16.	A
7.	A	17.	D
8.	B	18.	B
9.	C	19.	D
10.	B	20.	C

21. D
22. C
23. A
24. C
25. B

EXAMINATION SECTION
TEST 1

DIRECTIONS: Each question or incomplete statement is followed by several suggested answers or completions. Select the one that BEST answers the question or completes the statement. *PRINT THE LETTER OF THE CORRECT ANSWER IN THE SPACE AT THE RIGHT.*

1. Frost that appears on the evaporator coils of a direct expansion system

    A. should not be removed
    B. can be removed by passing hot vapor through the coils
    C. is best removed by using a fireman's axe
    D. can be removed faster by shutting down the coils

    1.____

2. On which system should a dehydrator be used?

    A. Sulphur dioxide   B. Freon 12
    C. Ammonia   D. Carbon dioxide

    2.____

3. In the absorption system, the flow of ammonia gas in relation to the strong liquid in the analyzer is _____ flow.

    A. cross   B. diagonal   C. parallel   D. counter

    3.____

4. In a commercial compressor refrigerating plant, there is a room thermostat that controls the liquid line solenoid valve.
   The part that stops and starts the compressor is the

    A. low pressurestat
    B. low temperature thermostat
    C. high pressurestat
    D. thermal expansion valve

    4.____

5. The general operating data for a vertical shell and tube ammonia condenser states that the rise in condenser water temperature is one degree per 30 gallons per minute per ton. If a condenser is installed to handle 60 tons, and 6 gallons per minute per ton of condenser water is provided at 80°, then water temperature leaving the condenser should be MOST NEARLY _____ °F.

    A. 110   B. 90   C. 85   D. 83

    5.____

6. The shaft seal is located on the

    A. compressor   B. condenser
    C. receiver   D. oil separator

    6.____

7. The strong liquor in an absorption system passes from the absorber to the heat exchanger, on to the

    A. analyzer and generator
    B. generator and receiver
    C. evaporator and suction line
    D. rectifier and condenser

    7.____

8. A definition for specific heat is the amount of heat needed to raise one _____ of a substance one _____.

   A. pound; degree
   B. half-pound; degree
   C. pound; BTU
   D. pound; half BTU

9. A refrigerant stored in a machinery room shall NOT be more than _____ % of the normal refrigerant charged, not more than _____ lbs. of the refrigerant, in addition to the charge in the system.

   A. 30; 300   B. 35; 350   C. 25; 325   D. 20; 300

10. A gauge reading on a compound gauge is 11" of vacuum. This would be _____ # Abs.

    A. 9   B. 14.7   C. 4   D. 7

11. The packing gland for a piston rod of a horizontal compressor should be

    A. sealed with syphon bellows
    B. loose for packing removal
    C. tight to prevent oil leaks
    D. tight enough to prevent leaks

12. The refrigerant is liquified in the compression system by the

    A. compressor
    B. evaporator
    C. receiver
    D. condenser

13. The piston rod of a horizontal ammonia compressor, when the cross-head is properly aligned, is MOST likely to wear

    A. at the crosshead end
    B. at the piston end
    C. at the middle of the rod
    D. on the side

14. If the liquid line is warmer than usual, this indicates

    A. too much refrigerant
    B. shortage of refrigerant
    C. receiver is full of liquid
    D. high head pressure

15. If the line between the king valve and the expansion valve begins to sweat, the cause is

    A. partially clogged liquid line
    B. air in the system
    C. completely clogged liquid line
    D. excessive oil in the system

16. There is a sight glass in the liquid line before the expansion valve. 16.____
Upon inspection, bubbles are seen, which indicates

   A. non-condensable gases in the receiver
   B. the purger will rectify this
   C. air is going to the expansion valve
   D. there is a shortage of refrigerant

17. If you were to put in line vibration eliminator in a Freon 12 system, to make the joints gas- 17.____
tight, you would use

   A. garloc packing
   B. red indian shellac
   C. silver solder or braze the joints
   D. litharge and glycerine

18. In order to pack an ammonia globe valve when the system is in operation, the valve 18.____
should be

   A. closed tight
   B. closed midway
   C. packed but renewed
   D. opened all the way and repacked

19. What color does red litmus testing paper turn with ammonia? 19.____

   A. Red   B. White   C. Blue   D. No change

20. What percentage of oil travels with the refrigerant in a system? 20.____

   A. 10   B. 40   C. 30   D. 50

21. In a refrigerating system with a pressure gauge where the needle points to 100 psig, 21.____
under normal operating conditions, the MINIMUM last number of the gauge should read

   A. 105   B. 110   C. 115   D. 120

22. In an ammonia plant, a manometer used to measure the amount of refrigerant being cir- 22.____
culated would NORMALLY be located between the

   A. compressor and condenser
   B. condenser and receiver
   C. receiver and expansion valve
   D. expansion valve and evaporator

23. In a calcium chloride brine tank of 1000 cubic feet, how many pounds of dichromate 23.____
would you use in the INITIAL charge?

   A. 20   B. 40   C. 100   D. 200

24. In a packaged air comfort cooler that uses Freon 12, the back pressure is 40 lbs. 24.____
This should be CLOSE to a temperature of _____ °F.

   A. 55   B. 112   C. 72   D. 45

25. In an ice plant, the agitation is air precooled because it 25.____

    A. lessens the load on the ice field
    B. increases air compressor capacity
    C. prevents the freezing of air lines
    D. decreases air pressure resistance

KEY (CORRECT ANSWERS)

1. B
2. B
3. D
4. A
5. C

6. A
7. A
8. A
9. D
10. A

11. D
12. D
13. C
14. B
15. A

16. D
17. C
18. D
19. C
20. A

21. D
22. C
23. C
24. D
25. C

TEST 2

DIRECTIONS: Each question or incomplete statement is followed by several suggested answers or completions. Select the one that BEST answers the question or completes the statement. *PRINT THE LETTER OF THE CORRECT ANSWER IN THE SPACE AT THE RIGHT.*

1. Under standard ton conditions, the liquid before the expansion valve should be

   A. 55° F
   B. 77° F
   C. 154° F
   D. 10° superheat

2. In reference to a solenoid valve, when the current is ON, the valve is

   A. open
   B. closed
   C. half open
   D. a quarter closed

3. Admiralty brass is NOT used with

   A. Freon 22
   B. Freon 12
   C. ammonia
   D. carbon dioxide

4. To tell if an R-12 system needs purging, close the king valve and pump the low side down to about 10 psig, stop the compressor, but let the water flow until the temperature of the liquid in the receiver and in the condenser remains constant. Determine the temperature for the condenser pressure. Determine the temperature of the Freon at the same pressure. If the temperature difference is more than 5° F, the system should be purged. This statement is

   A. true
   B. false
   C. at times true
   D. probable

5. Water leaving a horizontal shell and tube condenser is USUALLY

   A. somewhat warmer than the high side
   B. the same temperature as the discharge gases
   C. a little cooler than the discharge refrigerant gas
   D. always warmer than the high side

6. In a vertical shell and tube condenser with swirls on top of the tubes, if a few of these became blocked, the result might be a(n)

   A. slow down of the compressor
   B. drop in suction pressure
   C. increase in plant capacity if the suction pressure is constant
   D. need to increase water flow to prevent head pressure from rising

7. If Nessler's solution is added to a sample of salt brine, in the event of there being a trace of ammonia present in the brine, the color of the solution will turn

   A. blue
   B. red
   C. yellow
   D. pink

8. If you changed 115° Centigrade to Fahrenheit, the reading would be _____ ° F.

   A. 241
   B. 265
   C. 239
   D. 221

9. Automatic water regulating valves on condensers are activated by   9._____

   A. receiver temperature   B. condenser pressure
   C. suction temperature   D. suction pressure

10. In a large carbon dioxide plant, to detect leaks you would   10._____

    A. keep the plant in operation and use a soapy solution
    B. drain the entire system and use a trace of Freon 12
    C. use the hydrostatic test
    D. use Nessler's solution and a sulphur stick on the exposed pipes

11. In an absorption system, it is NOT necessary to have the   11._____

    A. analyzer, heat exchanger, and generator
    B. analyzer, rectifier, and condenser
    C. analyzer, rectifier, and receiver
    D. rectifier, heat exchanger, and absorber

12. A shaft seal of the bellows type construction is GENERALLY found in _____ compressors.   12._____

    A. Freon 12
    B. ammonia
    C. carbon dioxide
    D. absorption system generator

13. A large synchronous motor uses both AC and DC to turn it and is at constant speed. What current is used to start this motor?   13._____

    A. A single phase   B. Both AC and DC
    C. DC *only*   D. AC *only*

14. In an air conditioning system, for BEST operating efficiency, the finned coils should be   14._____

    A. dry   B. wet
    C. frosted   D. partly frosted

15. A pressure or temperature response mechanism for automatically stopping the operation of the pressure imposing element is a pressure   15._____

    A. relief valve   B. relief device
    C. limiting device   D. imposing device

16. _____ tons of refrigeration would be required to produce 100 blocks of ice, each weighing 400 pounds, daily.   16._____

    A. 40   B. 80   C. 120   D. 160

17. One of the effects of the presence of non-condensable gases in a refrigerating system is _____ pressure.   17._____

    A. low suction   B. high condensing
    C. high suction   D. low condensing

18. One difference between a flooded evaporator and a dry one is

    A. more refrigerant is needed in a dry evaporator
    B. more refrigerant is needed in a flooded evaporator
    C. a flooded system is never reused
    D. less refrigerant is required in a flooded system

19. A set of ammonia coils in a cold storage room used for storing meat has a low side float as a metering device. The bottom coil has no frost, but the top and center coils do.
    This is an indication of

    A. the system having low pressure
    B. the coil being air-bound
    C. the system having low back pressure
    D. excessive oil in the coil

20. A liquid seal in the refrigeration system

    A. keeps the refrigerant in the receiver
    B. prevents hot gas from going into the liquid line
    C. prevents hot gas from mixing with the foul gas
    D. all of the above

21. Refrigerant 718 is

    A. propane   B. water
    C. sulphur dioxide D. ammonia

22. If the suction pressure of an operating compressor were to read 30 pounds, what should the oil pressure gauge read?

    A. 10 psig   B. 50 psig
    C. 120 psig   D. The same

23. A refrigerant that will break down into phosgene and other compounds when exposed to a hot gas flame such as cooling gas is

    A. ammonia anhydrous   B. carbon dioxide
    C. aqua ammonia   D. Freon 11

24. In some ammonia plants, a unit is used which cools the gases being purged before they are passed over to the water bottle.
    This cooling is done in order to

    A. increase the rate of purging
    B. cool the gases before passing to the water bottle
    C. save the operator from manually purging the system
    D. recover ammonia which is still with the gas

25. An indication that the refrigeration system is SHORT of refrigerant is   25._____
    A. high head pressure and low suction pressure
    B. low suction pressure and low head pressure
    C. high suction pressure and low discharge pressure
    D. both pressures are equal

KEY (CORRECT ANSWERS)

1. B
2. A
3. C
4. A
5. C

6. D
7. C
8. C
9. B
10. A

11. C
12. A
13. D
14. B
15. C

16. A
17. B
18. B
19. D
20. B

21. B
22. B
23. D
24. D
25. B

TEST 3

DIRECTIONS: Each question or incomplete statement is followed by several suggested answers or completions. Select the one that BEST answers the question or completes the statement. *PRINT THE LETTER OF THE CORRECT ANSWER IN THE SPACE AT THE RIGHT.*

1. Refrigerating oil in a system should

    A. not have a low pour point
    B. be free from moisture
    C. not have a high flash point
    D. be acid and corrosive

    1._____

2. The safety head of a vertical compressor is held in place by

    A. twenty nuts and bolts
    B. twenty or more springs
    C. red indian shellac
    D. a strong helical spring

    2._____

3. The term *anhydrous* is used to indicate that the refrigerant has

    A. Freon present
    B. 20 or more pounds of Freon present
    C. no moisture
    D. moisture present

    3._____

4. If a float of a low pressure side float is punctured and sinks, the

    A. suction pressure is lowered
    B. head pressure is increased
    C. suction pressure is increased
    D. evaporator coils will frost

    4._____

5. Which of the following desiccants CANNOT be used in a refrigerating system?

    A. Drierite
    B. Calcium oxide
    C. Activated alumina
    D. Soda lime

    5._____

6. If a refrigeration system does NOT respond to the adjustments on the expansion valve, it may be due to

    A. incorrect motor speed
    B. low condenser water flow
    C. the incorrect refrigerant
    D. oil-clogged coil in the evaporator

    6._____

7. In a spray pond similar to a condenser, to kill algae in the water you would use

    A. silica gel
    B. chromite
    C. potassium permanganate
    D. potash

    7._____

8. A sign on the wall of a motor room contains pertinent information. Which one of the following can be omitted?

    A. Number of condensers
    B. Pounds of refrigerant required
    C. Name of installer
    D. Horsepower of prime movers

    8._____

9. A shell and tube type evaporator is designed so that it is

   A. full of liquid refrigerant with gas space at the top
   B. full of gas with a thin layer of liquid at the bottom
   C. completely submerged in a brine
   D. liquid brine covers the coil

10. The boiling temperature of R-22 compared with R-12 is

    A. 20° F lower
    B. 10° F lower
    C. 25° F higher
    D. 15° F higher

11. The type of constant speed motor generally used in large refrigerating plants is

    A. slip ring
    B. synchronous
    C. squirrel gauge
    D. double wound squirrel gauge

12. The capacity of an evaporative condenser will INCREASE if the

    A. wet bulb reading is high
    B. wet bulb reading is low
    C. capacity does not change
    D. amount of water used is less

13. The RPM of an 80 cycle, six pole, synchronous motor is

    A. 1200   B. 1500   C. 1800   D. 2000

14. One ton of refrigeration is equal to _____ BTU per _____ .

    A. 1200; minute
    B. 200; hour
    C. 12,000; hour
    D. 288,000; hour

15. What type of condenser could be used in winter without water?

    A. Submerged
    B. Shell and tube
    C. Shell and coil
    D. Atmospheric with drip

16. The evaporative coils in a cooler are along the ceiling, and one of these coils has insulating baffles.
    The baffles are to

    A. catch the dripping when the coils are defrosting
    B. supply gravity air to circulate in the cooler
    C. see that gravity air circulates over the coils
    D. none of the above

17. In methyl chloride systems, a dryer would PROBABLY be placed in the _____ near the _____.

    A. discharge; compressor
    B. liquid line; expansion valve
    C. suction line; compressor
    D. suction line; evaporator

18. A Freon 12 compressor used in an air conditioning system has a magnetic bypass. This is in order to

    A. equalize pressure in the cylinder
    B. relieve pressure when it becomes high
    C. regulate compressor capacity
    D. relieve oil from the cylinder to the crankcase

19. The formula $C = 0.6\, P_1 D^2$ is used for determining the capacity of a

    A. fusible plug   B. stop valve
    C. safety valve   D. venturi

20. A scale trap is placed in the suction line of a compression system to remove foreign matter.
    It would be MOST effective when the plant is

    A. new
    B. shut down for a long time
    C. old
    D. using only modern compressors

21. The one of the following refrigerants that USUALLY operates with a condenser pressure above 1050# is

    A. ammonia   B. sulphur dioxide
    C. carbon dioxide   D. Freon

22. The LARGEST size *threaded* pipe allowed in an NH_3 refrigeration system with a maximum of 250# pressure is _____ inches.

    A. 3   B. 3 1/2   C. 4   D. 4 1/2

23. When withdrawing refrigerant from a system into containers, in NO case can they be filled more than _____ %.

    A. 70   B. 75   C. 80   D. 85

24. If a system contains 400 pounds of Group 2 refrigerant, the number of REQUIRED breathing service masks is

    A. one   B. two   C. three   D. none

25. Carron oil (a liniment used for ammonia burns) is made up of equal parts of
   A. vaseline and picric acid
   B. lanolin and vinegar
   C. linseed oil and lime water
   D. sulphur dioxide and water

KEY (CORRECT ANSWERS)

1.	B	11.	B
2.	D	12.	B
3.	C	13.	A
4.	C	14.	C
5.	D	15.	D
6.	D	16.	C
7.	C	17.	B
8.	A	18.	C
9.	A	19.	A
10.	A	20.	A

21. C
22. A
23. B
24. A
25. C

TEST 4

DIRECTIONS: Each question or incomplete statement is followed by several suggested answers or completions. Select the one that BEST answers the question or completes the statement. *PRINT THE LETTER OF THE CORRECT ANSWER IN THE SPACE AT THE RIGHT.*

1. In order to detect F-12 leaks in a commercial system, you would use   1.____

    A. a sulphur stick B. litmus paper
    C. aqua ammonia D. a halide torch

2. With reference to a belt-driven compressor, if one of the four belts broke, you, as an engineer, would   2.____

    A. replace the four with a new set
    B. replace the broken belt
    C. operate with the three remaining belts
    D. pour on more belt grease

3. A plant refrigerating unit has 600 pounds of refrigerant in it. The CFM from the exhaust blower should be   3.____

    A. 1275   B. 1450   C. 1100   D. 600

4. If a paraffin base oil were to get into the evaporator used for low temperature work, you would remove it by   4.____

    A. heating up the coil and pumping it out
    B. putting a dehydrator in the liquid line
    C. letting it work its normal way back to the trap
    D. disposing of the coil, impossible to remove

5. A thermostatic expansion valve is USUALLY rated by   5.____

    A. BTU per minute B. BTU per hour
    C. tons of refrigeration D. I.M.E.

6. A rupture member can be substituted for a relief valve in a(n) _____ system.   6.____

    A. aqua ammonia B. sulphur dioxide
    C. carbon dioxide D. ammonia

7. An open vertical shell and tube condenser   7.____

    A. is suitable when the condensing water is not clean
    B. must use condensed water
    C. must use hydrant water
    D. has the ammonia vapor connection at the bottom

8. The degree of solubility, in reference to a refrigerating oil, is the LOWEST when using   8.____

    A. genetron 141 B. methyl chloride
    C. Preon 12 D. carbon dioxide

2 (#4)

9. On a compound gauge reading 9" of vacuum, the reading would equal

   A. ten pounds absolute
   B. two psig
   C. twenty pounds absolute
   D. 29.92 Hg

10. Which one of the following methods is NOT used to control the capacity of a compressor?

    A. A variable speed motor
    B. Cylinder bypass control
    C. Automatic capacity control
    D. Less water on the condenser

11. Silica gel is used as a dryer in Freon systems to

    A. keep air out of the system
    B. keep oil out of Freon
    C. keep evaporator coils from frosting
    D. remove moisture from Freon

12. Converting 15" Hg to the absolute pressure scale, it is equal to _____ lbs.

    A. 30   B. 8   C. 10   D. 14

13. The MAXIMUM capacity of humanly occupied space of Group 1 refrigerant such as carbon dioxide is _____ lbs.

    A. 3   B. 11   C. 21   D. 30

14. In a carbon dioxide system, you use bromthymol-blue.
    A leak is indicated by the color

    A. green   B. pink   C. yellow   D. blue

15. With a broken sight glass, what devices are used for safety and loss of refrigerant on a receiver?

    A. Automatic safety valve, piped to outside
    B. Metal guards about glass
    C. Manual hand valve
    D. Automatic shut-off valves and metal guards about glass

16. To remove water from an industrial ammonia system, you would

    A. drain from the high side
    B. drain from the low side suction
    C. use a regenerator
    D. drain the entire system

17. When testing high pressure side lines for leaks, you should keep this pressure test on for _____ minutes.

    A. 5   B. 10   C. 20   D. 30

18. Rupture members, when used in parallel with a relief valve, shall operate

    A. at pressures of 80% of design working pressure
    B. at pressures of 100%
    C. at pressures of 20%
    D. not to exceed 20% above the design working pressure

19. A halide torch would be used to

    A. solder copper tubing
    B. detect Freon leaks
    C. clear clogged carbon dioxide lines
    D. defrost a large evaporator

20. An oil lantern is used in the stuffing box

    A. to hold seal tight and rigid
    B. as a guiding light
    C. as a seal
    D. as a spacer to hold oil

21. An automatic oil trap is placed in an air conditioning system. When the float in the trap LIFTS, it allows

    A. hot gas to defrost the coils
    B. the oil out to drain
    C. oil to leave the trap to go back to the compressor crankcase
    D. the oil to go to the stuffing box

22. A good refrigerating oil should have _____ content.

    A. no moisture   B. no wax
    C. high flash   D. all of the above

23. When a refrigerant passes through the expansion valve, the temperature and the pressure drop.
    This is caused by

    A. some of the refrigerant evaporating as it passes through the expansion valve
    B. the rate of flow of the refrigerant through the system
    C. the superheat of the refrigerant
    D. the temperature and pressure of the refrigerant before it passes through the expansion valve

24. Sulphur dioxide may be discharged into

    A. carbonated brine   B. absorptive brine
    C. calcium chloride   D. water

25. A specification calls for the installation of a unit air conditioning system in the lobby of a building. This system is to contain 30# of Freon 12.
 In keeping with the rules, it can be said that the system may

 A. not be installed; no unit system can be placed in a lobby
 B. be installed if the system is reduced to 20#
 C. be installed
 D. not be installed as it contains a Group 2 refrigerant

25.____

KEY (CORRECT ANSWERS)

1. D
2. A
3. B
4. A
5. C

6. C
7. A
8. D
9. A
10. D

11. D
12. B
13. B
14. C
15. D

16. C
17. D
18. D
19. B
20. D

21. C
22. D
23. A
24. B
25. C

EXAMINATION SECTION
TEST 1

DIRECTIONS: Each question or incomplete statement is followed by several suggested answers or completions. Select the one that BEST answers the question or completes the statement. *PRINT THE LETTER OF THE CORRECT ANSWER IN THE SPACE AT THE RIGHT.*

Questions 1-10.

DIRECTIONS: Questions 1 through 10 are to be answered on the basis of the diagram shown below.

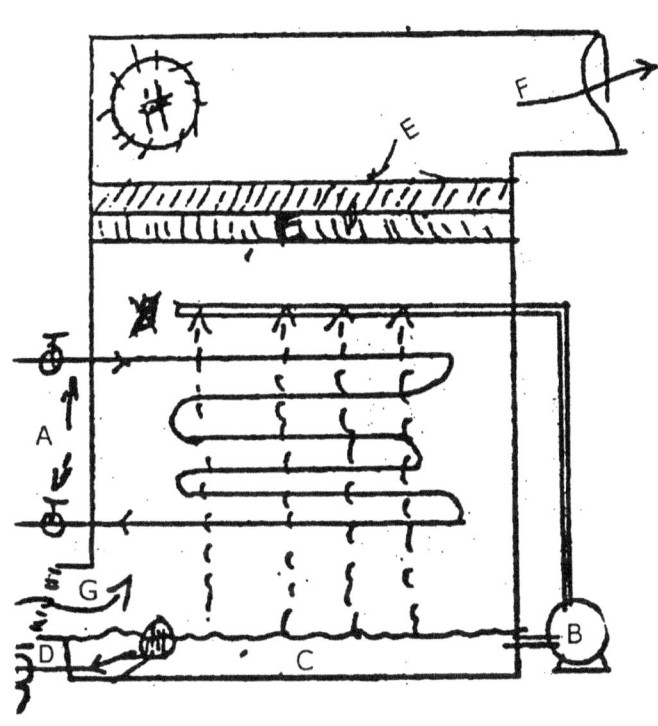

1. The diagram represents a(n)

    A. shell and tube condenser
    B. atmospheric condenser
    C. water cooling tower
    D. evaporative condenser

    1.____

2. It is used PRIMARILY to

    A. cut down overhead
    C. use air only
    B. save water
    D. save space

    2.____

3. Its principle of operation is the

    A. same as shell and tube
    C. sensible heat loss
    B. evaporation of some water
    D. latent heat gain

    3.____

4. It saves APPROXIMATELY _____ % of _____.   4.___

   A. 50; water B. 80; air C. 85; water D. 20; water

5. The pipes at A are _____ pipes.   5.___

   A. water
   C. baffle
   B. refrigeration condenser
   D. evaporator

6. The eliminators at E are for   6.___

   A. eliminating excessive air carry-over
   B. eliminating excessive moisture carry-over
   C. acoustic reasons
   D. saving electrical power *only*

7. The pump at B pumps from C.   7.___
   The liquid in the pan is

   A. brine
   C. water
   B. refrigerant
   D. sodium chloride

8. The ball at pipe D is for the   8.___

   A. water make-up line
   C. pressure alarm
   B. safety alarm
   D. syphon

9. The openings at G and F are for   9.___

   A. induced air from blower at H
   B. forced draft from fan at G
   C. natural draft air at G and F
   D. no purpose at all

10. If these water spray nozzles were to become clogged, it may cause _____ pressure.   10.___

    A. low suction
    C. high suction
    B. low head
    D. high head

11. In a Freon refrigeration system, a shell and coil condenser was replaced by a properly   11.___
    designed evaporative condenser.
    The city water to the condenser would

    A. decrease by 40-50%
    C. increase by 40-50%
    B. decrease by 85-90%
    D. increase by 85-90%

12. If the motor and compressor belts of a refrigeration unit are too tight, the   12.___

    A. motor and compressor will slow down
    B. unit will run normally
    C. capacity will go up
    D. motor will overheat

13. In comparing a waterless air conditioning unit to a regular water cooled type, under normal operating conditions, the

    A. head pressure for the waterless would be lower
    B. head pressure for the waterless would be higher
    C. aqua pump is lower than the condenser
    D. suction pressure is continually the same

14. In testing for ammonia leaks in a plant, red litmus paper was used.
    If ammonia is present, the color will change to

    A. blue   B. red   C. yellow   D. pink

15. If Nessier's solution is added to a sample of brine, in the event of ammonia being present, the color would change to

    A. blue   B. red   C. yellow   D. pink

16. The amount of power delivered by an electric motor depends ENTIRELY upon the

    A. type of motor   B. HP rating
    C. amount of electricity D. temperature of the motor

17. In a large cold storage plant, there are several calcium chloride brine coolers. These are shell and tube designed, each with an automatic float.
    The purpose of this float switch is to

    A. remove foul gases from the refrigerant
    B. remove water from the refrigerant
    C. control the refrigerant flow to the cooler
    D. remove oil and sludge from the refrigerant

18. How much liquid ammonia passes the expansion valve for 100 tons?

    A. 100#   B. 20#   C. 200#   D. 50#

19. _____ kind(s) of lubricant is(are) used in a horizontal, double-acting ammonia compressor.

    A. One   B. Two   C. Three   D. Four

20. A refrigeration system is operating at 100 psig on the high side.
    The dial of the pressure gauge on the high side of the system should have a full scale reading of

    A. 100   B. 110   C. 115   D. 120

21. At a given temperature, the ratio of the actual pressure of the vapor in the atmosphere to the saturation pressure is called

    A. relative humidity   B. absolute humidity
    C. humidifying effect   D. partial pressure

22. Of the following Freon refrigerants, the one which has the LOWEST refrigeration effect, in BTU per pound, is F-

    A. 12   B. 114   C. 11   D. 13

23. The solenoid valve is operated by _____ means.   23.____

    A. mechanical   B. electrical
    C. manual   D. hydraulic

24. The specific gravity of a supposed solution of calcium chloride is 0.9872.   24.____
    This would indicate that

    A. more salt should be added
    B. the sample is pure water
    C. more water should be added
    D. this is not a calcium chloride sample

25. Frost that appears on the evaporator coils of a direct expansion system is BEST removed   25.____

    A. with a scraper
    B. by passing hot vapor through the coils
    C. faster by shutting down the coils
    D. should not be removed

KEY (CORRECT ANSWERS)

1. D		11. B	
2. B		12. D	
3. B		13. B	
4. C		14. A	
5. B		15. C	
6. B		16. D	
7. C		17. C	
8. A		18. D	
9. A		19. B	
10. D		20. D	

21. A
22. B
23. B
24. D
25. B

TEST 2

DIRECTIONS: Each question or incomplete statement is followed by several suggested answers or completions. Select the one that BEST answers the question or completes the statement. *PRINT THE LETTER OF THE CORRECT ANSWER IN THE SPACE AT THE RIGHT.*

1. In the compression system with a low side float, the ball in the float is punctured and sinks.
   What would MOST likely happen?
   The

   A. low side would be falling with compressor running
   B. compressor would stop and head pressure would rise
   C. head pressure would fall
   D. low side would be rising with compressor running

   1.____

2. The capacity of a water-cooled condenser is LEAST affected by

   A. water temperature   B. amount of water
   C. refrigerant temperature   D. ambient temperature

   2.____

3. Where is the brine located in a shell and tube cooler?

   A. In the shell
   B. In the tube
   C. Alternates between the tube and the shell
   D. In the refrigerant in the tubes

   3.____

4. Assume the suction gas pressure in a system is 15" Hg. If this is converted to absolute pressure, it will be NEARLY

   A. 0#   B. 15#   C. 7#   D. 23#

   4.____

5. Sulphur dioxide may be discharged into

   A. carbonated brine   B. absorptive brine
   C. calcium chloride   D. water

   5.____

6. A vertical compressor has trunk type pistons and is single acting.
   If the oil rings leaked very badly, this would cause

   A. pounding upon starting
   B. a decreased capacity
   C. a slow start which speeds up
   D. scored and scratched cylinder walls

   6.____

7. Which of the following lists has items that are NOT part of a belt-driven compressor?

   A. Piston, cylinder, frame, and crankcase
   B. Stuffing box, suction valve, and frame
   C. Crankcase, discharge valve, and stuffing box
   D. Frame, crankcase, suction valve, valve rod, and piston

   7.____

121

8. The LOWEST operating temperature recommended for sodium chloride is _____ °F.   8.____
   A. 0   B. 5   C. 10   D. 20

9. What is the LOWEST operating temperature recommended for calcium chloride?   9.____
   A. -45° F   B. -60° F   C. -20° F   D. 0° F

10. Which of the following dessicants would change physically and/or chemically under the absorption process of water?   10.____
    A. Silica gel
    B. Activated alumina
    C. Calcium chloride
    D. Activated bauxite

11. In a spray pond similar to a condenser, to kill algae in the water, you would use   11.____
    A. silica gel
    B. chromite
    C. potassium permanganate
    D. potash

12. Lithium bromide absorption systems for use in air conditioning have the LOWEST possible water temperature of _____ °F.   12.____
    A. 31   B. 33   C. 35   D. 38

13. The CORRECT flow of refrigerant in the ammonia compression system is in the sequence of   13.____
    A. compressor, scale trap, condenser, expansion valve, evaporator
    B. compressor, oil trap, condenser, king valve, expansion valve, evaporator, scale trap
    C. generator, condenser, expansion valve, evaporator, absorber
    D. expansion valve, evaporator, condenser, oil trap, condenser

14. A rotary booster compressor has _____ bearing(s).   14.____
    A. one   B. two   C. three   D. four

15. Concerning the working pressures in ammonia and Freon compression systems,   15.____
    A. they are the same
    B. there is no comparison
    C. Freon is higher
    D. ammonia is higher

16. A sign on the wall of a motor room contains some pertinent information. The one of the following which can be omitted is   16.____
    A. number of condensers
    B. pounds of refrigerant required
    C. name of installer
    D. horsepower of prime movers

17. The strong liquor in the absorption system is formed in the   17.____
    A. generator
    B. evaporator
    C. condenser
    D. absorber

18. The refrigerant stored in a machine room shall NOT be more than _____ % of the normal charge or more than _____ pounds of refrigerant in addition to the charge in the system.

    A. 20; 300 B. 30; 300 C. 35; 350 D. 25; 325

19. A motor has a protection device to prevent burning out or damage, called a

    A. fusetron
    B. dual fuse
    C. circuit breaker
    D. thermal protector

20. In a calcium chloride brine tank of 1000 cubic feet, how many pounds of sodium diehromate would you use?

    A. 20 B. 40 C. 100 D. 200

21. Soldered joint is a gas-tight joint obtained by the joining of metal parts with metallic mixtures of alloys which melt at _____ °F and above _____ °F.

    A. 600; 250 B. 800; 300 C. 925; 350 D. 1000; 400

22. The _____ prevents the liquid refrigerant from returning to the compressor.

    A. oil trap
    B. scale trap
    C. accumulator
    D. king valve

23. A plant refrigerating unit has 600 pounds of refrigerant in it.
    The CFM from the exhaust blower should be

    A. 1100 B. 1275 C. 1450 D. 1800

24. Which of the following statements refers to a class *T* machine room?

    A. It must have a door opening into or under a fire escape.
    B. It must have a sealed room with no less than two hours of fireproof construction.
    C. All pipes must be sealed into the wall, ceiling, and floor.
    D. All pipes piercing the wall and ceiling should be tightly sealed with not less than one hour of resistance construction.

25. In general, a refrigeration system compressor is run to keep a meat storage room at 30° F.
    The horsepower per ton is GENERALLY

    A. 75 B. 2.0 C. 3.0 D. .90

KEY (CORRECT ANSWERS)

1.	D	11.	C
2.	D	12.	D
3.	B	13.	B
4.	C	14.	B
5.	B	15.	D
6.	D	16.	A
7.	D	17.	D
8.	A	18.	A
9.	A	19.	D
10.	C	20.	C

21. D
22. C
23. C
24. D
25. D

TEST 3

DIRECTIONS: Each question or incomplete statement is followed by several suggested answers or completions. Select the one that BEST answers the question or completes the statement. *PRINT THE LETTER OF THE CORRECT ANSWER IN THE SPACE AT THE RIGHT.*

1. Standard iron pipe size copper and red brass pipe and tubing may be used provided that the copper is NOT less than _____ %.   1._____

    A. 60   B. 75   C. 90   D. 80

2. How many stop valves are required in a system using 80# of Group 1 refrigerant and having two compressors and two receivers?   2._____

    A. 2   B. 4   C. 5   D. 6

3. Containers shall not be filled in excess of the permissible filling weight of containers and refrigerants as prescribed by the I.C.C., and in no case shall the container capacity be over _____ %.   3._____

    A. 90   B. 30   C. 60   D. 75

4. Refrigerant number 40 is   4._____

    A. ammonia
    C. ethylene
    B. sulphur dioxide
    D. methyl chloride

5. Water leaving a horizontal shell and tube condenser is USUALLY   5._____

    A. somewhat warmer than the high side
    B. the same temperature as the discharge gases
    C. a little cooler than the discharge refrigerant gas
    D. always warmer than the high side

6. In testing condenser water for carbon dioxide leaks, you would use   6._____

    A. Nessier's solution
    C. a halide torch
    B. bromthymol-blue
    D. litmus paper

7. The specific heat of a substance is generally defined as a ratio of the quantity of heat required to raise a given quantity of a substance through a given temperature range to the quantity of heat required to raise the same weight of water through the same temperature range.   7._____
    This statement is

    A. true
    C. partly true
    B. false
    D. none of the above

8. The properties of a good refrigeration oil include: 8._____

    A. low flash point
    B. non-corrosive and non-harmful quality to metals
    C. 5% by proportion to the weight of paraffin
    D. emulsifies and mixes readily with the refrigerant

9. Sensible heat is detected by means of a

   A. pressurestat
   B. hydrostat
   C. thermometer
   D. gauge

10. Carron oil (a liniment used for ammonia burns) is made up of equal parts of

   A. vaseline and picric acid
   B. linseed oil and lime water
   C. lanolin and vinegar
   D. sulphur dioxide and water

11. A plant is equipped with a bank of shell and tube vertical condensers.
    To INCREASE the capacity of any of the condensers, the operator would

   A. *increase* the flow of water and refrigerant to the condenser
   B. *increase* the flow of refrigerant to the system
   C. *decrease* suction pressure and head pressure
   D. *increase* the suction pressure and the condenser pressure

12. The purpose of the high side float in an ammonia system is to feed the

   A. evaporator when condenser supplies enough refrigerant
   B. evaporator when refrigerant is needed
   C. condenser when refrigerant is needed
   D. compressor when needed

13. Silica gel and activated alumina are used as a dryer in an R-12 system to

   A. keep air out of the system
   B. keep oil out of Freon
   C. keep evaporator coils from frosting
   D. remove moisture from Freon

14. In a properly designed system, it is decided to reduce the condenser exit water temperature from 12° F to 9° F.
    In order to do this,

   A. *decrease* the condenser water by 25%
   B. *increase* the refrigerant flow
   C. *decrease* the condenser water by 25%
   D. *decrease* refrigerant flow

15. In respect to R-12 system piping, hard copper and black iron streamline fittings should be made by

   A. welding
   B. soldering or brazing
   C. flanging
   D. flaring

16. In the lubrication of a compression system, it is found that

   A. vegetable oil is preferred for best results
   B. Freon has the same degree of miscibility with oil as does ammonia
   C. a chemical reaction between Freon and oil occurs
   D. the refrigerant mixes with lubricating oil

17. If the feeler bulb was placed right after the expansion valve, it would

    A. be incorrect
    B. be right
    C. run normally
    D. get higher efficiency

18. The MAXIMUM capacity of humanly occupied space of Group 1 refrigerants, such as carbon dioxide, is _____ lbs.

    A. 3   B. 11   C. 21   D. 30

19. In an ammonia system, the suction gas pressure is 0 psig.
    What temperature is the evaporator gas?

    A. 0°   B. -10°   C. -8.73°   D. -23°

20. A fusible plug is set to melt at _____ °F.

    A. 180   B. 280   C. 380   D. 144

21. The MOST accurate characteristic pertaining to a brine is:

    A. it is not corrosive when treated with carbon dioxide
    B. acid will not corrode zinc piping
    C. alkaline will not corrode bronze piping
    D. it is preferable to maintain it neutral

22. Of the following water-cooled condensers, the one that consists of one or more assemblies of two tubes, one within a tube, is called a(n) _____ condenser.

    A. atmospheric
    B. shell and tube
    C. shell and coil
    D. double pipe

23. The MAIN reason for purging a Freon centrifugal refrigeration system is to remove

    A. Freon
    B. water vapor
    C. non-condensable gases
    D. gas lubrication oil

24. A compressor in a refrigerating system may lose oil if

    A. there is air in the system
    B. the velocity of the refrigerant in the risers is too low
    C. there are medium pressure drops in the evaporator
    D. there are small load variations in the system

25. The expansion valve is built MOST NEARLY like a _____ valve.

    A. shut-off
    B. pressure reducing
    C. blow-off
    D. double-seated globe

KEY (CORRECT ANSWERS)

1. D
2. D
3. D
4. D
5. C

6. B
7. A
8. B
9. C
10. B

11. A
12. A
13. D
14. A
15. C

16. D
17. A
18. B
19. D
20. B

21. D
22. D
23. C
24. B
25. B

TEST 4

DIRECTIONS: Each question or incomplete statement is followed by several suggested answers or completions. Select the one that BEST answers the question or completes the statement. *PRINT THE LETTER OF THE CORRECT ANSWER IN THE SPACE AT THE RIGHT.*

1. In order to determine the actual operating capacity of a chilled water cooler, it is essential that an operator know the specific heat of the water as well as the poundage of water flow per unit of time.
   With respect to the specific heat of water, in the normal liquid temperature range, it can be properly said that the specific heat of water is

   A. the same at all temperatures from 30° to 212° F
   B. high at low temperatures and low at high temperatures
   C. high at low temperatures and high at high temperatures
   D. low at low temperatures and high at high temperatures

   1.____

2. A Freon refrigerating plant is being used in an air conditioning system to remove sensible heat from the air in a two stage after-cooler to a silica gel air dehydrating unit.
   If the outside surface of the coils in the after-cooler were to operate wet, the probability is that the

   A. suction pressure is too high
   B. refrigerant is wet
   C. coils in the after-cooler are not properly vented
   D. none of the above

   2.____

3. The use of screwed joints in refrigeration systems for refrigerant pressures above 250 psi is permitted, provided that the nominal size of the pipe is NOT more than _____ inches.

   A. 1 1/4   B. 1 3/4   C. 2 1/4   D. 3

   3.____

4. Which of the following is Refrigerant 718?

   A. Propane   B. Ammonia   C. Water   D. Air

   4.____

5. Thirty gallons of water per minute are to be reduced from 80° F to 40° F.
   How many tons of refrigeration are required to do this?

   A. 10   B. 30   C. 50   D. 70

   5.____

6. When attempting to read the high side pressure gauge on an operating ammonia compressor, it is noted that the pointer *hunts,* or has a wide and relatively slow back and forth movement.
   This would MOST likely indicate that the compressor

   A. is overloaded
   B. valve action is sluggish
   C. suction valves are stuck open
   D. is operating normally

   6.____

7. If an absorption system was to be placed in operation, and the low and high sides were to be 16# and 150# of steam, how much would be required per ton of refrigeration?

   A. 70#   B. 20#   C. 200#   D. 10#

8. In reference to a synchronous motor, it is NOT correct that it

   A. is a constant speed motor
   B. can be run using 220, 440, or 2300 volts
   C. is usually run with a lagging field current
   D. is excited by direct current

9. The concentration of a brine which is used in an indirect system is determined by

   A. Orsat meter   B. Nessler's reagent
   C. manometer   D. hydrometer

10. A 200 ton air conditioning plant is set up with Freon compressors.
    Assuming that neither of the compressors is equipped with bypass solenoids, then in order to be able to get at LEAST four steps of capacity with these two machines, they should be driven by _____ motors.

    A. synchronous   B. repulsion and induction
    C. capacitor type   D. wound rotor induction

11. In a flooded shell and tube brine cooler, the brine is USUALLY pumped through the

    A. tubes and shell alternately by means of a program device
    B. tubes
    C. shell
    D. tubes and shell

12. The volume of cylin, in cubic feet, having a diameter of 8 inches and a total length of 150 feet is MOST NEARLY

    A. 25   B. 50   C. 75   D. 100

13. The scale trap is located between the

    A. compressor and condenser
    B. condenser and receiver
    C. evaporator and compressor
    D. evaporator and condenser

14. The safety head of a vertical compressor is held in place by

    A. twenty bolts and nuts   B. twenty springs or more
    C. red indian shellac   D. a strong helical spring

15. Refrigerant 717 is NOT corrosive to

    A. iron   B. copper   C. brass   D. bronze

16. Which of the following refrigerants is in Group 2?

    A. F-12   B. Methyl chloride
    C. Isobutane   D. Ethane

17. A shaft seal (of the bellows type construction) is found on _____ compressors. 17._____

    A. Freon 12   B. ammonia
    C. carbon dioxide   D. absorption

18. In an evaporative condenser, for each pound of water that evaporates, _____ BTU of 18._____
    heat is required.

    A. 565   B. 144   C. 970   D. 790

19. The gas pressure in a refrigeration system is 9" Hg. 19._____
    If this was converted to absolute pressure, it would be

    A. 2   B. 8   C. 12   D. 16

20. In a certain compression type refrigeration system, the Freon compressor is running con- 20._____
    tinuously.
    As the load on the evaporator DECREASES, the suction pressure

    A. increases
    B. decreases
    C. first decreases, then steadily increases
    D. remains steady, regardless of changes in load

21. Refrigerant passing through a condenser coil at 180° F could only condense if the cool- 21._____
    ing medium were at a temperature of _____ ° F.

    A. 120   B. 180   C. 220   D. 260

22. R-12 refrigerant at 80° F exerts _____ psig. 22._____

    A. 84.2   B. 161.2   C. 143.6   D. 80.0

23. The cost of operating a 40 HP motor per hour at 0.6 KWH and running at 80% efficiency 23._____
    is

    A. $3.73   B. $4.06   C. $2.98   D. $2.23

24. In a compression cycle, a multi-cylinder, single-acting compressor operates automati- 24._____
    cally on room temperature (the *on and off cycle*). Upon starting, it pounds a while.
    The MOST likely reason for this would be

    A. a worn wrist-pin bushing
    B. oil pumping due to overcharge of oil
    C. piston slap
    D. worn crankcase bearing

25. What type of condenser can be used WITHOUT water in winter weather? 25._____

    A. Shell and coil   B. Atmospheric drip
    C. Sulphuric acid   D. Vertical shell and tube

KEY (CORRECT ANSWERS)

1.	A	11.	B
2.	C	12.	B
3.	D	13.	C
4.	C	14.	D
5.	C	15.	A
6.	B	16.	B
7.	B	17.	A
8.	B	18.	C
9.	D	19.	C
10.	D	20.	B

21. A
22. A
23. D
24. B
25. B

AIR CONDITIONING CONCEPTS AND SYSTEMS

TABLE OF CONTENTS

	Page
I. CHILLED WATER SYSTEMS	1
A. Introduction	1
B. Chilled Water Chart	1
C. Components	1
II. AIR CIRCULATION	5
A. Introduction	5
B. Natural Air Flow	5
C. Forced Air Flow	5
D. Ventilation and Air Conditioning Systems	8
E. Duct Work	8
F. Filters	10
III. PSYCHROMOETRY AND HEAT LOAD	12
A. Psychrometrics	12
B. Heat of the Air	13
C. Three Air Temperatures	13
D. Humidity	16
E. Factors Affecting Human Comfort and Efficiency	20
F. Figuring Heat Loads	22
IV. STEAM JET SYSTEM	27
A. Introduction	27
B. Operating Cycles	27
C. Operating and Maintenance	29
V. ABSORPTION SYSTEM	30
A. Introduction	30
B. The Lithium Bromide Test	30
C. Operating Cycles	31
D. Equilibrium Diagrams	40

AIR CONDITIONING CONCEPTS AND SYSTEMS

CHAPTER 1
CHILLED WATER SYSTEMS

A. INTRODUCTION

The process of air conditioning by the use of chilled water is one of several applications of the indirect expansion system. When several remote locations are to be conditioned by the same compressor, the chilled water system is most economical. By using a centrally located machine to chill the water and then circulate the water by means of pumps, pipes, and valves through cooling coils located in or at the spaces to be conditioned, a large amount of air conditioning is accomplished with a small amount of refrigerant. This reduces (1) the possibility of losing large amounts of refrigerant in case of a leak, (2) the length of expensive copper tubing required for direct expansion systems, and (3) the inaccessibility to refrigerant tubing which is common in direct expansion systems.

A chilled water system as used in conjunction with a reciprocating refrigerant compressor and the water chiller is described in this chapter. The chilled water system for this type unit is also used with the jet steam system, absorption system, and large centrifugal air conditioning plants. The basic difference in these systems is the manner in which the water is chilled. How the water is chilled in each of these systems can be seen by referring to the drawings and diagrams in the applicable chapter in this text. The remaining components in these chilled water systems, such as pumps, piping, valves and cooling coils, are all basically the same.

B. CHILLED WATER CIRCUIT

The flow of chilled water can be traced throughout its circuit by referring to figure 1. The water is cooled in the chiller to a temperature between $40°$ and $45°$ F. The circulating pump takes a suction from the chiller and discharges the water through the main balancing valve into the chilled water supply main.

As shown, the water is fed to the cooling coil through a stop valve, solenoid valve, and a coil balancing valve. As the water circulates through the tubes in the cooling coil, heat is absorbed from the surrounding air. The heat laden water is returned to the water chiller through the chilled water return main. In the chiller, the refrigerant absorbs the heat from the water and it is ready to repeat the cycle.

COMPONENTS

C1. Water Chiller.-The water chiller used in conjunction with a reciprocating type refrigerant unit, as shown in figure 1, is of the tube-shell type.

The refrigerant enters the tubes from the thermal expansion valve and makes four passes through the chiller. The expansion bulb for the expansion valve is located in the refrigerant outlet line from the chiller. The end plates or headers are designed to direct the refrigerant through half of the tubes in the lower section on the first pass, back through the other half on the second pass, through half of the tubes in the upper section on the third pass, and back through the other half on the final pass.

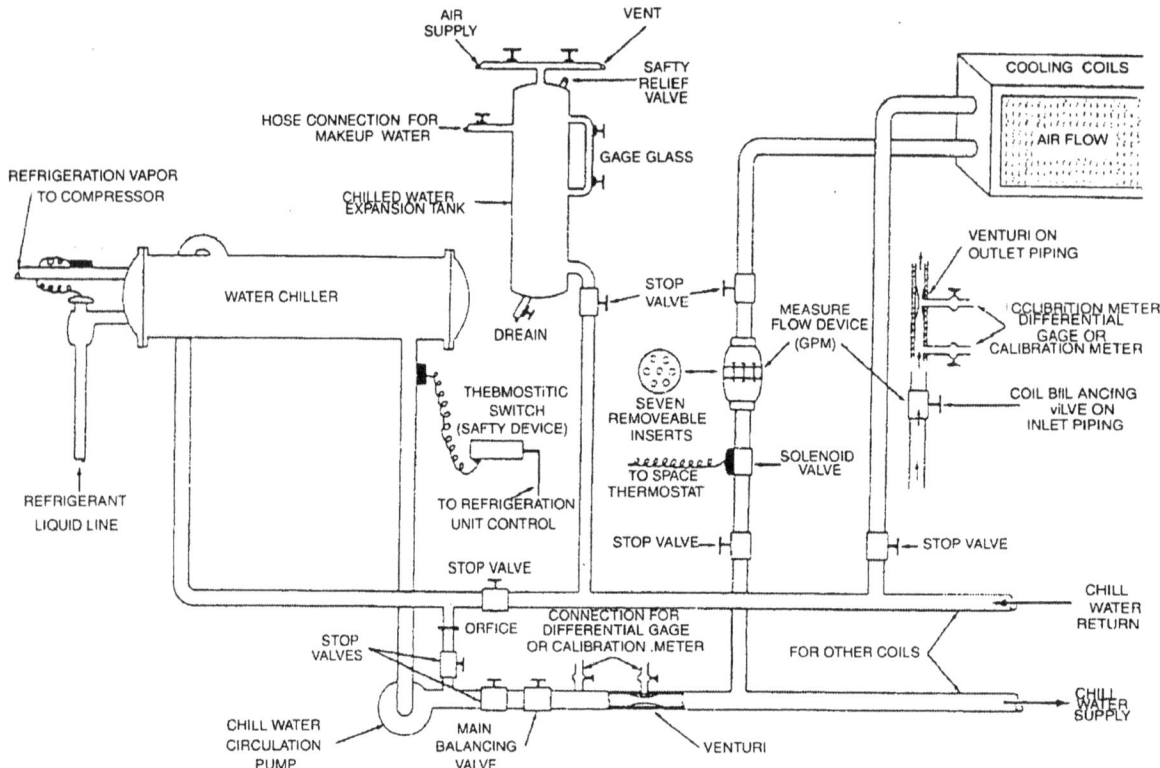

Figure 1. - A chilled water air conditioning circuit.

The water enters the shell at one end of the chiller and is directed by baffles to flow around all the tubes before leaving from the other end of the chiller. The water always enters the chiller at the outlet of the refrigerant so as to create what is called "counterflow." By making the refrigerant and water flow through the chiller in opposite directions, more heat is transferred over a given area.

C2. Thermostatic Switch. -The sensing bulb of the thermostatic switch is located in the chill water line from the water chiller. The switch is a safety device; its primary function is to stop the refrigeration unit or units if the temperature of the chilled water approaches the danger of freezing.

The switch is wired into the pilot control circuit and, during normal operation, the contacts are closed to complete the circuit. When the temperature of the water reaches a predetermined temperature, the fluid in the sensing element contracts allowing the contacts of the switch to open. This action opens the pilot circuit which in turn allows the main contacts in the refrigeration unit motor control panel to open, stopping the compressor. Normally the compressor motor is controlled by the low pressure switch which is actuated by pressure in the refrigerant suction line.

C3. Chilled Water Circulating Pumps.- Chilled water systems are designed to use either one or two centrifugal pumps to circulate the chilled water; the number used depends on the size of the installation. The system shown in figure 1 uses only one such pump.

The pump is driven by an electric motor and is designed to deliver a gallon per minute flow rate slightly above the total flow rate of all the cooling coils the pump supplies. This eliminates the possibility of reduced flow to any of the coils.

The pump takes suction from the water chiller and discharges into the chilled water supply line. The small line on the discharge side of the pump is connected to the chilled water return line. Installed in the small line is an orifice to allow some leakage through to the return line. This enables any air which may get into the system, such as through pump packings, to work its way back to the chilled water expansion tank.

C4. Main Balancing Valve. - The main balancing valve is installed in the chilled water supply line near the circulating pump, with a distance of at least ten pipe diameters distance of straight pipe on each side. The main balancing valve is, in reality, a constant flow regulator. It is a throat-type collar insert that fits in the water pipe and is so designed in shape and size as to regulate the flow of water in gpm over a variable inlet pressure and outlet pressure.

Venturi tubes are located on the inlet or outlet sides of the valve with one tube extracting from the insert, as shown in figure 2. The tubes are connected to a dial-type differential pressure gage calibrated in gpm.

Main balancing valves are stamped with their rated capacity when tested. The flow rate required for a specific valve or regulator should be stamped or marked externally for reference. When no markings appear in the area of the flow control device, the manufacturer's technical manual must be consulted and adhered to.

C5. Cooling Coil Controls. - Each cooling coil in the system is attached to the supply and return mains by branch lines. The controls for the chilled water to the coils are located in these branch lines. Each branch supply line and branch return line has a manually operated stop valve installed to isolate the cooling coil from the rest of the system.

In the branch supply line between the stop valve and the cooling coil is an electrically operated solenoid valve. This valve is wired into the space thermostat. As the temperature of the space increases, the electrical contacts of the thermostat close, energizing the solenoid. The electrical current passing through the coil in the solenoid causes the valve to open; this allows the chilled water to circulate through the cooling coil. When the temperature of the space is lowered to the thermostatic setting, the electrical contacts in the thermostat open; this action breaks the electrical circuit and allows the solenoid valve to close and stop the flow of chilled water through the cooling coil.

The coil balancing valve is normally located in a straight section of the pipe which supplies the cooling coil. Valves of this type are similar to the main balancing valve, except they are smaller and regulate the flow for the individual cooling coil. Where space will not permit these fittings in the supply line, they can be installed on the outlet side of the cooling coil. Regardless of where they are installed, they must have at least ten pipe diameters distance of straight unobstructed pipe on each side of them.

The venturi taps are installed on each side of the coil balancing valve with stop valves and caps. The rate flow indicator, as shown in figure 2, is not attached; a portable unit should be available to check the flow rate.

Some coil balancing valves are of a type that can be adjusted externally by a key and valve stem. The name plate data of the cooling coil specifies the design flow rate of the coil and these valves should be calibrated as close as possible to the designed rate. The range factor is plus or minus 10 percent over a pressure range from 10 to 150 psi.

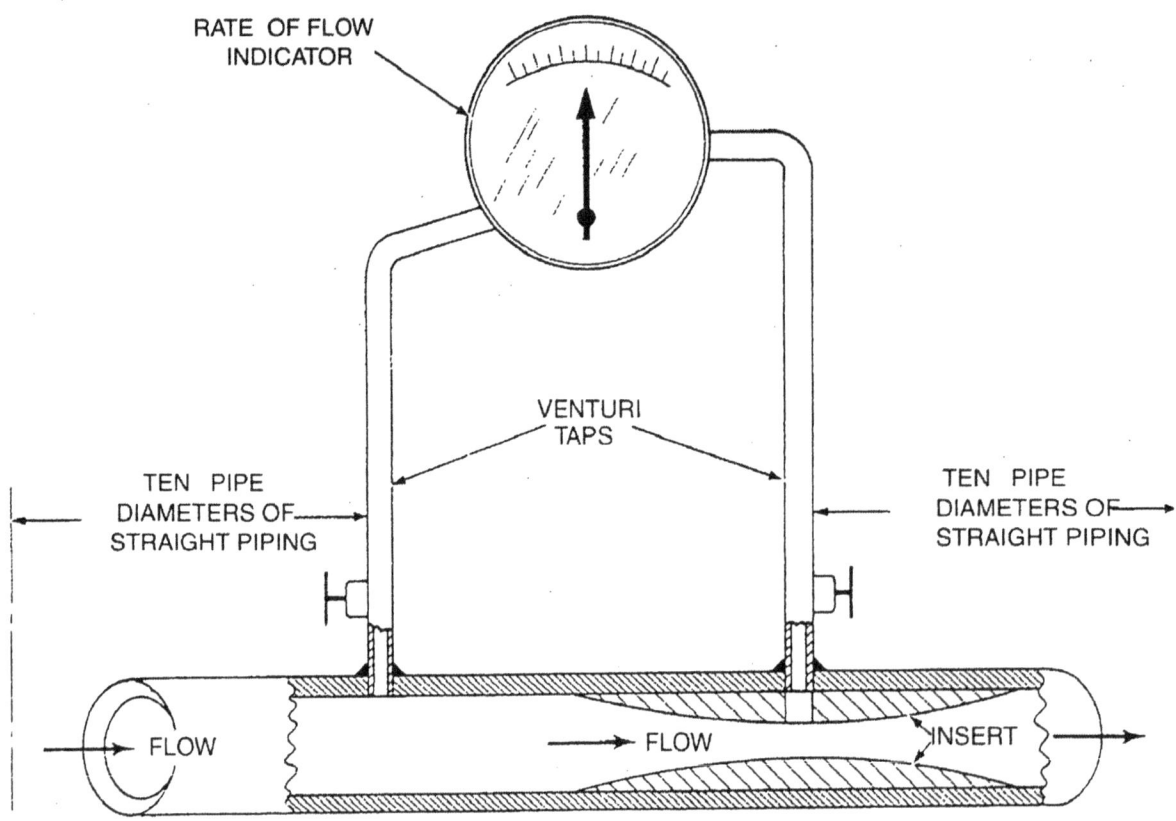

Figure 2.-Balancing valve or flow regulator.

C6. Expansion Tank. - The expansion tank is located near the water chiller and the chilled water circulation pump. The functions of the tank are to (1) collect any air that may leak into the system, (2) maintain a constant pressur on the return chilled water main so the circulation pump will have a positive suction pressure, and (3) provide a space to allow for the expansion of the chilled water when the plant is secured and the water temperature increases.

The tank is equipped with various fittings, one of which is a safety relief valve. This valve is installed in the upper section of the tank; if pressure becomes excessive, the valve permits air in the tank to escape.

The fitting for adding makeup water is a hose connection. This too is a safety device because the hose should be connected only when adding water. This prevents the possibility of the chilled water being forced back through the hose into the supply water system.

An air supply fitting is located in the upper section of the tank for the purpose of adding air to maintain the constant suction pressure on the chilled water return to the circulating pump.

A sight glass/gage arrangement on the side of the tank indicates the water level. This level should be maintained between 1/3 and 1/2 of a tank when the plant is in operation.

A drain valve is installed in the very bottom of the tank for drainage and also to remove sediment.

CHAPTER 2
AIR CIRCULATION

A. INTRODUCTION

Air circulation is one of the most important factors essential for satisfactory refrigeration and air conditioning. Without some means to circulate the air, one area of a space would become colder than other areas and an unequal temperature condition would exist within the space. Because air currents are used to transport the heat within a space to the cooling element, care should be used not to block these currents with the stowage of such as boxes and lockers, or by partitions. Air flow, as it applies to refrigeration and air conditioning, and the means of creating a circulation of air are considered in this chapter.

B. NATURAL AIR FLOW

The three methods of heat transfer conduction, convection, and radiation were discussed in an earlier chapter of this text. Convection is the conveying of heat from one point to another by the movement of a circulating medium; it is this method that is very important in refrigeration and air conditioning. For example, if the warm air in a room rises and comes in contact with the cooler surface of an air conditioning cooling coil, the air will lose some its heat to the cooler surface. The cooled air will then settle and absorb heat from the warmer air; this action creates what is known as natural circulation. The area in the vicinity of the coil will become cool, but the air would be progressively warmer the farther you move from the coil due to the minimum air movement caused by natural circulation. It is for this reason that some form of forced circulation of the air is needed.

C. FORCED AIR FLOW

C1. Types of Fans (Blowers). - Fans used in plants in conjunction with supply and exhaust systems may be divided into two general classes: AXIAL FLOW AND CENTRIFUGAL. Most fans in duct systems are of the axial flow type because fans of this type require less space for installation.

Bracket fans are used in warm weather to provide local circulation. These fans are usually installed in living, hospital, office, commissary issuance, and berthing spaces on ships which are not air conditioned. Where mechanical cooling is employed, bracket fans are sometimes used to facilitate proper circulation and direction of the cooler air.

C2. Centrifugal Fans.-Centrifugal fans are generally preferred for exhaust systems handling explosive or humid vapors. The motors of these fans, being outside the air stream, cannot ignite the explosive vapors. The motors are subject to insulation failure to a lesser degree than the motors of the vaneaxial fans, when fans exhaust very humid air or steam as in sculleries. If the temperature of the vapors being handled is very high, the heat can be transmitted through the shaft to the motor and cause bearing damage and insulation breakdown. Figure 1 shows the construction of a centrifugal fan.

The housing of the fan is designed so it may be adjusted to any one of eight different discharge angles. The fan wheels are of three types as shown in figure 2.

Backward curved blades are deeper than other types, and the wheels have fewer blades and operate at a higher speed. Most shipboard centrifugal fans have wheels with backward curved blades because of favorable pressure and speed characteristics. Since the wheel is overhung on the motor shaft (not belt driven permitting use of lower powered motors, and the continually rising pressure characteristic from free delivery to no delivery, permitting a much broader use of standard fans.

High pressure, low volume fans such as gland exhausters, usually have cast radial blades to obtain strength at a low cost.

C3. Axial Fans. - There are three general types of the axial fanspropeller, vane-axial and tubeaxial.

Two styles of the vaneaxial fans are shown in figure 3. The fan shown in view A has flanged fittings at each end for permanent installation in the duct work. The fan shown in view B is a portable unit commonly called, in plants, a "Red Devil." It is fitted with a screen at one end and a half connector at the other to which flexible duct can be attached. The general term for this duct is "elephant trunk." The fittings on each end of the portable unit are interchangeable so the unit can be used as either a supply or exhaust fan, permitting use of the fan in the space being ventilated or remote from the space.

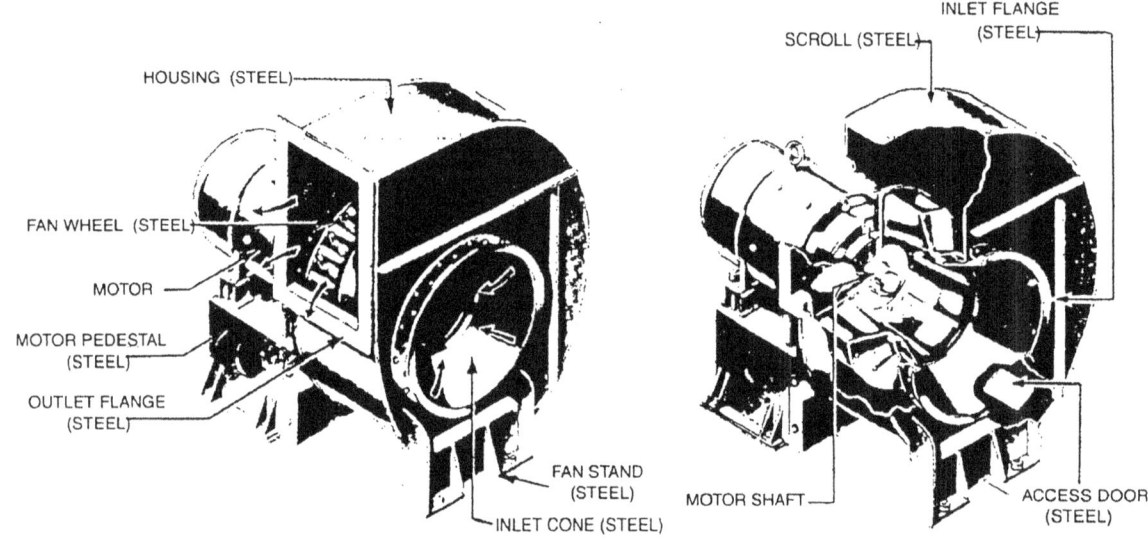

Figure 1.—A centrifugal fan; exterior and cutaway views.

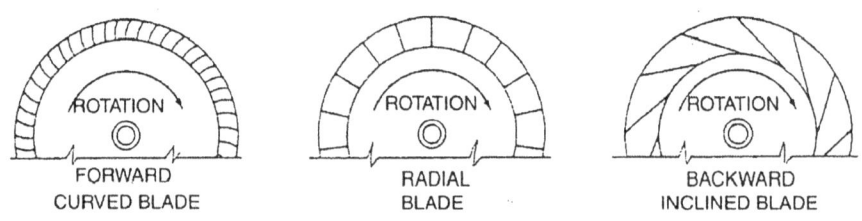

Figure 2.—View of types of blading used on centrifugal fans.

The name vaneaxial is derived from the vanes which are usually located downstream from the impeller and between the motor and fan housing and the axial flow of the air through the unit. The vanes are designed to straighten out the spiraling flow of the air from the impeller blades and to increase the efficiency.

The tubeaxial fan is the same as the vane-axial fan except it has no vanes. Fans of this type operate at low pressure and are usually installed so as not to discharge through duct work. They are used in unit heaters and coolers, in very short duct systems, and in bulkheads.

Axial fans are very susceptible to unbalance, resulting in noise and reduced bearing life. Blades must be cleaned frequently with approved solvent. Care is of great importance when installing new bearings.

The propeller fan consists of a stamped or cast wheel located in an orifice ring and is either motor or belt driven. A window fan is a common example of this type fan.

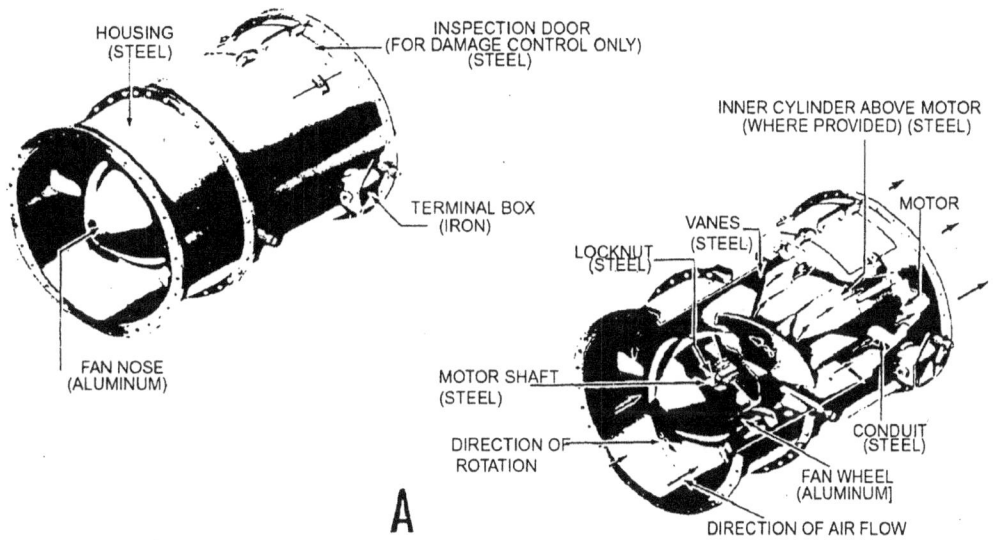

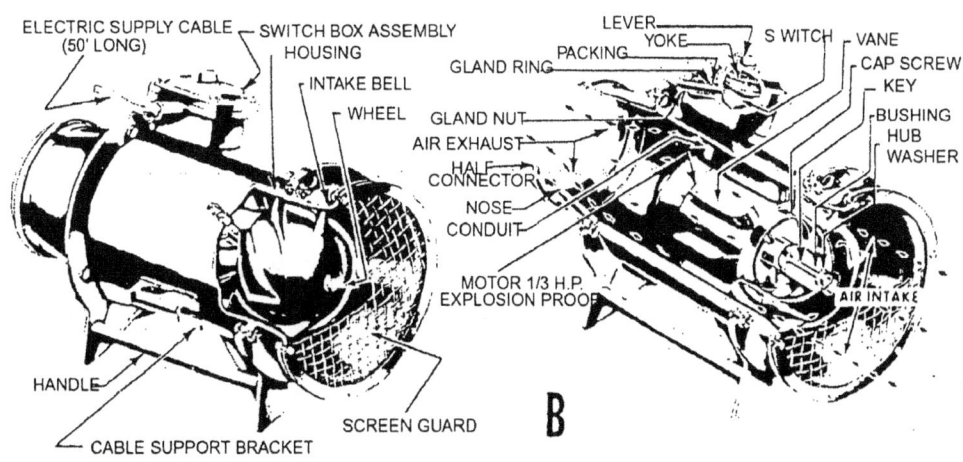

Figure 3.—Vane-axial ventilating fans.
  A. For duct installations.
  B. For portable use.

D. VENTILATION AND AIR CONDITIONING SYSTEMS

There are two types of systems generally used in power plants to maintain desired environmental control. These are ventilation systems (supply and exhaust), and recirculating systems (air conditioning). Duct heaters may be used in either or both systems, while mechanical cooling is used exclusively in air conditioning systems.

A ventilation system is generally regarded as a system where the air used is drawn from the weather, circulated through the space and exhausted back to the weather.

An air conditioning system is a system where all or part of the air from spaces being served is recirculated, and the air is cooled by mechanical means. Where only part of the air is recirculated due to personnel needs, the system is provided with replenishment air (fresh air) from the weather as shown in figure 4.

E. DUCT WORK

E1. Ducts. - Air is carried to the numerous spaces in plants and distributed as needed to maintain a specific space condition through air passages called ducts. Ducts (air passages) are also used to exhaust air to the weather.

These ducts are round, square, flat, oval, or rectangular in shape and are sized in accordance with the capacity of the fan (blower) in the system. Ducts are designed to carry a relatively high speed airflow but the flow is not to exceed an average 3500 feet per minute.

The round duct provides the most efficient air flow and requires less material to construct than comparable square or rectangular ducts. However, rectangular ducts are used more often because they can be better fitted into restricted areas and along the overhead where space is available.

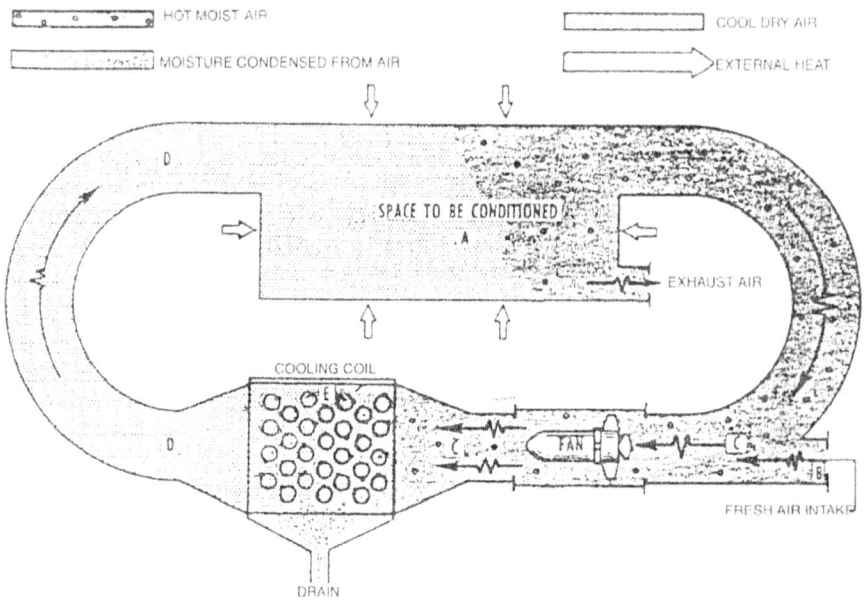

Figure 4.—A mechanical air-cooling cycle using the partially replenished air system.

Duct work is divided into three sections the main duct, the main branch duct, and the branch duct. The main duct is the section that begins at the air inlet and continues to the most remote outlet. A main branch duct is a branch from the main duct that has two or more outlets. The branch duct is a branch from either the main or the main branch duct and has only one outlet.

E2. Waterproof Ventilators (surface ships only). - When the main duct begins on an exposed weather deck, some means must be used to prevent the entry of water during driving rains and heavy weather. This is accomplished by the use of waterproof ventilators. (See fig. 5.)

The waterproof ventilator shown consists of an outer housing, an inner ventilator shaft extending up to the outer housing, and a bucket-type closure supported over the ventilator shaft by a compression spring. The bucket is provided with drain tubes extending into a sump between the ventilator shaft and the outer housing. The sump is provided with scupper valves, which drain onto the weather deck.

The ventilator operates automatically, and is normally open. Small quantities of water which enter the ventilator fall into the bucket and drain out through the drain tubes and scuppers. In heavy seas, when water enters the bucket faster than it drains out, the weight of water forces the bucket down against the top of the ventilator shaft. Thus, a watertight seal is formed and maintained until sufficient water drains out to permit the force of the spring to raise the bucket to the open position. Operating gear is generally provided to permit manual closing of the ventilator. With slight variations in construction, this ventilator is used for both the supply and exhaust of air,

E3. Ventilation Duct Fittings. - To ensure a smooth and even flow of air for proper distribution, the duct work is equipped with devices to distribute and direct the air flow. These fittings and their purpose and use are as follows:

Dampers. Dampers are usually located in the branch duct although sometimes they can be found in the supply duct. Their purpose is to make temporary adjustments of the air flow.

Diffusion terminals. These fittings are used to direct the flow of air as it leaves the duct work and to ensure draft free ventilation.

Vane duct turns. These are vanes installed in the duct work where the duct makes a turn. As the flow of air is traveling at a forward velocity, the vanes direct the flow through the turn to reduce a turbulence in the air stream.

Splitters. Splitters are used to proportion air to a branch duct. They are more or less a vane designed to direct a certain amount of the air in the main or main branch duct to the branch duct.

Plenum chamber. Used in recirulating ventilation systems, the plenum chamber is the mixing area. It is the only area in the system where turbulence of the air is desired and is usually found just prior to the fan. The recirculated air and the replenished air are mixed in this chamber to equalize the temperature.

E4. Cleaning and Care. - The duct workfor ventilation and air conditioning systems in plant has been designed and fabricated by the contractor in accordance with specifications established by code . No changes should be made in design such as adding more outlets or blanking off of return ducts or exhaust ducts. This will cause a change in the operating efficiency of the system. To ensure efficient operation, it is equally important that duct work and fittings be kept clean in accordance with the Planned Maintenance System program.

F. FILTERS

F1. Electrostats. - The electrostatic filter keeps practically all the dust and foreign matter from entering a ventilation system so equipped. This is accomplished by suspending a very high positive voltage wire between two grounded wires. The electrons in the air space around the wires put a positive electrical charge on any particle that passes the ionized field. Grounded plates with a negative potential as high as 13,000 volts are used to draw the positive charged particles to them.

Electrostatic filters are available in different sizes and capacities. The model number designates the air flow and efficiency of the filter. For example, model number 76D106-93 indicates that the filter will treat a maximum of 7600 cubic foot of air per minute and will remove a minimum of 93 percent of all foreign matter. These filters can be cleaned by washing with cold water and detergent.

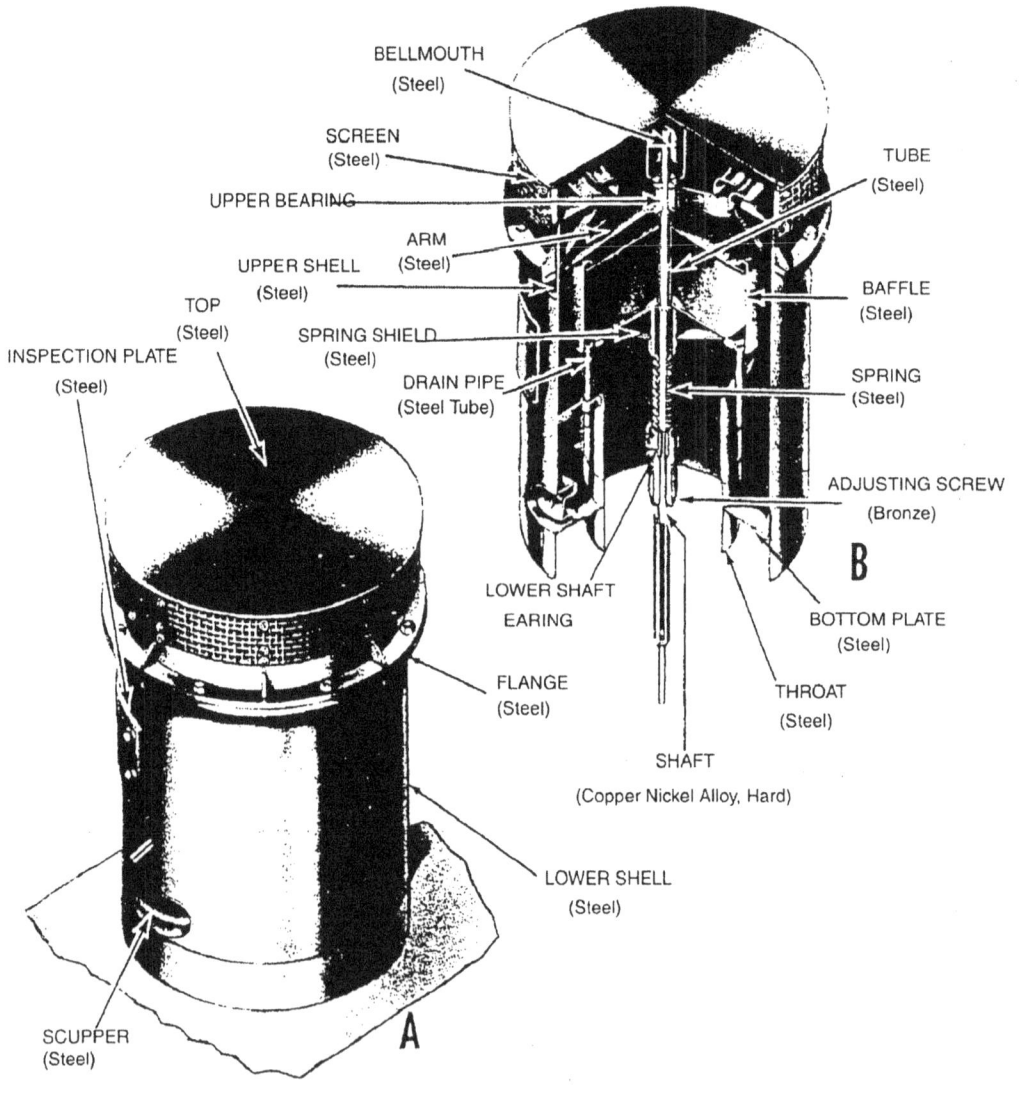

Figure 5.—Waterproof ventilator
A. Exterior view
B. Cutaway view

F2. Carbon Filters. - Carbon filters are used where odor causing gases and bacteria are to be removed. The carbon is in the form of activated charcoal and is commonly processed from coconut shells. It has a filtering capacity of about 50 percent of its weight. By baking the filter at 1000° F, it can be made reusable.

F3. Disposable Filters. - The most common of all filters for shore based application is the disposable or throw away type. Filters of this type are made of wire re-enforced cardboard frames and filled with various fiber materials such as wool, spun glass, and so forth.

As the air is forced through the filter, the fibers trap and hold about 90 percent of all the dust particles. These filters should be replaced when the pressure drop across the filter exceeds the pressure drop indicated on the label plate for dirty filter conditions. Usually, replacement is necessary about twice a year, but may be more often if conditions warrant.

F4. Cleanable High-Velocity Filters. - These are the filters used in air conditioning systems in plants. They are of the cleanable, viscous, impingement, high-velocity type.

The filter is installed ahead of the cooling coils in air conditioning systems and unit coolers. Newer installations have pressure taps on either side of the filter bank. By the use of a portable differential pressure gage, the pressure drop across the filter may be quickly read. When the pressure drop increases to three times that of a clean filter, in the same location, the filter should be cleaned.

When practicable, the filters can be cleaned by use of the galley dish washing machine. Use the specified amount of washing compound and run the filter through the machine with the dirty side up. When the filter is clean and dry it should be reoiled. Spray or dip the filter with an approved oil.

Set the filter on end and allow to drain for at least 18 hours. It is preferable to allow the filter to set and drain in an area where the temperature is higher than the temperature of the air to be filtered.

CHAPTER 3

PSYCHROMETRY AND HEAT LOAD

A. PSYCHROMETRICS

A1. Definition. - Psychrometry (sy-krom-etry) means literally the measurement of cold, from the Greek psychros, cold. It is the special name that has been given to the modern science that deals with air and water vapor mixtures. The amount of water vapor in the air has a great influence on human comfort. Such atmospheric moisture is called humidity, and the common expression, "It isn't the heat, it's the humidity," is an indication of the popular recognition of the discomfort-producing effects of moisture-laden air in hot weather.

A2. Air and Humidity, a Physical Mixture. - The water vapor in the air is not absorbed or dissolved by the air. The mixture is a simple physical one, just as sand and water are mixed. The temperature of the water vapor is always the same as that of the air.

If a tin can is filled with sand to the top, there is still room into which water can flow between the grains of sand. If the can is then filled with water to the top, that sand is holding all the water it is able to hold. It is said that the sand is saturated with water.

In the same way, air can hold different amounts of water vapor, and when it is holding all the vapor it is able to hold, it is called saturated air. The amount of moisture at the saturation point varies with the temperature of the air; the higher the temperature, the more moisture the air can hold.

A3. Dewpoint. - The saturation point is more often called the dewpoint, for if the temperature of the saturated air falls below its dew-point, some of the water vapor in it must condense to liquid water, generally in drops. The dew that appears early in the morning on foliage when there is normally a drop in temperature, if the air is moist, is such a condensation, and is readily recognized. The sweating of cold water pipes, with which almost everyone is familiar, is also the condensation of dew from moist air on the cold surfaces of the pipes.

A4. Condensation of Saturated Air. - Condensation of water vapor from the air can take place when the air temperature is below the dew-point. In nature, moisture is condensed on foliage and other surfaces as dew if the air temperature is above $32°$ F. If the temperature of the surface is below freezing, the moisture condenses as frost. Above the earth's surface it is mist, and when the mist is very thick, it is called a fog. If such condensation on dust particles is high in the air, the fog is then called a cloud. Under certain conditions of sudden cooling with much condensation, the droplets grow so large they can no longer float in the air, and then they fall as rain. Sometimes a layer of air at a temperature below $32°$ F exists high in a storm area; through this cold layer, raindrops may be carried up and down several times by air currents until they freeze and fall as hail. In cold weather, when the temperature is below $32°$ F, condensation on the dust in the air forms snowflakes.

A5. Difference Between Water Vapor and Water Drops. - The question is sometimes asked: If the air contains moisture, why does the moisture not freeze when the temperature is below $32°$ F? The answer is that only a liquid can freeze and a vapor is not a liquid. Drops of water, however small they may be, are merely small masses of liquid. In a mist or fog, the drops are so small that they float in the air, but they are nevertheless liquid. Air moisture does indeed freeze sometimes, if that moisture is in the state of liquid drops, and then it takes the form either of hail or of sleet which is partially frozen moisture. Liquid moisture in the air (for example, mist) may exist in the form of drops subdivided so small as to be imperceptible to the human eye as individual drops; yet each single drop is formed of a great multitude of molecules. In a vapor or gas, the subdivision actually consists of single molecules.

A6. Intermolecular Distance Determines State. - The fundamental difference between the three states of matter-solid, liquid, and gaseous is the distance between the molecules. In a solid, they are close and hold to one another so that each has little or no freedom of motion. In a vapor or gas, the molecules are so far apart that all mutual attraction is lost and each has complete freedom of motion, except as bounded by a container. Solids and liquids are visible to the human eye, but vapors and gases, with few exceptions, are invisible. Water vapor is invisible. The visible white cloud arising from a tea-kettle or steam pipe is not really vapor or steam, although it is usually called steam, but is formed of minute liquid droplets that have condensed on striking the cooler air. They re-evaporate in a few minutes and are invisible again.

A7. Formation of Frost. - When molecules of water vapor come into contact with a cool surface they may condense and appear in the liquid state as dew.

Water vapor can, however, pass directly to the solid state without going through the liquid phase; this process is called crystallization. For crystallization to take place, the surface condition must be at or below the freezing temperature. The water vapor arranges itself on the surface in solid geometrical forms or designs, called crystals. If the cold surfaces are extended to large areas, such as the ground, glass windows, and so forth, the crystals are called frost. Frosting always appears on the cooling coils (evaporators) of mechanical refrigerating systems. This frost must be removed periodically since it has some insulating quality and lessens the refrigerating capacity.

B. HEAT OF THE AIR

B1. Sensible Heat of Air. - The heat of air is considered from three standpoints. First, sensible heat is that measured by household, or dry-bulb, thermometers. This is the temperature of the air itself, without regard to any humidity it may contain. It may be well to emphasize this by stating that sensible heat is the heat of dry air.

B2. Latent Heat in Air. - Second, air nearly always contains more or less moisture. Conditions of complete absence of moisture rarely occur, perhaps only in desert regions. Any water vapor present, of course, contains the latent heat which made it a vapor. Such latent heat of the moisture in the air may be spoken of as the latent heat in the air.

B3. Total Heat of Air. - Third, any mixture of dry air and water vapor, that is, air as we usually find it, does contain both sensible heat and latent heat. The sum of the sensible heat and the latent heat in any sample of air is called the total heat of the air. It is usually measured from zero degrees as a convenient starting point.

C. THREE AIR TEMPERATURES

C1. Need for Three Air Temperatures. - In as much as air conditioning deals with these various heats of air and the condensation of the moisture in it as well, three different temperatures are needed to understand and control the operations. These are the dry-bulb, wet-bulb, and dew-point temperatures.

C2. Dry-Bulb Temperature. The dry-bulb temperature is the temperature of the sensible heat of the air, as measured by an ordinary thermometer. Such a thermometer is called in psychrometry or in air conditioning engineering a dry-bulb thermometer, because its bulb is dry, in contrast to the wet-bulb type next described.

C3. Wet-Bulb Temperature. - A wet-bulb thermometer is an ordinary thermometer with a cloth sleeve, of wool or flannel, placed around its bulb and then wet with pure water. The cloth sleeve should be clean and free from oil and thoroughly wet with clean fresh water (preferably distilled water). The water in the cloth sleeve is caused to evaporate by a current of air at high velocity, and the evaporation, withdrawing heat from the thermometer bulb, lowers the temperature, as then measured, a certain number of degrees. The difference between the dry-bulb and wet-bulb temperatures is called the wet-bulb depression. If the air is saturated, evaporation cannot take place and the wet-bulb temperature is the same as the dry-bulb.

Complete saturation, however, is not usual and a wet-bulb depression is normally to be expected.

C4. Wet-Bulb Temperature Measures Total Heat. - The wet-bulb thermometer indicates the total heat of the air being measured. If air at several different times or different places is measured and the wet-bulb temperatures found to be the same for all, the total heat would be the same in all, though their sensible heats and respective latent heats might vary considerably. Again, in any given sample of air, if the wet-bulb temperature does not change, the total heat present is the same, even though some of the sensible heat might be converted to latent heat, or vice versa.

C5. Sling Psychrometer. - In air conditioning work, the two thermometers, wet-bulb and dry-bulb, are mounted side by side on a frame, to which a handle and short chain is attached. (See fig. 1.) The thermometers are whirled in the air, thus providing the high velocity air currents for evaporation. Such a device is called a sling psychrometer.

The procedure for using the sling psychrometer follows:

1. Soak the wick with distilled water.

2. Whirl the instrument for about one minute at a speed which will provide an air speed of at least 1000 feet per minute over the bulbs. To cover the greatest area, move about the room.

3. Stop whirling the instrument and immediately read the wet-bulb temperature.

4. Without re-wetting the wick, whirl the instrument for another 10 seconds. Repeat steps 3 and 4 until the lowest temperature is obtained. Use this lowest temperature as the wet-bulb reading.

The foregoing procedure is for use when temperatures are above freezing. If the temperature is below freezing, then the wick is only dampened and the instrument is whirled for 2 minutes. Then follow steps 3 and 4 as before.

C6. Hand Electric Psychrometer. - The hand electric psychrometer is a handheld-portable instrument used to obtain free air temperature, dewpoint, and relative humidity. (See fig. 2.)

The two thermometers comprising the psychrometer have a range from plus $10°$ F to plus $110°$ F. The psychrometer comes with a carrying case and three water bottles. With the exception of the three standard flashlight batteries which supply the power, it is ready for operation as issued. Figure 3 shows the complete unit.

For operating at temperatures above $50°$ F, the following procedures apply.

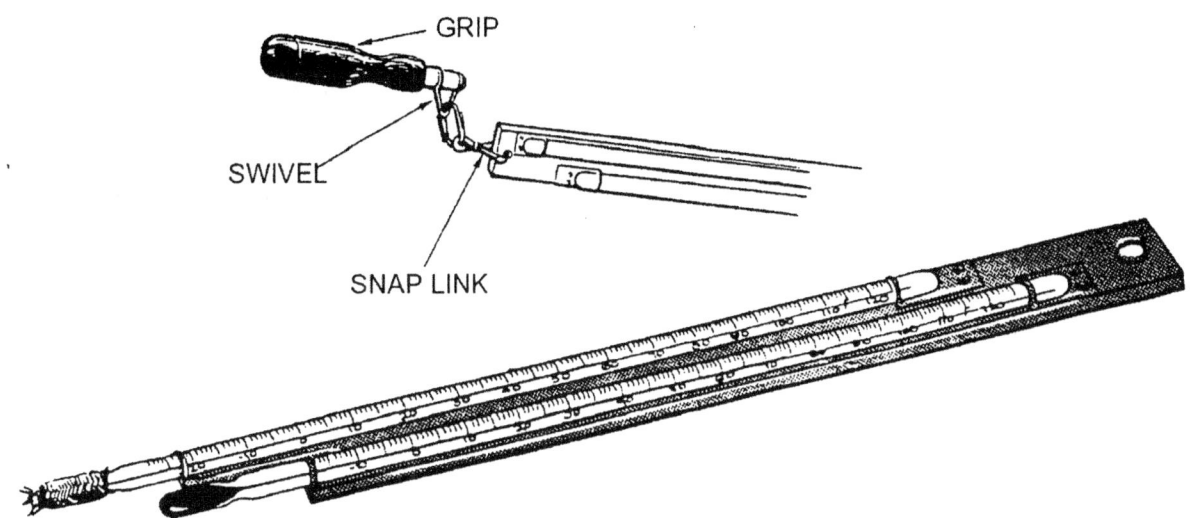

Figure 1.—A standard sling psychrometer.

Expose the psychrometer to the air for at least 5 minutes before using it for readings.

Open the sliding door halfway, remove the water bottle and close the sliding door.

Saturate the wick with distilled water by using one of the following methods. Method 1 is recommended.

Method 1. Remove the sliding air intake and thoroughly saturate the wet-bulb wick, taking every precaution to prevent water from contacting either thermometer tube or the dry-bulb. Any moisture which may have contacted the dry-bulb must be removed.

Method 2. Without removing the sliding air intake, hold the psychrometer so that the bulbs point upward. Carefully apply water, a drop at a time to the wet-bulb wick, so as not to cause the thermometer tube to become wet from an overly saturated wick. Any moisture which may have contacted the dry-bulb must be removed.

If method 1 was followed, replace the air intake, being sure that the small circular holes in the air intake are positioned against the thermometer holder. Replace the water bottle.

Either of the following positions may be used during operation.

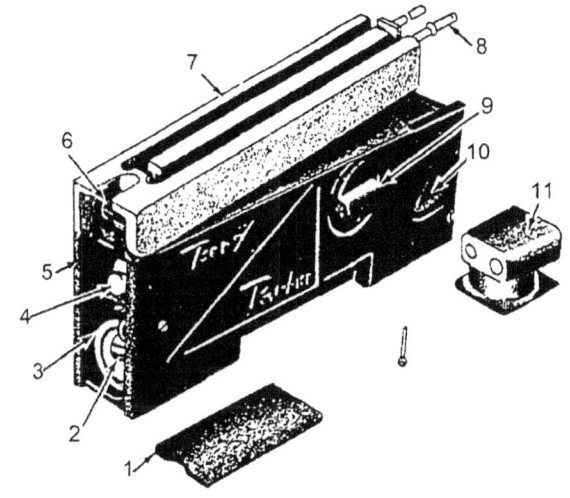

1. Sliding door.
2. Spring contact.
3. Battery compartment
4. Water bottle.
5. Bottle compartment.
6. Hinge pin.
7. Thermometer holder.
8. Wet-bulb wick, ment.
9. Knob.
10. Exhaust parts,
11. Sliding air intake.

Figure 2. - Exposed view of hand electric psychrometer

1. Place the instrument on a flat surface with the graduations of the thermometer facing upward and the air intake pointing to the left and into the wind; or

2. Grasp the instrument in the left hand with the fingers fitting the curved portion of the case, the graduations of the thermometers facing the operator, and the air intake pointing to the left and into the wind.

CAUTION: In either position, the air intake and both exhaust ports must be entirely free of obstruction and far enough away from the operator's body or any other source of moist air or temperature that may cause a false reading.

Turn the switch knob clockwise to start aspiration. If thermometer illumination is desired, continue turning the knob until sufficient light intensity is obtained.

When the wet-bulb temperature stabilizes at a minimum value, note the readings of both thermometers and turn off the switch by turning the knob counterclockwise.

Evaluate the readings using the tables supplied with the instrument.

The following precautionary measures should be observed to ensure accurate performance when temperatures are below 50° F.

1. The instrument should be stored in its case and at a suitable location to keep it at approximately ambient temperature.

2. If brought from a warm room to outside temperature below 50 °F, special care should be taken to point the instrument into the wind and to ensure that an equilibrium temperature is reached by letting the fan run for 5 to 10 minutes.

3. If brought from cold to warm temperature for a reading, ensure that condensation on the dry-bulb does not give an erroneous reading due to wet-bulb effect.

The remaining steps in the operation of the hand electric psychrometer are identical with those already mentioned.

C7. Dewpoint temperature.- The dewpoint depends upon the amount of water vapor in the air. If air at a certain temperature is not saturated, that is, if it does not contain the full quantity of water vapor it can hold at that temperature, and the temperature of that air falls, a point is finally reached at which the air is saturated for the new, lower temperature and condensation of the moisture then begins. This point is the dewpoint temperature of the air for the quantity of water vapor present.

C8. Relation of Dry-Bulb, - Wet-Bulb, and Dewpoint Temperatures. The definite relationships between the three temperatures should be clearly understood. These relationships are:

1. When the air contains some moisture but is not saturated, the dewpoint temperature is lower than the dry-bulb temperature, and the wet-bulb temperature lies between them.

2. As the amount of moisture in the air increases, the differences between the temperatures grow less.

3. When the air is saturated, all three temperatures are the same.

D. HUMIDITY

D1. Humidity. The word humidity is often used in speaking generally of the moisture, or water vapor, in the air. It has, besides, two technical meanings: absolute humidity and relative humidity.

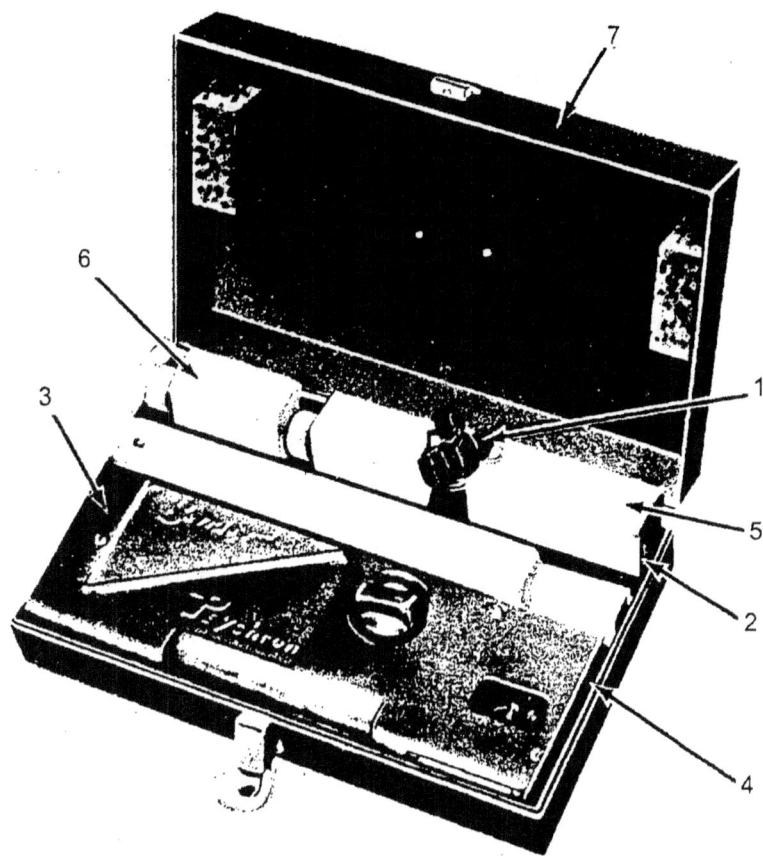

1. Neck strap.
2. Sparethermometers.
3. Psychrometer.
4. Instructions and tables
5. Box (extra wick, thread, and lamp).
6. 2-oz. bottle.
7. Carrying case.

Figure 3.- Hand electric psychrometer with carrying case

D2. <u>Absolute Humidity and Specific Humidity</u>. Humidity in air is expressed according to its weight. The weight of the moisture that air can contain depends upon the temperature of the air, and is independent of the pressure of the air. This weight is usually given in grains; there being 7,000 grains to the pound. <u>Absolute humidity is the weight of water vapor in grains per cubic foot of air. Specific humidity is the weight of water vapor in grains per pound of dry air.</u> This second form is more generally used. It should be understood that the weight of moisture in grains refers only to moisture in the actual vapor state, and not in any way to any moisture that may be present in the liquid state, such as fog, rain, dew, or frost.

D3. Relative Humidity. - Relative humidity is the ratio of the weight of water vapor in a sample of air to the weight of water vapor that same sample of air contains when saturated. This ratio is usually stated as a percentage. For example, if the air is fully saturated, its relative humidity is 100 percent. If the air contains no moisture at all, its relative humidity is zero. If the air is half saturated, its relative humidity is 50 percent.

D4. Importance of Relative Humidity. - As far as comfort and discomfort resulting from humidity are concerned, it is the relative humidity and not the absolute or specific humidity that is the important factor. This can be more easily understood by an example.

It should be understood that moisture always travels from regions of greater wetness to regions of lesser wetness, just as heat travels from regions of higher temperatures to regions of lower temperatures. If the air above a liquid is saturated, the two are in equilibrium and no moisture can travel from the liquid to the air; that is, the liquid cannot evaporate. If the air is only partially saturated, some evaporation can take place and some moisture will travel into the air.

Suppose the specific humidity of the air to be 120 grains per pound of dry air. This is the actual weight of the water vapor in that air. If the dry-bulb temperature of the air is 76° F, the relative humidity is nearly 90 percent; that is, the air is nearly saturated. The body perspires but the perspiration does not evaporate quickly because the air already contains nearly all the moisture it can hold. The general feeling of discomfort is a warning that the environment under such conditions is not suitable for the best maintenance of health. Nature has, however, given the human body extraordinary powers of resistance, and the body can take a great deal of punishment without permanent harm, though its efficiency drops for the time being.

But if the dry-bulb temperature is 86° F, the relative humidity is only 64 percent. That is, although the absolute amount of moisture in the air is the same, the relative amount is less, because at 86° F the air can hold more water vapor than it can at 78° F. The body is now able to evaporate its excess moisture and the general feeling is much more agreeable, even though the air temperature is ten degrees hotter.

In both cases, the specific humidity is the same, but the ability of the air to evaporate liquid moisture is quite different at the two temperatures. This ability to evaporate moisture is indirectly indicated by the relative humidity. It is for this reason that extreme importance is placed upon control of relative humidity in air conditioning.

D5. Psychrometric Chart. - There is a relationship between dry-bulb, wet-bulb, and dewpoint temperatures, and specific and relative humidity. Given any two, the others can be calculated. However, the relationship can be shown on a chart, and in air conditioning it is customary to use the chart, since it is far easier than calculating. Such a chart is called a pschrometric chart; a simple form of it is given in figure 4. In this chart, note that the wet-bulb temperature scale and dewpoint temperature scale lie along the same line, which is, of course, the 100 percent relative humidity line. But note that the dewpoint temperature lines run horizontally to the right, and the wet bulb temperature lines run obliquely down to the right.

To use the chart, take the point of intersection of the lines of the two known factors, interpolating if necessary. From this intersection point, follow the lines of the unknown factors to their numbered scales and read the measurement.

Example 1. Given a dry-bulb temperature of 70° F and a wet-bulb temperature of 60° F, what are the dewpoint temperature and the relative humidity? From the intersection, follow horizontally along the dewpoint line to the dewpoint scale. Answer: The dewpoint temperature is 53. 6° F. The relative humidity will be found to be 56 percent, read at the intersection of the lines of the two curved relative humidity lines.

Example 2. If the dewpoint remains at 53. 6° F, what is the relative humidity if the air is heated to a dry-bulb temperature of

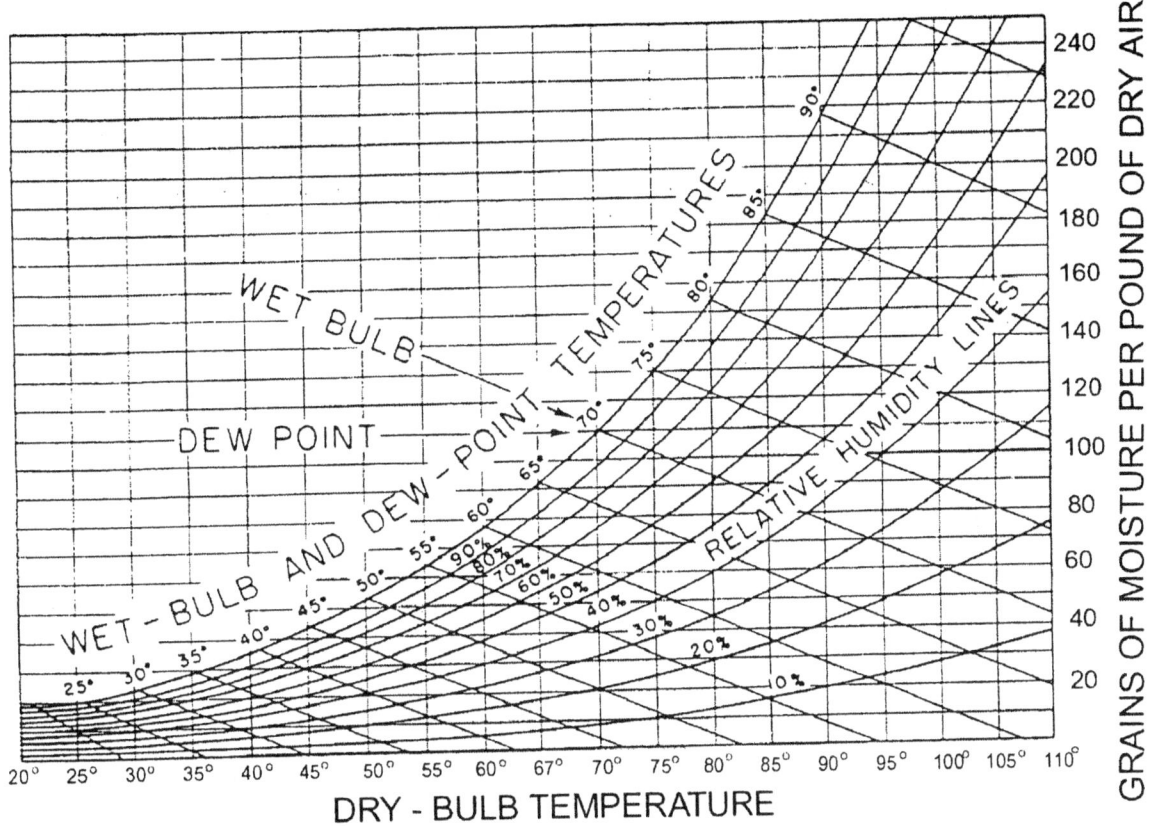

Figure 4. - Simplified psychrometric chart.

80° F? Answer: Follow the dewpoint line horizontally to the 80° F dry-bulb temperature line, where interpolation reads 40.5 percent.

Example 3. Given a dry-bulb temperature of 80° F and a dewpoint temperature of 70° F, what is the relative humidity if the dry-bulb temperature of the air is then raised to 90° F? Answer: Note the intersection of the dew-point 70° F line running horizontally from the dewpoint scale to the vertical 80° F dry-bulb line. Follow from this line, horizontally to the 90° F dry-bulb line and read the relative humidity which is 52 percent.

The actual weight of any amount of water vapor in the air at any temperature can be read on the chart from the scale at the right hand side. For example, take the 70° F dry-bulb temperature line. The intersection on this line of the various relative humidity percentage lines, followed horizontally to the right, gives the number of grains of water vapor per pound of the air. At the bottom is zero moisture, or completely dry air. At the top is 100 percent saturation, such as air at 70° F holding a maximum of 110.5 grains per pound. The various weights of water vapor that air at 70° F holds for any percentage of saturation can be found by following horizontally to the right from any relative humidity percentage point on the 70° F dry-bulb line.

Example: What is the actual weight of water vapor in air at 85° F dry-bulb and 70° F wet-bulb temperatures? Answer: About 85.5 grains per pound of dry air.

Large detailed psychromatic charts that are convenient for the accurate solution of problems are usually free from various manufacturers of air conditioning equipment. Such charts are one of the most valuable tools an air conditioning man can have when used properly.

E. FACTORS AFFECTING HUMAN COMFORT AND EFFICIENCY

E1. Comfort.- In air conditioning practice, the term comfort is used to mean not comfort in the sense of mere pleasure, such as relaxing in a soft arm chair, but rather comfort in the sense of physiological well-being and general efficiency of mind and body.

E2. Humidity Requirements for Good Health. - If air is too dry, the mucous membranes of the mouth, nose, and lungs are adversely affected, and not only feel parched and uncomfortable, but are also more susceptible to germs. If air is too moist, the body is constantly in a state of perspiration, cannot maintain a proper rate of evaporation, and clothing stays damp. It has been found that for best health conditions, a relative humidity of 40 to 60 percent is desirable. Even within this range, a distinction can be made between winter and summer conditions, for the best possible results. A range of 40 to 50 percent relative humidity is considered best in cold weather; in hot weather, the best range is 50 to 60 percent.

E3. Temperature Regulation of the Human Body. Ordinarily, the body is at a fairly constant temperature of $98.6°$ F. This, of course, refers to the interior of the body and not to the skin surfaces, which vary in temperature. Nature has so evolved the human body that any serious departure from this normal temperature of $98.6°$ F is dangerous to health. Even a change of one degree, up or down, is noticeable. But since the body is continually receiving a heat gain from surrounding and interior processes, there must also be a continuous output of heat to keep a balance. Fortunately, the body is equipped to maintain this balance automatically, and on the whole does an extraordinarily good job.

E4. Body Heat Gains. - The body gains heat by the following methods:

1. Radiation. The heat radiation gain comes from our surroundings, but since heat always travels from regions of higher temperature to regions of lower temperature, such surroundings must have a temperature higher than $98.6°$ F for the body to receive heat from them. Indoor heat radiation is gained from heating devices, stoves, operating machinery, hot pipes, and electric light bulbs. The greatest source of heat radiation is the sun.

2. Convection. The heat convection gain comes from currents of heated air only, and is usually found around operating machinery or other heat producing equipment.

3. Conduction. The heat conduction gain comes from objects which the body comes in contact with from time to time, such as when one touches a hot cup of coffee or uses hot water to wash.

4. Body heat production. Most of the body's heat comes from within the body itself. Heat is being continuously produced inside the body by the oxidation of foodstuffs and other chemical processes, by friction and tension within the muscle tissues, and by other causes as yet not well known.

E5. Body Heat Losses. - The heat given off by the body is of two kinds, sensible heat and latent heat. Sensible heat is given off by three methods—radiation, convection, and conduction. Latent heat is given off by evaporation.

1. Heat radiation loss. The body is usually at a higher temperature than that of its surroundings and, therefore, radiates heat to walls, floors, and other objects. The temperature of the air does not influence this radiation, except as it may alter the temperature of surrounding objects.

2. Heat convection loss. Heat is carried away from the body by convection currents, both by the air coming out of the lungs and by exterior air currents moving about the body. These may exist in the air itself moving or be caused by a person's movement through the air.

3. Heat conduction loss. Since the body is usually at a higher temperature than that of its surroundings, it gives up heat by conduction through bodily contact with the cooler objects.

4. Heat loss by evaporation. Under normal air conditions, the body gets rid of much of its excess heat by evaporation. When the body perspires, liquid emits from the pores to the outer surface of the skin. There it immediately begins to evaporate, and it does so by withdrawing heat from the body. Inside the body the heat is sensible heat but, in the process of evaporation, it becomes latent heat. The rate of evaporation and, hence, of heat loss, depends upon the temperature, relative humidity, and the motion of air.

Ordinarily with air at not too high a temperature and relative humidity, and when not too active, the body gets rid of its excess heat by radiation, convection, and conduction. When engaged in work or exercise, the body develops much more internal heat and perspiration begins. But perspiration rapidly evaporates if the relative humidity is not high. If, however, the relative humidity of the air is high, the moisture cannot evaporate, or does so only at a slow rate. In such cases, the excess heat cannot be removed by evaporation, and the body is dependent on radiation, convection, and conduction to eliminate its excess heat. This, of course, it cannot do and discomfort follows.

E6. Amount of Body Heat Loss. - The amount of heat given off by the body varies according to its activity. When seated at rest, the average adult male gives off about 390 Btu per hour. When working at fullest exertion, the body gives off about 1500 Btu per hour.

E7. Comfort Zones. - Extensive research has shown that a normal feeling of comfort is experienced by most persons in air at different temperatures, relative humidities, and air motion, within not too great a range. The average temperature within a range in which the greatest percentage of persons feel comfortable has been given the name comfort line, and the range itself is called the comfort zone. Since summer and winter weather conditions are markedly different, the summer comfort zone varies from the winter comfort zone. The human body is able to adapt itself automatically to the summer and winter conditions. Air conditions, indoors, that are quite comfortable in summer are decidedly uncomfortable in winter, and vice versa.

All the information gathered in the test has been compiled on a chart called the comfort chart shown in figure 5.

By using these charts to plot the dry-bulb temperature, the wet-bulb temperature, or the relative humidity, the effective temperature (E.T.) can be found.

The effective temperature is not a temperature that can be measured on a thermometer, but an experimentally determined index of a various combinations of temperature, humidity, and air movement that induce the same feeling of comfort for the average person.

Referring to the chart in figure 5, a dry-bulb temperature of 79° F and a relative humidity of 30 percent would give the same effect of comfort as a dry-bulb temperature of 75° F and a relative humidity of 60 percent, as they both fall on the E.T. line of 71. As shown in the upper left portion of the chart, 98 percent of the subjects tested preferred this line for summer comfort. The winter comfort average is shown in the lower section of the chart.

These charts provide an authentic guide for air conditioning, and if the air is maintained within the zones shown, it is found that general comfort is experienced.

E8. Heat and Humidity as Affected by Air Motion. - In this chapter it has been necessary to explain individually the action of the various factors of heat and humidity. In reality, they act simultaneously and, moreover, the motion or lack of motion of the air itself influences their effects considerably.

F. FIGURING HEAT LOADS

B1. The definition of heat load is the total amount of heat expressed in Btu which must be removed by the cooling coils to maintain the desired conditions and temperature within a space.

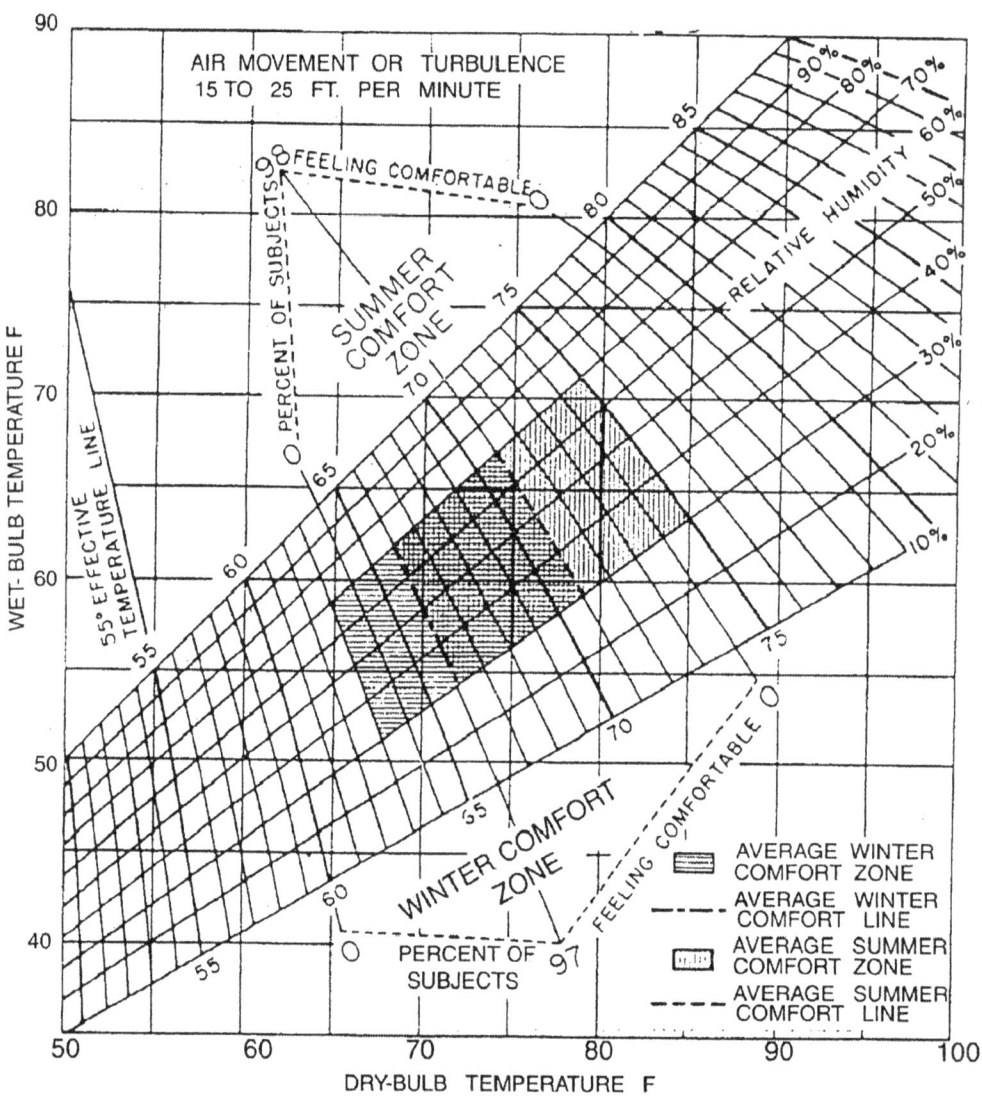

Figure 5.—Comfort index chart.

As all things contain heat, everything in the space must be taken into consideration when figuring the heat load. Some of the things that are common in both refrigeration and air conditioning that effect the heat loads are:

1. The temperature difference between the desired temperature of the space and the surrounding temperature outside the walls of the space.

2. The number and size of the fans, lights, and motors installed in the space to be cooled.

3. The type and thickness of the insulating materials installed in the walls, floor, and ceiling or overhead of the space.

As these are only three of the things to be considered, it can be seen that the total heat load can only be a calculated figure and cannot be the same at all times. Take the difference between the inside and outside temperatures for an example. The inside temperature is a set value of so many degrees but the outside temperature will always be changing, such as from summer to winter or even from day to night. Even with these defaults, extreme care must be used and all heat producing elements must be taken into consideration.

If a refrigeration unit or an air conditioning unit with insufficient capacity is installed, it would run continually and not be able to cool or maintain the area at a sufficiently low enough temperature. Whereas, an oversized unit would be an unnecessary expense to the owner.

F2. Figuring Heat Loads for Refrigeration. In refrigeration, there are three types of heat loads to be considered in finding the total heat load. The three types of heat loads are:

1. Product load. The product load is the amount of heat, measured in Btu, which must be removed from the product to lower the temperature of that product over a given range.

2. Maintaining load. Maintaining load is the amount of heat, measured in Btu, which must be removed each twenty-four (24) hours to maintain the desired temperature in the refrigerated space.

3. Pull down load. The pull down load is the amount of heat, measured in Btu, which must be removed from the product and the space during the time required to bring the product down to a given temperature.

By referring to charts that are made available by leading refrigeration manufacturers and in most refrigeration booklets, the specific heat, latent heat, and freezing temperatures of all food products can be found.

Also available are charts for the heat gains through the various insulating materials. These are factors that have been determined by scientific studies, over periods of time, and compiled on all types of building materials and constructions. This heat is referred to as the "K" factor and is expressed in the number of Btu that will penetrate one square foot of surface area, per degree temperature difference, per each twenty-four (24) hour period.

By the use of a hypothetical problem, the steps can be more clearly understood as to how these heat loads are figured.

Example problem: Find the pull down load for 1000 pounds of fresh lean beef received at a temperature of 65° F, to be stored at a temperature of 0° F, with an ambient temperature of 78° F. The refrigerator space is 10 feet wide, 20 feet long, and 10 feet high. The refrigeration compressor has a capacity of three (3) tons.

The construction of the refrigerator box must be determined to find the amount of heat that penetrates the materials.

Suppose the box construction is made of materials and thicknesses as shown in figure 9-6. The door is made of the same material and thickness as the rest of the box.

By referring to charts such as the one in chapter 2, section 212, the "K" factor can be found for the materials. The "K" factor for the composite structure can be found by using the formula:

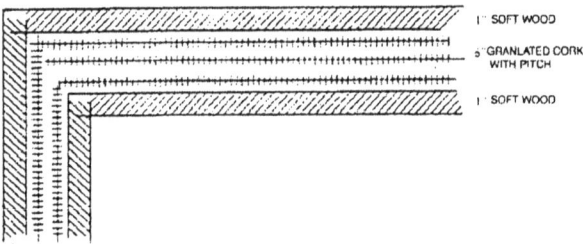

Figure 6. Composite structure for a refrigeration box.

$$K = \cfrac{1}{\cfrac{\text{Thickness 1}}{\text{"K" for 1}} + \cfrac{\text{Thickness 2}}{\text{"K" for 2}} + \cfrac{\text{Thickness 3}}{\text{"K" for 3}}}$$

Then, by substituting the values in the formula and working the problem, the final results are found.

$$"K" = \cfrac{1}{\cfrac{1}{.80} + \cfrac{1}{.428} + \cfrac{1}{.80}} = \cfrac{1}{1.25 + 14.018 + 1.25} =$$

$\dfrac{1}{16.5} = .06$ which is the unit of conductivity for the panel.

Next, the product load must be determined and the formula and steps are:

Step 1 is to remove the sensible heat of the product and lower its temperature to its freezing temperature. By reference to charts on frozen products, it is found that the specific heat of fresh lean beef above freezing is .77 and the freezing temperature is 29° F.

By the formula, step 1 is:

PL = W (T1-T2) x SH   PL = Product load
                               W = Weight of the product
PL = 1000 (65-29) x .77   T1 = Temperature of product
PL = 1000 x 36 x .77   T2 = Freezing temperature of product
PL = 26,720 Btu   SH = Specific heat of product

Formula, step 2:
PL = W x LHF   LHF = Latent heat of fusion for beef which is 100
PL = 1000 x 100
PL = 1000,000 Btu

Formula, step 3: This is the same as for step 1, except the product is now frozen and the temperatures will be from the freezing point to desired temperature. Also, the specific heat value for frozen beef is changed to .40

PL = 1000 (29-0) x .40
PL = 1000 x 29 x .40
PL = 11,600 Btu

By adding the findings of steps 1, 2, and 3, the total product load is found to be 138,320 Btu.

At the same time the meat is being refrigerated to remove the 138,320 Btu, heat has penetrated the space through the insulation and must also be removed. This is the maintaining load and is found by the following method:

$$ML = \frac{A(T1-T2) \times (K+K1)}{24}$$

Values to be substituted are:

A. = External area of the refrigerated space
T1 = Ambient temperature surrounding the space
T2 = Desired temperature inside the space
K = Conductivity factor for the composite material
Kl = The value of one (1) Btu which, when added to K, will serve to compensate for heat introduced due to door traffic

$$ML = \frac{1000(78-0) \times (.060+1)}{24}$$
$$= \frac{78,000 \times 1.06}{24}$$

ML = 82,680 Btu per twenty-four (24) hours
ML = 3,445 Btu per hour

The final step in obtaining the pull down load is:

$$PDL = ML\frac{(PL)}{(CCP-ML)} + PL$$

These values and meanings are:

ML = Maintaining load per hour = 3,445 Btu
PL = Total product load = 138,320 Btu
CC = Compressor capacity, 3 ton = 36,000 Btu

$$PDL = 3,445\frac{138,320}{(36,000-3,445)} + 138,320$$

$$PDL = 3,445\frac{(138,320)}{(32,555)} + 138,320$$

PDL = 3,445 x 4.25 + 138,320
PDL = 152,961.25 Btu

This is then the number of Btu the compressor must remove from the space and the product to bring the temperature of the product down to 0° F.

F3. **Figuring Heat Loads for Air Conditioning.** The methods used for determining the size air conditioning unit for a given space or building are somewhat the same as those used for refrigeration.

Here, also, air conditioning manufacturers have charts available that have been compiled by research and study. Such charts will give:

1. The Btu per hour each occupant will "give-off" while engaged in rest, work, or play.

2. The Btu per hour for different size electrical appliances, such as motors, toasters, lights, etc. This can best be figured by finding the total amount of watts used by all appliances and multiplying by 3.4.

3. The design temperature conditions of various regions throughout the United States.

4. The amount of Btu per hour, per square foot, per degree temperature difference for all types of walls, floors, ceilings, roofs, partitions, and windows. The values of the external walls and roofs will vary

according to their color and the direction in which they face.

By the use of these charts, the amount of heat, in Btu, that is generated inside the space and the amount that penetrates the structure can be determined.

This heat load must be based on the temperature of an average summer day. It must be remembered, however, that when the outside temperature remains above average for long periods of time (three or four days), the load created may be more than that for which the unit is designed. Even then, the removal of the humidity will furnish a fairly comfortable feeling for the occupants.

CHAPTER 4

STEAM JET SYSTEM

A. INTRODUCTION

A1. Advantages. - Where high pressure steam and fresh water are readily available, the steam jet air conditioning system has many advantages. It has no vibration, and no moving parts except the centrifugal pumps used to circulate the chilled water and the float control valve to maintain the proper water level in the flash tank. Because water is the refrigerant, the steam jet system is especially suitable in places where leaks of the chemical refrigerant gases could be hazardous.

A2. Principles of Operation. - How the temperature of a liquid and its vapors vary with different pressures is explained in chapter 2. It is this principle that enables the steam jet cooling unit to perform its function.

The steam jet system uses only fresh water as the refrigerant and employs the well known principle of cooling by flash evaporation. The water to be cooled is admitted to a flash tank wherein a predetermined absolute pressure is maintained by a system of ejectors. The absolute pressure to be maintained in the flash tank is the vapor pressure of the water corresponding to the desired temperature of chilled water to be produced. For example, if it is desired to produce a chilled water temperature of 50° F, it is necessary that an absolute pressure of 0.363 inches of mercury be maintained in the flash tank.

The incoming water from the air conditioning system enters the flash tank at a temperature higher than 50° F; the actual temperature depends on the amount of heat absorption and the rate of flow of the water. The instant this water at the elevated temperature is exposed to the reduced pressure in the flash tank, a portion of the water flashes into vapor, the latent heat of vaporization, being absorbed from the main body of the water. This absorption of heat by the vapor accordingly cools the main body of water to the desired final chilled water temperature.

The vapor developed within the flash tank is at such a low temperature that it is impossible to directly condense these vapors with a cooling medium at a normal temperature and it becomes necessary to withdraw these vapors by means of a large ejector, called a booster ejector. This booster ejector is designed to withdraw all of the vapors from the flash tank at the desired absolute pressure and compress them to a higher absolute pressure, with a resultant higher temperature, so that these vapors can then be condensed by a mdeium such as sea water at the usual temperature. The booster ejector accordingly discharges to a surface condenser for this purpose. The surface condenser is fitted with a two stage ejector for maintaining the required vacuum in the condenser.

Since the flashed vapors withdrawn from the flash tank result in a continual loss of water from the chilled water system, an equal amount of fresh water must be added to the chilled water system as make-up. Part of the condensate discharged from the condenser condensate pump is used for this purpose.

B. OPERATING CYCLES

B1. Steam Cycle. - A schematic drawing of a jet steam water cooling unit is shown in figure 1. This unit normally operates with a minimum steam supply pressure of 500 psig. However, by changing the ejector nozzles in the booster ejector and the first and second stage condenser ejectors, the unit can operate on shore steam with a pressure of at least 40 psig at a reduced capacity.

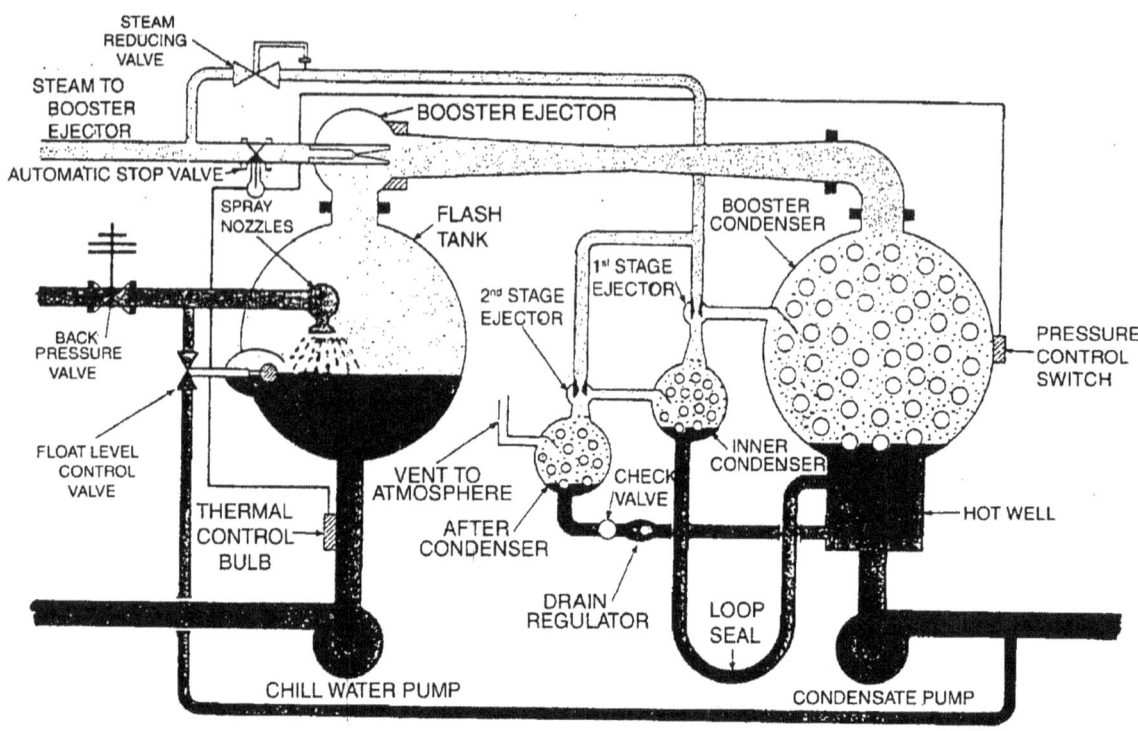

Figure 1. - Schematic drawing of a stem jet water cooling unit.

Under normal operation, steam at a minimum pressure of 500 psig enters the unit through the automatic steam stop valve to the booster ejector. This valve is controlled by the chilled water temperature and the pressure in the booster condenser. The valve is either fully opened or fully closed. A sensor bulb (thermal control) installed in the chilled water line from the flash tank will cause the valve to close if the temperature of the water becomes too cold. Also, a pressure switch in the booster condenser will cause the valve to close if an undue rise in pressure occurs. Closing the valve will stop the steam supply to the booster ejector stopping the cooling effect on the water. Under emergency conditions, the valve can be opened by a hand wheel.

With normal operating temperature and pressure, the valve is opened and the steam is admitted to the booster ejector nozzle. The steam attains a high velocity as it passes from the nozzle. The high velocity steam jet from the nozzle creates a suction and draws in the vapors and non-condensable gases (air) from the flash tank. This creates a vacuum in the flash tank of approximately .148 psia or 29.62 inches of mercury (Hg).

The vapors and noncondensables from the nozzle and the flash tank are carried through the diffuser tube to the booster condenser. As the vapors pass over the cooler tubes in the condenser, their heat is removed and carried away. Most of the vapors are condensed by the cooler tubes and the liquid drains to the bottom of the condenser and collects in the hot-well. From the hot-well, some of the condensate is returned to the boiler water system and some to the flash tank to maintain a constant water level.

Because the booster condenser must operate under a vacuum of .946 psia or 27.99 Hg in order for the booster ejector to perform its function, an air ejector system of two stages is connected to the condenser shell. Steam is supplied to these ejectors at a minimum pressure of 135 psig (40 psig when operating on shore steam).

The source of steam can be either an auxiliary steam supply line or the supply line to the booster ejector through a pressure reducing valve. As the steam passes the nozzle in the first stage ejector, it draws the noncondensed gases from the booster condenser in the same manner as the booster ejector does from the flash tank.

These gases, along with the steam from the first stage nozzle, are subjected to the cool surfaces of the tubes in the inner cooler. The condensed liquid drains from the inner cooler through a loop seal to the hot-well of the booster condenser. The greater vacuum in the booster condenser will enable the condensate to flow through the loop seal to the hot-well. If there was a direct connection between the inner cooler and the hot-well of the booster condenser, the vacuum would be equalized. Since the booster condenser carries a higher vacuum than the inner cooler, it is necessary that some form of seal be maintained in the drain line to prevent this equalization of vacuum. The water in the U-shaped loop seal line provides this seal.

The steam passing through the second stage ejector draws the noncondensed gases from the inner cooler and subjects them to the cool surfaces of the tubes. All noncondensables, such as air that may have entered the system through the pump packings or other small leaks, are vented to the atmosphere. The gases that are condensed are drawn to the hot-well through a check valve and drain regulator; then the condensate is dumped overboard or returned through the steam drain system.

B2. Chilled Water Cycle.-The chilled water at a temperature of about 50° F is drawn from the lower side of the flash tank by a centrifugal pump and discharged into the chilled water piping system that feeds the various cooling units. The pump and chilled water system is similar to the one described in chapter 1. The pump operates with approximately 55 psig discharge pressure.

The chilled water is circulated through the cooling coils and absorbs heat from the air and returns at a temperature of approximately 55° F.

A back pressure regulating valve is located in the chill water return line prior to its entry into the flash tank. The valve is adjusted to maintain the pressure to the spray nozzles in the flash tank at a pressure of 35 psig. The water at 35 psig is sprayed from the spray nozzles in a fine mist. Because of the pressure drop from 35 psig at a temperature of about 55° F to a pressure of .148 psig, some (about 1 percent) of the water mist will flash or change into a vapor. In order to flash or change state, a latent heat must be added to the water mist. This heat is absorbed from the surrounding water and lowers its temperature. Approximately 1000 Btu's are required to change one pound of water at the vaporizing temperature into water vapor (steam). To cool water, the removal of about one Btu is required to lower the temperature of one pound of water one degree. Therefore, the amount of vapors that is flashed off and carried over to the booster condenser will be small compared to the amount of water cooled.

To maintain a constant level of water in the flash tank and to replace the water flashed into vapor, a supply line is installed from the discharge side of the condensate pump to a float control valve attached to the side of the flash tank. When the water level decreases, the valve will open and allow water to enter the flash tank through the spray nozzles.

C. OPERATING AND MAINTENANCE

As the operating procedures and maintenance will vary with the different models, sizes and makes, the manufacturers' instruction manuals must be consulted and adhered to. No unit should be considered as being a complete installation unless the instruction manual is provided.

CHAPTER 5
ABSORPTION SYSTEM

A. INTRODUCTION

The absorption type air conditioning system used in plant installations chills fresh water which is circulated through cooling coils. The absorption cycle differs from the compression cycle in that heat energy instead of mechanical energy is used to effect the change in conditions necessary to complete the refrigeration cycle. A heater or generator is used instead of a compressor. Gas, steam, an electric heating element, or a chemical may be used as a source of heat. Inmost plants systems which operate on the absorption principle, a solution of lithium bromide serves as an absorbant that maintains the necessary vacuum for chilling the water which is pumped to the cooling coils.

B. THE LITHIUM BROMIDE UNIT

B1. General Explanation. - The lithium bromide unit is an absorption machine that uses water as a refrigerant and lithium bromide as an absorbent. The cycle of the machine is based on the facts that:

1. Lithium bromide has the ability to absorb great quantities of water vapor.

2. Water will boil (vaporize) and absorb heat at a low temperature when subjected to a high vacuum.

The jet steam system described in the previous chapter operates on basically the same principle. However, instead of using steam to create a vacuum and remove the water vapors, a chemical is used in the lithium bromide unit.

B2. Description of the Machine. - In the lithium bromide unit, the absorber and the evaporator are combined in a single shell because they operate at nearly the same temperature and pressure. The evaporator occupies the upper portion of the shell and contains the refrigerant (water) spray nozzles, chilled-water tube bundle, baffle eliminators, and the refrigerant water pan. The absorber occupies the lower section of the shell and contains the lithium bromide solution spray nozzles, condensing water tube bundle, and a divided semicircular sump which serves as a collecting container and reservoir for both the strong and weak lithium bromide solutions.

The evaporator and absorber are partially separated by the refrigerant water pan between the chilled-water tube bundle and the condensing tube bundle and partially by the eliminator baffels that extend upward in an inverted "V" shape from the sides of the water pan.

In addition to the absorber and evaporator, the lithium bromide unit contains several other essential parts including several pumps and controls. A brief description of these parts follows.

The refrigerant water storage tank serves as a reservoir for the water from the refrigerant water pan. The solution heat exchanger consists of a set of coils which transfer heat from the strong solution to the weaker solution of lithium bromide. The generator contains a weak solution spray nozzle, steam heated tube bundle, a baffle eliminator, and a collecting reservoir in the bottom to collect the strong solution. The condenser, as the name indicates, has a tube bundle for the condensing water and a collecting area in the bottom for the condensate to collect. The purge tank is a reservoir for a small amount of lithium bromide and contains the level control probes. Attached to the tank is a vent to the atmosphere through an activated charcoal filter, a pump, and a jet exhauster (eductor).

Like the jet steam plant, the unit's only moving parts which cause vibration or wear, are the pumps used to circulate the liquids. These are the refrigerant water pump, purge pump, sealing water pump, strong solution pump, and the weak solution pump.

Note: The following explanation is for a specific type of application. Some plants are equipped with hermetic pumps which eliminates the need for a sealing pump. Not all units are equipped with the standby pump, and the plant must be shut down in the event of a casualty to any pump.

The refrigerant water pump is actually two pumps with motors, mounted on the same base. (See fig. 1.) The piping is arranged to allow for the use of one pump at a time and have the other pump as a standby.

There are two sets of solution pumps (fig. 2) mounted so they are driven by the same motor. A pump is mounted on each end of the motor shaft. One pump handles the strong solution and is called the absorber pump; the other pump handles the weak solution and is called the generator pump. The pumps are so arranged to allow the use of one set at a time and have one set as a standby unit.

The purge pump is used to circulate the solution from the purge tank through the jet exhauster and back to the purge tank. (See fig.3.)

The water sealing pump is used to maintain a water seal to pump stuffing boxes to ensure a positive seal and eliminate the entry of air to the system.

The lithium bromide unit also includes various controls such as thermostats, water and steam regulating valves, and thermocouples.

C. OPERATING CYCLES

C-1. Lithium Bromide Cycle. - The cycle of the lithium bromide solution as well as the other liquids and vapors can be followed by reference to the schematic flow diagram, figure 4.

The lithium bromide cycle starts as a strong solution from the strong solution reservoir. The absorber pump takes a suction from the strong solution reservoir and delivers the strong solution to the spray nozzles in the absorber section of the shell. As the solution is sprayed from the nozzles, it absorbs the refrigerant vapors from the evaporator section; this action weakens the solution due to the absorption of the vapors. The weakened solution is collected in the weak solution chamber where the generator pump takes its suction and discharges the solution to the heat exchanger.

As the weak solution passes through the heat exchanger, it is heated by the hot strong solution. The heated weak solution then flows to the weak solution spray nozzles in the generator. As the solution is sprayed over the hot steam heated tube bundle, the water vapors are separated from the lithium bromide solution. The solution, being heavier than the vapors, collects in the bottom of the generator as a strong solution.

From the generator, the hot strong solution flows through the heat exchanger where it gives up some of its heat to the weak solution, and hence back to the absorber. In the absorber, it is discharged so as to flow over the condensing water tube bundle, which absorbs more of the heat to be carried away. The solution then drains into the strong solution reservoir and is ready to commence another cycle.

C2. Refrigerant Water Cycle. - The refrigerant water is pumped by the refrigerant water pump from the refrigerant water storage tank to the spray nozzles in the evaporator section. As the sprayed droplets of water come in contact with the chilled water tube bundle, a portion of the droplets are flashed into vapors. The heat absorbed from the chilled water tubes and in turn from the chilled water within the tubes causes the droplets to vaporize.

The vapors rise to the baffle eliminators where any droplets are trapped and drained into the refrigerant water pan. The vapors, being attracted to the lithium bromide, flow through the baffles to the absorber section where they are absorbed by the strong solution of lithium bromide being sprayed from the nozzles.

The vapors are then carried by the weak solution to the generator as explained in the lithium bromide cycle. When the weak solution is heated by the steam passing through the tube bundle in the generator, the water vapors are separated from the solution and rise through the eliminator baffles and flow to the condenser.

In the condenser, the water vapors flow across the condensing coils, or tube bundle, and are condensed. The condensate drains from the condenser to the refrigerant water pan in the evaporator section.

The refrigerant water that does not flash into vapors when sprayed from the nozzles in the evaporator also drains into the refrigerant water pan. The pan is connected to drains that carry the water back to the refrigerant storage tank to commence another cycle.

Figure 1. - Refrigerant pump.

Figure 2. - Absorber-generator, or solution pumps

Figure 3. - Purge pump.

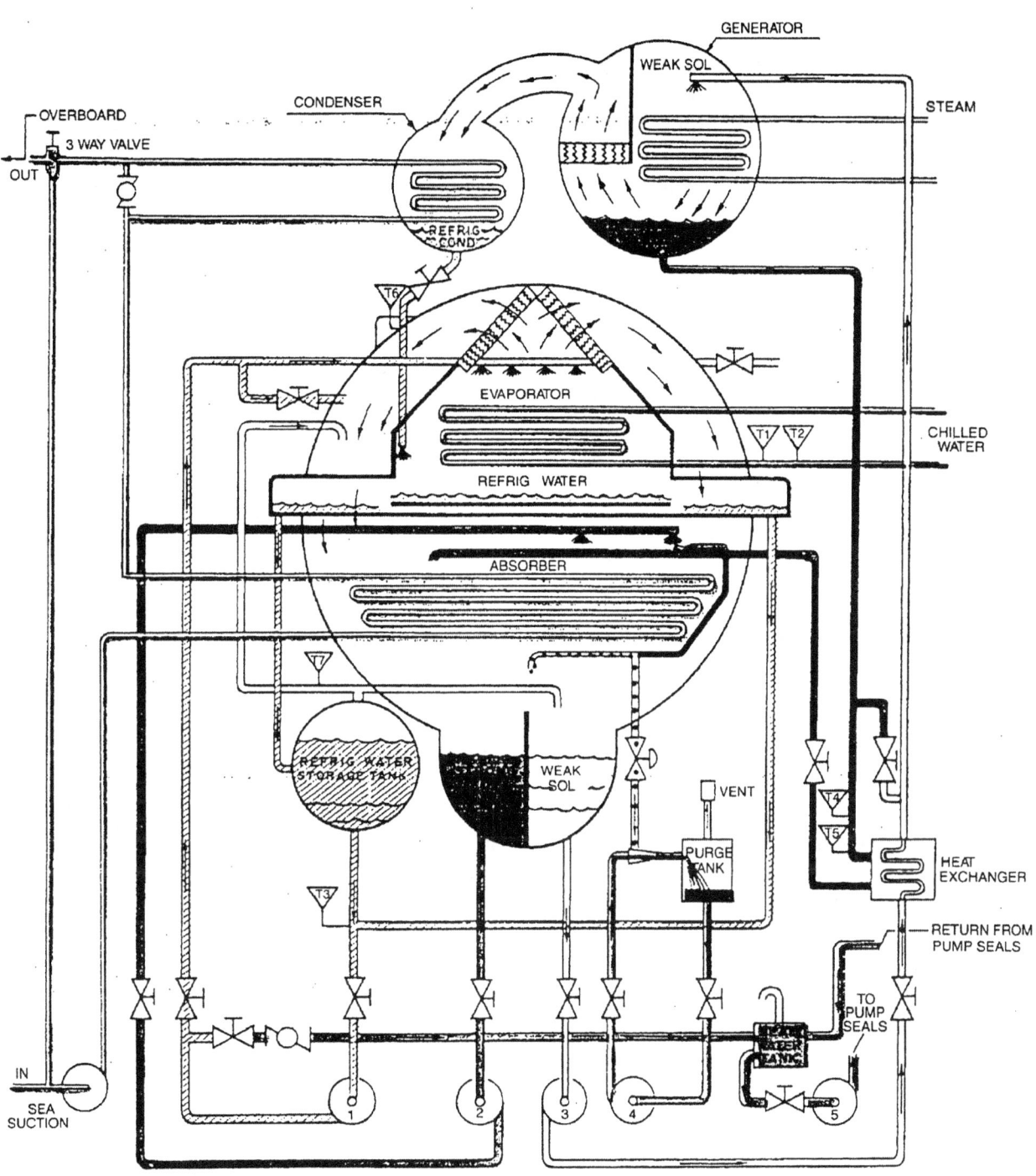

Figure 4.- Schematic flow diagram for a lithium bromide machine.

C3. Purge Cycle.- The purge system circulates lithium bromide solution from the purge tank through a jet exhauster and back to the tank by the use of the purge pump. When the pump discharges through the nozzle in the exhauster, the velocity head is increased and the static head decreased; this action creates an area of low pressure at the nozzle throat. A purge tube from the absorber section is connected so that the low pressure will induce the flow of noncondensables from the absorber. The gases carried back to the tank are vented through an activated charcoal filter to the atmosphere and any water vapors carried over and through the exhauster are absorbed by the lithium bromide solution.

With the circuit energized, the pump is cycled by the level control probes in the purge tank. (See fig. 5.) In the operating range, the pump is running and the pump control valve in the line from the absorber to the exhauster is open. When the level rises enough to contact the high operating probe, a relay is energized to open a contact and stop the pump. The purge control valve, however, will remain open. Because of the difference between the atmospheric pressure in the purge tank and the pressure (about 0.2 inch Hg absolute) in the absorber section, the solution in the tank flows back through the jet exhauster and the purge control valve to the absorber.

When the level in the purge tank drops and the low operating probe is uncovered, the relay is deenergized to close the contact and start the pump. The high and low safety probes stop the pump and cause the purge control valve to close if the level rises above or falls below the operating range. When this occurs, lithium bromide solution must be added or removed to restore the normal operating range before the purge unit will resume its automatic cycle.

The discharge from the exhauster is divided so the largest part enters the tank under the surface of the liquid in the tank to prevent turbulence which would cause a false level on the control probes. The lighter gases enter near the top of the surface and are vented to the atmosphere.

The purge tube is connected internally to a solution drip tube. The drip tube collects small amounts of lithium bromide solution from the spray pattern above the absorber tube bundle and directs it into the purge tank. If a small amount of solution is not supplied to the tank, the concentration of the solution in the tank will eventually approach zero percent because of water vapors being carried with the noncondensables out of the machine when the purge pump is running.

The concentration and temperature of the solution in the purge tank determine the vapor pressure which can be maintained in the system. The higher the concentration and lower the temperature, the lower the vapor pressure. The temperature of the solution is kept low by the chilled water circulating through the cooling coils in the purge tank. The concentration is maintained by the amount of solution drawn from the absorber through the drip tube. The open end of the drip tube should be turned so that it collects enough solution from the spray to raise the level in the purge tank at a rate of one inch every 15 minutes. This will maintain a concentration of approximately 55 percent. The position of the drip tube is controlled with an external actuating rod which is set and locked with a set screw.

MARINE APPLICATIONS

C4. Condensing or Salt Water Cycle. Salt water enters the salt water circulating pump from the sea through strainers. The water is discharged from the pump to the tube bundle in the absorber. As the water passes through the tubes, heat is absorbed from the strong lithium bromide solution returning from the generator and from the heat caused by the lithium bromide solution absorbing the water vapors from the evaporator.

From the absorber tube bundle, the water flows through the tube bundle in the condenser and condenses the refrigerant water vapors from the generator. Absorbing more heat in the condenser, the salt water is then directed overboard through a discharge line. This line includes a 3-way valve as shown in figure 6. This valve is controlled by a thermostat located in the discharge line from the salt water circulating pump to the absorber tube bundle and is operated by air pressure. The function of the valve is to maintain the salt water at a constant temperature of 85° F as it enters the absorber tube bundle. This is accomplished by diverting some of the warmed overboard water back to the suction side of the salt water circulating pump.

C6. Steam Cycle. Steam is admitted to the tube bundle in the generator through a steam control valve. The steam is used for heating the weak solution of lithium bromide to a temperature that will cause some of the refrigerant vapors to separate from the solution.

The affinity of lithium bromide solution for water vapor increases with the solution concentration; therefore, the higher the concentration the more refrigerant vapors absorbed, the specific volume in the evaporator is decreased (the vacuum is higher), and the refrigerant can remove more heat from the chilled water because a greater quantity will vaporize at a fixed temperature.

The concentration is a function of the amount of refrigerant vapors separated from the solution in the generator, and this in turn is a function of the amount of heat supplied by the steam.

By the use of a temperature sensing device in the chilled water system to position the steam control valve in accordance

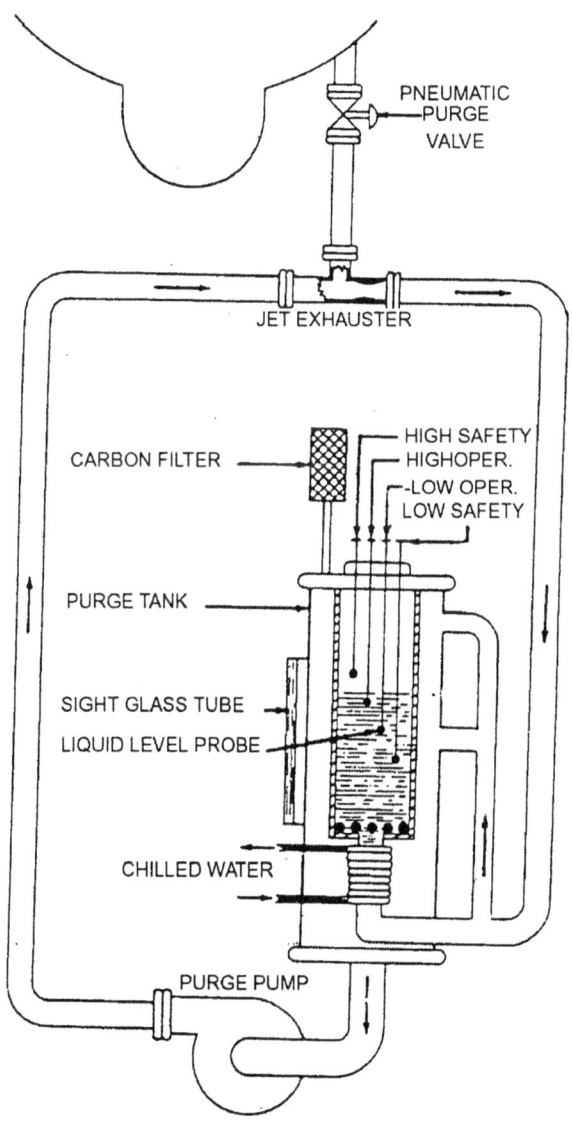

Figure 5.—Schematic diagram of the purge system

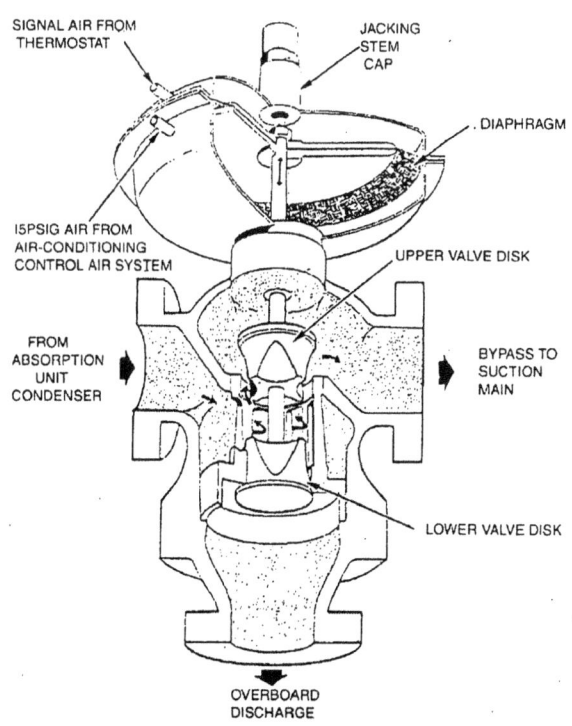

Figure 6.—Temperature regulating, 3-way valve.

with the temperature variations, the output of the machine can be controlled to meet varying demands of the air conditioning loads.

The steam control valve is a diaphragm and spring operated throttling valve; an increase in air pressure causes the valve to open and a decrease in air pressure causes the valve to close. A cutaway view of a typical steam control valve is shown in figure 7.

At 15 psig control air pressure, the valve is fully open; at 3 psig air pressure, the spring holds the valve shut. The control air is supplied from the air conditioning control air system to the steam control valve, electric-pneumatic relay, the chilled water thermostat, the strong solution tem-

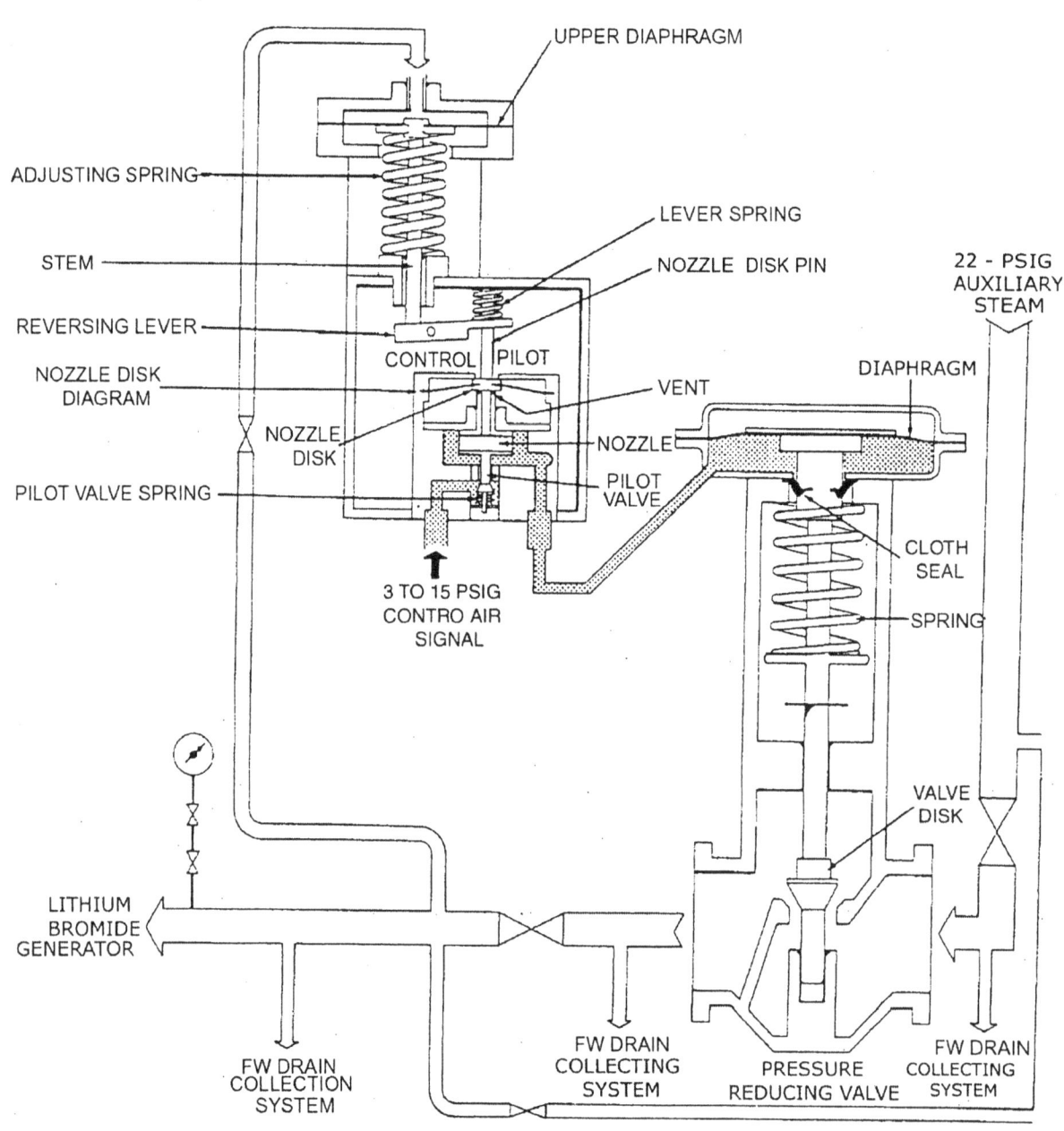

Figure 7. - Steam control valve.

perature limit control, and the steam valve control pilot. The schematic drawing, figure 8, shows the paths of the steam and control air systems. Under normal operating conditions, only the chilled water thermostat changes the control air signal to the steam valve.

The sensing bulb at the outlet of the chilled water coil from the evaporator positions the thermostat as the chilled water temperature changes. As the temperature of the water rises and more refrigerating capacity is required, the thermostat increases the air signal to the valve and

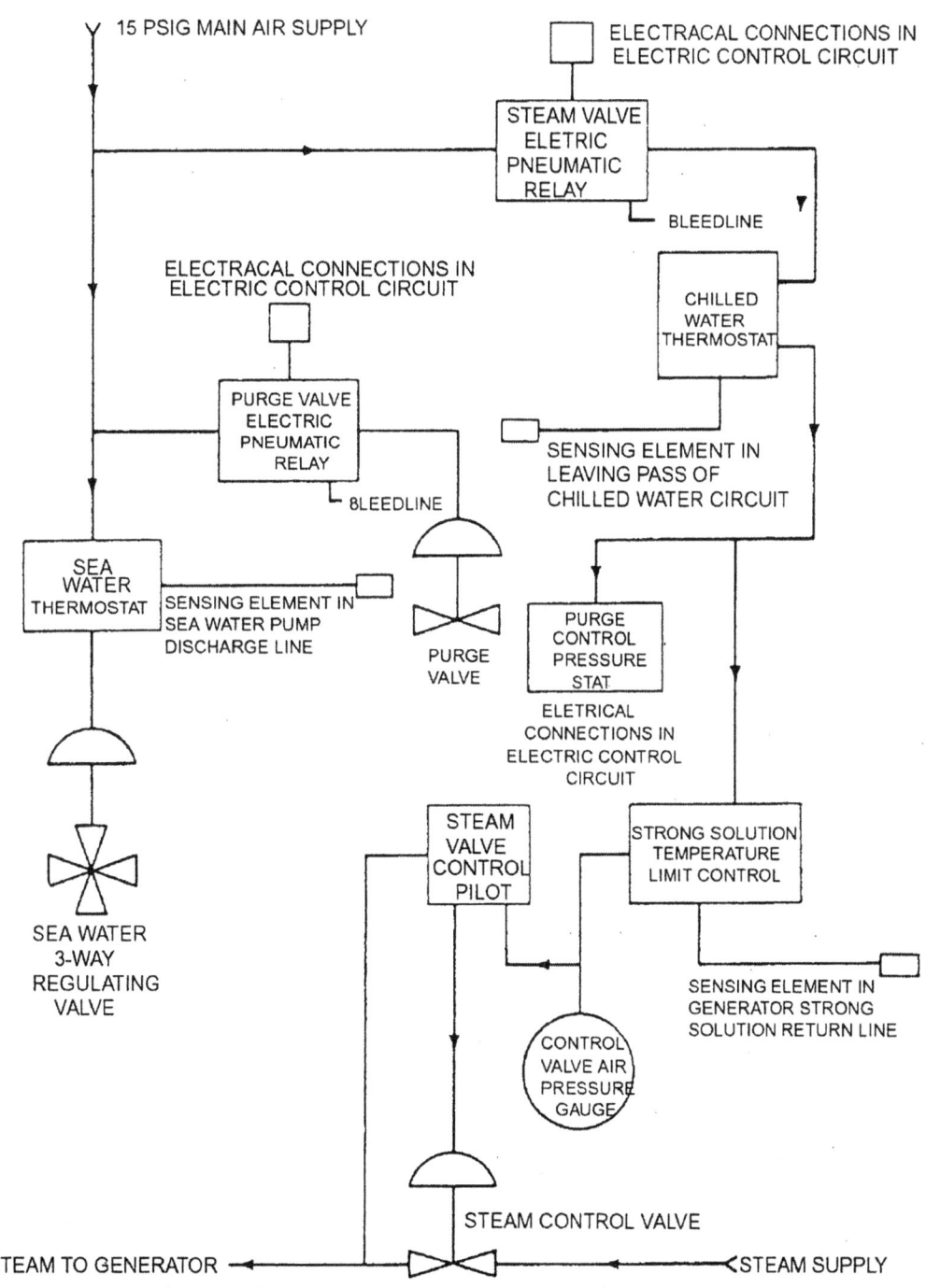

Figure 8. - Control air and steam supply system.

permits a greater flow of steam to the generator tube bundle.

The range of the thermostat is 5 F. At a chilled water temperature of 40 F, the air signal is 3 psig and the valve is fully closed. At a chilled water temperature of 45 F, the air signal is 15 psig and the valve is fully opened. An intermediate temperature of the chilled water will cause the valve to be partly opened.

With an inlet pressure of 22 psig, the steam pressure at the outlet of the valve is 18 psig with the valve fully opened. The pilot valve in the control pilot is open permitting air flow from the thermostatically controlled electric-pneu- matic relay. To prevent pressure in the steam coils from exceeding 18 psig, the control pilot repositions the steam control valve to throttle the steam flow and maintain the desired pressure.

The control pilot, as shown in figure 7, is a diaphragm-operated lever and nozzle which positions the pilot valve to regulate the flow of control air to the steam control valve. The control pilot consists of an upper diaphragm and adjusting spring, a reversing lever and spring, and a lower diaphragm assembly. The lower assembly includes the spring actuated pilot valve and the air actuated bleed-off nozzle. The sensing line steam pressure acts on the upper side of the upper diaphragm, pushing it against the adjusting spring. When the steam sensing line pressure is below 18 psig, the reversing lever spring forces the reversing lever down on the nozzle disk pin. The pin bears down on the nozzle which moves the pilot valve down, thus opening the port to allow air flow to the steam valve diaphragm. When the steam sensing line pressure exceeds 18 psig, the pressure on the upper diaphragm overrides the adjusting spring and reversing lever spring pressure. This removes the pressure on the nozzle disk pin and the nozzle. Air pressure from the control air signal then forces the nozzle disk off its seat, thus bleeding off the operating pressure through the atmospheric vents. With the nozzle no longer bearing against the pilot valve, the pilot valve spring pressure is sufficient to shut the pilot valve to air flow. The air continues to bleed off until the steam valve takes a new position and the steam sensing line pressure drops to normal. Then the adjusting spring and lever spring close the nozzle disk and reopen the pilot valve.

D. EQUILIBRIUM DIAGRAMS

D1. Using the Equilibrium Diagrams for Lithium Bromide. - The pressure, temperature, and concentration relation of the solution in the various stages of the cycle can be plotted on a diagram or chart such as shown in figure 9. When any two conditions are known, the third can be found by the use of the diagram. For example, if you have the temperature and the specific gravity of the lithium bromide solution, by plotting these points on the diagram the percentage of concentration can be found. The cycle of operation can be drawn on the diagram by plotting the pressures, temperatures, and concentrations which exist throughout the machine;

In figure 9, the scale on the left (straight horizontal lines) is for the vapor pressure of the solution, or evaporator water at equilibrium conditions.

The scale on the right side (horizontal lines) is for pure water corresponding to the vapor pressures of the left hand scale.

At the bottom is the scale (vertical lines) for the solution concentration in percent by weight. For example, a solution of 60 percent is 60 percent lithium bromide and 40 percent water by weight.

The curved lines running across the chart are the solution temperature lines. These should not be confused with the saturation temperature.

The slightly curved lines that extend upward from the bottom of the chart are the specific gravity lines. They are used to determine the concentration of the solution. By measuring the specific gravity with a hydrometer and finding the temperature with a thermometer, the percentage of con-

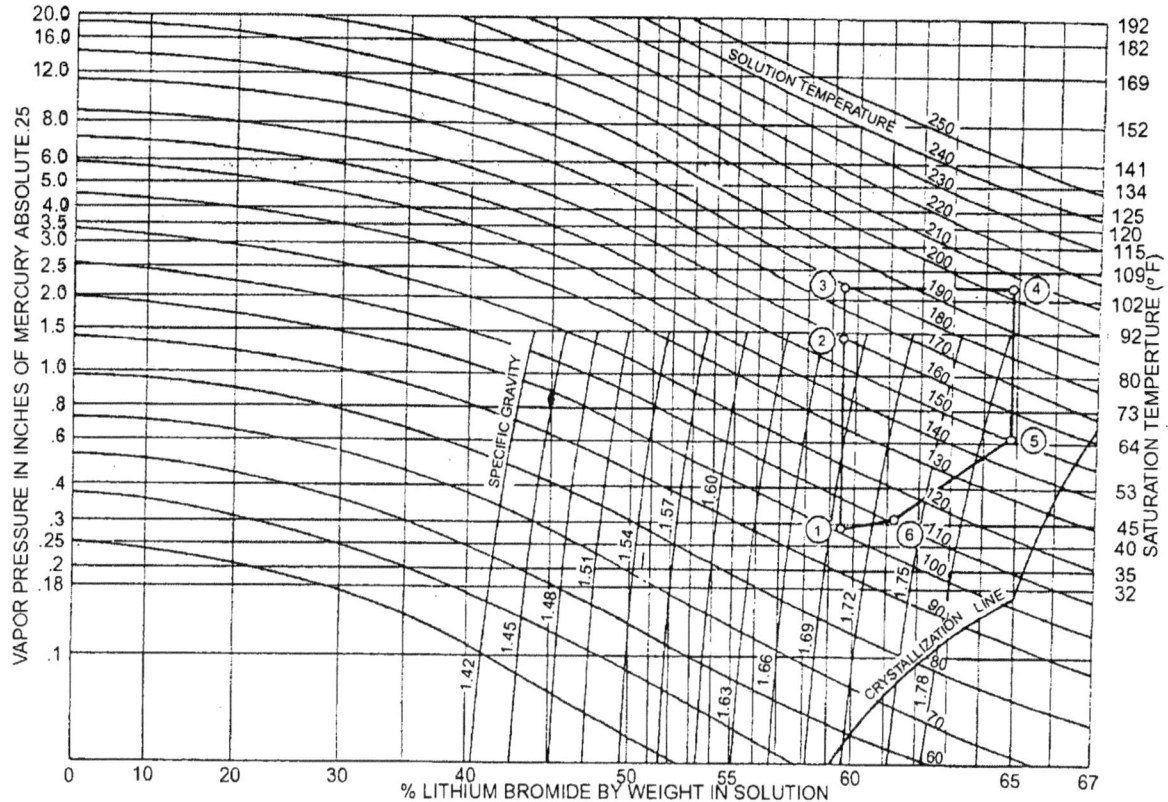

Figure 9. - Equilibrium diagram for lithium bromide.

centration for the solution can be determined by plotting these two points. For example: if the solution temperature is 120 °F, and the specific gravity is 1.72, the concentration of the solution will be 61 percent.

The curved line in the lower right hand corner is the crystallization line. It indicates the point at which the solution will begin to change from a liquid to a solid state and sets the limits of the cycle. Crystallization of a solution is quite different from the freezing of a single substance such as water. When water is subjected to a temperature of 32° F or lower, eventually all of it will freeze. In contrast, when the lithium bromide solution temperature is reduced below the solidification point for that particular concentration, only a portion of the salt will crystallize or freeze. The remainder will become more dilute or less concentrated and will remain in the liquid state.

Crossing the crystallization line does not necessarily result in "freeze-up" providing the subcooling does not progress too far. Crystallization of the solution will not harm the machine, but it will interrupt service. Satisfactory operation is designed to take place above the crystallization line.

D2. Operating Cycle Table. The table of the operating cycle conditions in figure 10 lists the temperatures, pressures, and concentrations which exist in a lithium bromide machine when it is operating at theoretical full load design conditions of 45° F chilled water, 85° F condensing water, and 18 psig steam. The points described below are also represented on the equilibrium diagram in figure 9.

Point 1 is the weak solution as it leaves the absorber and enters the heat exchanger.

Point 2 is the same solution after it passed through the heat exchanger and before it enters the generator. Lines 1 and 2 represent the temperature increase due to the effect of the heat exchanger.

Point 3 is the temperature at which the solution begins to boil in the generator. Lines 2 and 3 represent the amount of heat required to raise the temperature of the solution to the boiling point.

Point 4 is where the solution reaches 64.7 percent at 204° F after some of the refrigerant has been boiled out. Lines 3 and 4 are the amount of heat required to boil off the refrigerant vapors and reconcentrate the solution.

Point 5 is the drop in solution temperature due to the effect of the heat exchanger. This is the same amount of heat that was picked up by the weak solution as it passed through the heat exchanger on its way to the generator. (Lines 1 and 2)

Point 6 is the intermediate solution which is pumped from the absorber sump into the spray nozzles. It is solution at point 5 after it has passed over the absorber tube bundle. The intermediate solution is then pumped through the spray nozzles where it absorbs refrigerant vapors and is diluted back to a weak solution (Point 1).

These temperatures and pressures exist in the machine at design full load conditions. As the load decreases, the cycle diagram on the equilibrium diagram is moved to the left because the solution is less concentrated, and downward because the steam pressure is reduced; therefore, the temperature in the generator will be lower. Because of the reduction in steam, the amount of re concentration will become less and the cycle diagram will become more narrow.

Point	Solution Temp (°F)	Vapor Press.("Hg.)	Concentration (%)	Saturated Temp. (°F)
1	106.0	.29	59.4	44.8
2	160.0	1.40	59.4	.90
3	178.0	2.20	59.4	104
4	204.0	2.20	64.7	104
5	150.0	.60	64.7	65
6	112.6	.31	61.2	.46

Figure 10. - Operating cycle conditions.

BASIC FUNDAMENTALS OF AIR CONDITIONING AND REFRIGERATION

TABLE OF CONTENTS

	Page
I. Operation	1
A. Using the Dehydrator	1
B. V-Belt Drive	1
C. Checking Compressor Oil	2
II. Maintenance	3
A. Compressor Maintenance	3
B. Removing Shaft Seal	5
C. Installing Shaft Seal	5
D. Lapping Shaft Seal	6
III. System Maintenance	6
A. Charging the System	6
B. Purging Air from the System	7
C. Cleaning Suction Strainers	7
D. Cleaning Liquid Line Strainer	7
E. Cleaning Oil Filters and Strainers	7
IV. Condensers	8
A. Checking Condenser Performance	8
B. Cleaning Condenser Tubes	8
C. Cleaning Air-Cooled Condensers	9
D. Testing for Leaks	9
E. Retubing Condensers	9
V. Expansion Valves	10
A. Thermostatic Expansion Valve	10
B. Automatic Expansion Valve	12
C. Hand Expansion Valve	13
D. Switches	13
E. Evacuating and Dehydrating the System	13
F. Reactivating the Drying System	14
G. Cleaning the System	16
VI. Detecting and Correcting Troubles	16
A. Trouble-Diagnosis Chart	17

BASIC FUNDAMENTALS OF AIR CONDITIONING AND REFRIGERATION

I. OPERATION

Proper operation of any unit of machinery is an important part of maintaining it. To ensure proper operation of the refrigeration plant, it is necessary to understand the principles of operation of the unit. It is also necessary to make periodic inspections and tests. It is good practice to make an hourly check of all temperatures and pressures throughout the system and to check the oil level in the compressor crankcase.

One of the best methods, and probably the easiest, for checking plant operation is to compare the temperatures and pressures of the plant with corresponding temperatures and pressures which were recorded during a period when the plant was known to be operating properly. The value of the comparison will depend on the similarity of the conditions existing when each set of readings was taken.

A daily operating log for refrigeration equipment should be maintained and used for a continuous analysis of the operating conditions found in a refrigeration plant.

Refrigeration plants are equipped with automatic controls and once the plant is in normal operation, very little attention is required. However, these plants are, like all units of machinery, liable to casualties, so periodic checks must be made to ensure that the plant is operating normally. The main purpose of the operating log is to ensure that abnormal operating conditions do not go undetected.

Usually the personnel assigned to operate and maintain refrigeration plants are graduates of an air conditioning and refrigeration school. However, in small shops, the men assigned to make the periodic checks on the refrigeration plants may or may not have attended this school. These men must be properly indoctrinated as to how to take and record the temperatures and pressures in a refrigeration plant and also as to why these readings are important for the operation of the plant.

A. USING THE DEHYDRATOR

A dehydrator is installed in the liquid line between the receiver and the expansion valve to absorb moisture that has entered the system. The dehydrator is installed with a bypass so that it may be cut in or out of the system. The dehydrator should be put into use when the system is being charged, at any time the system is opened for repairs, or at any time the presence of moisture is suspected.

Dehydrators can absorb only small quantities of moisture and are installed to minimize the effects of moisture. If large quantities of moisture are present in the refrigeration system, more than one dehydrator must be used, or other means must be taken to rid the system of moisture. Another drying-out process is described in this chapter under "Evacuating and Dehydrating the System."

B. V-BELT DRIVE

Belts must be properly tightened. Excessive looseness will cause slippage, rapid wear, and deterioration of V-belts. On the other hand, a belt that is too tight will result in excessive wear of both the belt and main bearing of the compressor. In extreme cases, it may cause a bad seal leak. If a belt is properly tightened, it should be possible to depress it, by the pressure of one finger, as much as 1/2 to 3/4 inch, at a point midway between the flywheel and motor pulleys.

When replacement of one belt of a multiple V-belt drive is necessary, a complete new set of matched belts should be installed. Belts stretch considerably during the first few hours of operation. Replacement of a single belt will upset the load balance between the new and old belts and be a potential source of trouble. It is better practice to run the unit temporarily with a defective belt removed than to attempt to operate a new belt in conjunction with two or more seasoned belts.

V-belts, motor pulleys, and compressor flywheels should be kept dry and free of oil. Belt dressing should never be used.

C. CHECKING COMPRESSOR OIL

If the apparent oil level observed immediately after a prolonged shutdown period is lower than normal, it is almost certain that the actual working oil level is far too low. After a sufficient quantity of oil has been added to raise the apparent oil level to the center of the bull's-eye sight glass, on the side of the compressor, the actual oil level should be checked as follows:

1. Operate the compressor or manual control for at least one hour. Then slowly close the suction line stop valve. If the compressor is operating on a water cooler or other coil which is apt to freeze, observe the temperature and interrupt compressor operation as necessary to prevent freezing. Repeat cycling until the total running time (one hour) is obtained.

2. Stop the compressor, turn the flywheel until the crankshaft and connecting rod ends are immersed in the lubricating oil, and immediately observe the oil level in the sight glass.

To check the oil level when the compressor has been running on its normal cycle, with no abnormal shutdown, proceed as follows:

1. Wait until the end of a period of operation; if the operation is continuous, wait until the compressor has been in operation at least 1/2 hour.

2. As soon as the compressor stops, turn the flywheel until the crankshaft and connecting rod ends are immersed in the lubricating oil, and observe the oil level in the sight glass.

Do not remove oil from the crankcase because of an apparent high level unless it is known that too much oil has been previously added, or unless it is apparent that oil from the crankcase of one compressor of the plant has been inadvertently deposited in the crankcase of another.

However, if the oil level is lower than its recommended height on the glass, additional oil should be added. Do not add more oil than is necessary to obtain the desired level. Too much oil can result in excessive oil transfer to the cooling coils.

Adding Oil

There are two common methods of adding oil to a compressor. In one type of installation a small oil-charging pump is furnished for adding oil to the compressor crankcase. In another type, oil is placed in the compressor by means of a clean, well-dried funnel. In either case, care must be taken to prevent the entrance of air or foreign matter into the compressor.

When performing hourly checks of the compressors, you may observe no oil in the crank-case, or a very low oil level on the sight glass. This indicates that the oil has left the compressor and is circulating in the system; and that it will be necessary to add oil to the normal level and operate the system. After the compressor has reclaimed the excessive oil in the system, the added oil should be drained.

Removing Oil

To remove oil from the compressor crank-case, reduce the pressure in the crankcase to approximately 1 psi by gradually closing the suction line stop valve. Then stop the compressor, close the suction and discharge line valves, loosen the lubricating oil drain plug near the bottom of the compressor crankcase, and allow the required amount of oil to drain out. Since the compressor crankcase is under a slight pressure, do not fully remove the drain plug from the compressor, but allow the oil to seep out around the threads of the loosened plug.

When the desired amount of oil has been removed, tighten the drain plug, open the suction and discharge line valves, and start the compressor. If an oil drain valve is provided in lieu of a plug, the required amount of oil may be drained without the necessity of pumping down the compressor.

Changing Oil

When clean copper tubing is employed for the mains and evaporators, and reasonable care has been taken to prevent the entrance of foreign matter during installation, the oil in the compressor crankcase will probably not become sufficiently contaminated to require renewal. When iron or steel pipe and fittings are used in the system, a sample of oil from the compressor crankcase should be withdrawn into a clean glass vessel every three months. If the sample shows contamination, the entire lubricating oil charge should be renewed. It is good practice to check the cleanliness of the lubricating oil after each cleaning of the compressor suction scale trap.

II. MAINTENANCE

In order for you to perform the required maintenance you must understand the proper operating and maintenance procedures. In most instances, personnel who are assigned to maintain refrigeration plants are graduates of an Air Conditioning and

Refrigeration School. While this school teaches most operating and maintenance procedures, the manufacturer's technical manuals should be referred to for the details of the plants on your ship.

A. COMPRESSOR MAINTENANCE

Refrigeration compressors vary to such an extent that this training course could not cover each type. The manufacturer's technical manuals must be referred to for details of any specific unit. Compressors range from small reciprocating types (for drinking water coolers) to very large centrifugal units used for air conditioning on large ships. Compressors may be splash lubricated or forced-feed lubricated. Centrifugal compressors are seldom used on plants smaller than 110 tons. They operate on the same principle as a centrifugal pump, except that they are designed to pump a gas instead of a liquid. Reciprocating compressors are used for air conditioning on most ships.

If a compressor cannot be pumped down and is damaged to the extent that it has to be opened fox repairs, it is necessary to first close the suction and discharge valves and then allow all refrigerant in the compressor to vent to the atmosphere, through a gage line.

To service a compressor correctly, it is necessary to be familiar with the manufacturer's technical manual. These manuals usually give a step-by-step procedure for disassembling the compressor and for renewing any part of the unit.

Before disassembling a compressor, make certain that the faulty operation of the unit is not caused by trouble in some other part of the system. Disassemble only the part of the compressor that is necessary to correct the fault. As internal machined parts are removed, every precaution should be taken to protect them from being damaged in handling and from corrosion.

Before starting to reassemble a compressor, all partsincluding replacement parts should be carefully washed in an approved solvent and permitted to dry in air. The final rinse should be made with clean solvent. The parts should be wiped with a lintfree cloth before the unit is assembled. Every precaution should betaken to prevent dirt, lint, water, or other foreign matter from entering the compressor during reassembly.

When it becomes necessary to remove, replace, or repair internal parts of the compressor, the following precautions should be observed:

1. Carefully disassemble and remove parts, noting the correct relative position so that errors will not be made when reassembling.

2. Inspect all those parts that become accessible due to the removal of other parts requiring repair or replacement.

3. Make certain that all parts and surfaces are free of dirt and moisture.

4. Apply compressor oil freely to all bearing and rubbing surfaces of parts being replaced or reinstalled.

5. If the compressor is not equipped with an oil pump, make certain the oil dipper on the lower connecting rod is in correct position for dipping oil when the unit is in operation.

6. Position the ends of the piston rings so that alternate joints come on the opposite side of the piston.

7. Care should be taken not to score gasket surfaces.

8. Renew all gaskets.

9. Clean the crankcase and renew the oil.

Whenever repairs to a compressor are of such a nature that any appreciable amount of air enters the unit, the compressor should be evacuated, after assembly is completed. The proper procedure is as follows:

1. Disconnect a connection in the compressor discharge gage line, between the discharge line stop valve and the compressor.

2. Start the compressor and let it run until the greatest possible vacuum is obtained.

3. Stop the compressor and immediately open the suction stop valve slightly in order to blow refrigerant through the compressor valves and purge the air above the discharge valves through the open gage line.

4. Close the discharge gage line and open the discharge line stop valve.

5. Remove all oil from the exterior of the compressor, and test the compressor joints for leakage, using the halide leak detector.

Testing Suction and Discharge Valves

A compressor should not be opened for inspection or repair until it has definitely been determined that the faulty operation of the system is or is not due to leaky suction or discharge valves.

Faulty compressor valves may be indicated either by a gradual or a sudden decrease in the normal compressor capacity. Either the compressor will fail to pump at all, or else the suction pressure cannot be pumped down to the designed value, and the compressor will run for abnormally long intervals or even continuously. If the compressor shuts down for short periods, the compressor valves may be leaking.

If the refrigeration plant is not operating satisfactorily, it will be best to first shift the compressors and then check the operation of the plant. If the operation of the plant is still not satisfactory when the compressors have been shifted, the trouble is in the system, and not in the compressor.

The compressor discharge valves may be tested by pumping down the compressor to 2 psig, and then stopping the compressor and quickly closing the suction and discharge line valves. If the discharge pressure drops at a rate in excess of 3 pounds in a minute and the crankcase suction pressure rises, there is evidence of compressor discharge valve leakage. If it is necessary to remove the discharge valves with the compressor pumped down, open the connection to the discharge pressure gage in order to release discharge pressure on the head. Then remove the compressor top head and discharge valve plate, being careful not to damage the gaskets.

If the discharge valves are defective, the entire discharge valve assembly should be replaced. Any attempt to repair them would probably involve relapping, and would require highly specialized equipment. Except in an emergency, such repair should never be undertaken aboard ship.

The compressor internal suction valves may be checked for leakage as follows:

1. Start the compressor by using the manual control switch on the motor controller.

2. Close the suction line stop valve gradually, to prevent violent foaming of the compressor crankcase lubricating oil charge.

3. With this stop valve closed, pump a vacuum of approximately 20 inches Hg. If this vacuum can be readily obtained, the compressor suction valves are satisfactory.

Do not expect the vacuum to be maintained after the compressor stops, because the Refrigerant-12 is being released from the crankcase oil. Do not attempt to check compressor suction valve efficiency of new units until after the compressor has been in operation for a minimum of 3 days. It may be necessary for the valves to wear in.

However, if any of the compressor suction valves are defective, the compressor should be pumped down, opened, and the valves inspected. Defective valve(s) or pistons should be replaced with spare assemblies.

Crankshaft Seal Repairs

On reciprocating compressors, the crankshaft extends through the compressor housing to provide a mount for the pulley wheel. At this point the shaft must be sealed to prevent leakage of lubricating oil and refrigerant. There are several types of crankshaft seals, depending on the manufacturer. The crankshaft seal is bathed in lubricating oil at a pressure equal to the suction pressure of the refrigerant. The first indication of crankshaft failure is excessive oil leaking at the shaft.

When the seal requires replacement, or signs of abnormal wear or damage to the running surfaces are present, a definite reason for the abnormal conditions exists and an inspection should be made. It is very important to locate and correct the trouble or the failure will reoccur.

Seal failure is very often the result of faulty lubrication, usually due to the condition of the crankcase oil. Dirty or broken oil is generally caused by one or both of the following conditions:

1. Dirt or foreign material in the system or system piping. Dirt frequently enters the system at the time of installation. After a period of operation, foreign mate rial will always accumulate in the compressor crankcase, tending to concentrate in the oil chamber surrounding the shaft seal. When the oil contains grit, it is only a matter of time until the highly finished running faces become damaged, causing failure of the shaft seal.

2. Moisture is frequently the cause of an acid condition of the lubricating oil. Oil in this condition will not provide satisfactory lubrication and will promote failure of the compressor parts. If the presence of moisture is suspected, a dryer should be used when the compressor is put into operation. At any time foreign mate rial is found in the lubricating oil, the entire system (piping, valves, and strainers) should be cleaned thoroughly.

B. REMOVING SHAFT SEAL.— In the event a shaft seal must be repaired or renewed, proceed as follows:

If the seal is broken to the extent that it permits excessive oil leakage, do not attempt to pump the refrigerant out of the compressor, air (containing moisture) will be drawn into the system through the damaged seal. Moisture in the air may cause expansion valves to freeze. If oil is leaking excessively, close the compressor suction and discharge valves and relieve the pressure to the atmosphere by loosening a connection on the compressor discharge gage line. If the condition of the seal does permit, pump down the compressor as previously explained in this chapter.

Next drain the oil from the compressor crankcase. Since the oil contains refrigerant, it will foam while being drained. The oil drain valve or plug should be left open while you are working on the seal, so that refrigerant escaping from the oil remaining in the crankcase will not build up a pressureand unexpectedly blow out the seal while it is being removed.

Remove the compressor flywheel (or coupling) and carefully remove the shaft seal assembly. If the assembly cannot be readily removed, build up a slight pressure in the compressor crankcase by slightly opening the compressor suction valve, taking the necessary precautions to support the seal to prevent it from being blown from the compressor and damaged.

C. INSTALLING SHAFT SEAL.— When the replacement is made, the entire seal assembly should be replaced. The parts should be clean and should be replaced in accordance with the manufacturer's instructions.

Wipe the shaft clean with a linen or silk cloth, do not use a dirty or lint-bearing cloth. Unwrap the seal, being careful not to touch the bearing surfaces with the hands. Rinse the seal in an approved solvent and allow to air-dry. (Do not wipe the seal dry.) Dip the seal in clean refrigerant oil. Insert the assembly in accordance with the instructions found in the manufacturer's technical manual and bolt the seal cover in place, tightening the bolts evenly. Replace the flywheel and belts and test the unit for leaks by opening the suction and discharge valves and using a halide leak detector.

D. LAPPING SHAFT SEAL.— Due to the difficulty of properly lapping the rubbing surfaces of a shaft seal, a seal leak should be corrected by renewing the assembly. If, however, a new shaft seal is not available, and it is possible to use the existing seal by refinishingthe rubbing surfaces, the seal can be lapped as follows:

1. Thoroughly clean the surfaces of the shaft shoulder and seal collar.

2. Lap the back of the shaft seal collar to the crankshaft shoulder. This joint must form an absolute seal so the importance of this lapping cannot be overemphasized. Only jeweler's rouge or the equivalent should be used for the lapping. The abrasive must be used sparingly to avoid getting it into the shaft bearings or crankcase. As the lapping proceeds, use less and less abrasive and finish the lapping with compressor lubricating Oil.

3. After the lapping has been completed, thoroughly clean the shaft shoulder and permit it to dry without wiping. With the shaft seal shoulder and collar dry and clean, lap the two surfaces together as a final lapping operation.

4. The surfaces are properly lapped when the surface of both the shaft shoulder and the shaft seal collar form a perfect contact and are free of all mars, scratches, or other imperfections. It is good practice to make the final examination with the aid of a good magnifying glass.

5. In some instances, a molded synthetic rubber gasket is provided instead of the metal-to-metal joint between the shaft seal collar and the crankshaft shoulder. In any case, it is extremely important that these parts be properly fitted and that the gasket be kept in good condition in order that a tight seal be maintained at this point.

When a shaft seal is lapped in, it should be regarded as a temporary repair and a new assembly should be installed as soon as possible.

III. SYSTEM MAINTENANCE

A refrigeration system that has been properly installed and properly operated will need little maintenance. However, certain tests, inspections, and maintenance procedures must be carried out to ensure that the system will operate at its rated capacity.

Learning to start and secure a refrigeration system is not enough to do your job properly. As a mechanic you must know the operating principles of the entire system, how each unit of the system operates, and why it is necessary; how each control and safety device works, and the reason for its being installed on the system. This understanding can be attained only through study, either by attending an Air Conditioning and Refrigeration School or by studying the manufacturer's technical manuals.

For men who have not attended an Air Conditioning and Refrigeration School, a training program should be set up to ensure an adequate number of qualified personnel to operate and maintain the air conditioning and refrigeration equipment.

A. Charging the System

Information concerning the charging of refrigeration systems mav be found in a technical manual. The amount of refrigerant charge must be sufficient to maintain a liquid seal between the condensing and evaporating sides of the system. When the compressor stops, under normal operating conditions, the receiver of a properly charged system is about 85 percent full of refrigerant. The proper charge for a specific system or unit can be found in the manufacturer's technical manual or on the blueprints.

A refrigeration system should not be charged if there are leaks or if there is reason to believe that thereisaleakinthe system. The leaks must be found and corrected. Immediately following or duringthe process of charging, the system should be carefully checked for leaks.

A refrigeration system must have an adequate charge of refrigerant at all times; otherwise its efficiency and capacity will be impaired.

B. Purging Air From The System

Operate the system for 30 minutes. Observe the pressure and temperature as indicated on the high pressure gage. Read the thermometer in the liquid line, and compare it with the temperature conversion figures shown on the discharge pressure gage. If the temperature of the liquid leaving the receiver is more than 15° F lower than the temperature corresponding to the discharge pressure, the system should be purged. While the system is still operating, slightly open the purge valve on the condenser. Purge very slowly, at intervals, until the air is expelled from the system and the temperature difference drops below 15° F.

C. Cleaning Suction Strainers

When putting a new unit into operation, the suction strainers should be cleaned after a few hours of operation. Refrigerants have a solvent action and will loosen any foreign matter in the system. This foreign matter will eventually reach the suction strainers. After a few days of operation, the strainers will need another cleaning. They should be inspected frequently during the first few weeks of plant operation, and then cleaned as found necessary.

The suction strainers are located in the compressor housing or in the suction piping. The procedure for cleaning the strainers is as follows:

1. Pump down the compressor.
2. Remove the strainer and inspect it for foreign matter.
3. Clean the strainer screen by dipping it in an approved solvent and then allow it to dry.
4. Replace the strainer and evacuate the air from the compressor.
5. Test the housing for leaks by wiping up all oil and then using a halide leak detector.

D. Cleaning A Liquid Line Strainer

Where a liquid line strainer is installed, it should be cleaned at the same intervals as the suction strainer. If a liquid line strainer becomes clogged to the extent that it needs cleaning, a loss of refrigeration effect will take place. The tubing after the strainer will be much colder than the tubing ahead of the strainer.

To clean the liquid line strainer, secure the receiver outlet valve and wait a few minutes to allow any liquid in the strainer to flow to the cooling coils. Then close the strainer outlet valve and very carefully loosen the cap which is bolted to the strainer body. (Use goggles to protect the eyes.) When all of the pressure is bled out of the strainer, remove the cap and lift out the strainer screen. Clean the strainer screen, using an approved solvent and a small brush. Reassemble the spring and screen in the strainer body, then replace the strainer cap loosely. Purge the air out of the strainer, by blowing refrigerant through it, then tighten the cap. After the assembly is complete, test the unit for leaks.

E. Cleaning Oil Filters and Strainers

Compressors arranged for forced feed lubri-' cation are provided with lubricating oil strainers in the suction line of the lube oil pump and an oil filter may be installed in the pump discharge line. A gradual decrease in lubricating oil pressure indicates that these units need cleaning. This cleaning may be accomplished in much the same manner as described for cleaning suction strainers.

When cleaning is necessary, the lubricating oil in the crankcase should be drained from the compressor and a new charge of oil should be added before restarting the unit.

When the compressor is put back into operation, the lube oil pressure should be adjusted to the proper setting by adjustment of the oil pressure regulator.

IV. CONDENSERS

The compressor discharge line terminates at the refrigerant condenser. In shipboard R-12 installations, these condensers are usually of the multipass shell-and-tube type, with water circulating through the tubes. The tubes are expanded into grooved holes in the tube sheet so as to make an absolutely tight joint between the shell and the circulating water. Refrigerant vapor is admitted to the shell, and condenses on the outer surfaces of the tubes.

Any air which may accidentally enter the refrigeration system will be drawn through the piping and eventually discharged into the condenser with the R-12 gas. The air accumulated in the condenser is lighter than the refrigerant gas and will rise to the top of the condenser when the plant is shut down. A purge valve, for purging accumulated air from the refrigeration system (when necessary), is installed at the top of the condenser, or at a high point in the compressor discharge line.

A. Checking Condenser Performance

An overall check for water-cooled condenser performance may be used after, AND ONLY AFTER, the condenser has been properly purged. After the condition of the condensing surface has been determined, make preliminary preparations to the system as outlined in the procedure, discussed earlier in the chapter, used to check for noncondensable gases. Then proceed as follows:

1. Record the condensing temperature which corresponds to the pressure in the condenser, while the compressor is in operation.

2. Record the temperature of the water leaving the condenser.

3. Subtract the temperature of the water leaving the condenser from the condensing temperature obtained in (1). The temperature of the water leaving the condenser will be several degrees below the condensing temperature of pure R-12.

4. Clean the water side of the condenser, if the difference between the temperature of the outlet circulating water and the temperature corresponding to the condensing pressure increases 5° F to 10° F above the temperature difference obtained when the condenser was in good condition and operating under similar heat loads, and if this difference is not caused by an overcharge of refrigerant or noncondensable gases.

B. Cleaning Condenser Tubes

In order to clean the condenser tubes properly, it is necessary first to drain the cooling water from the condenser and then to remove the water connections and water chests. When the water chests are removed, be careful not to damage the gaskets between the tube sheet and the water side of the water chest. Tubes should be inspected as often as practicable and be cleaned as necessary by the use of an approved method for cleaning steam condenser tubes.

Rubber plugs and an air or water lance should be employed when necessary to remove foreign deposits. It is essential that the tube surfaces be kept clear of particles of foreign matter; however, care must be taken not to destroy the thin protective coating of corrosion products on the inner surfaces of the tubes. If the tubes become badly corroded, they should be replaced in order to avoid the possibility of losing the R-12 charge and admitting salt water to the R-12 system.

C. Cleaning Air-Cooled Condensers

Although the large plants are equipped with water-cooled condensers, auxiliary units are commonly provided with air-cooled condensers, and this eliminates the necessity for circulating water pumps and piping.

The exterior surface of the tubes and fins on an air-cooled condenser should be kept free of dirt or any matter that might obstruct heat flow and air circulation. The finned surface should be brushed clean with a stiff bristle brush as often as necessary. When installations are exposed to salt spray and rain through open doors or hatches, care should be taken to minimize corrosion of the exterior surfaces. The finned surface is usually coated with solder and should never be painted; it may be retinned if necessary.

D. Testing for Leaks

To prevent serious loss of refrigerant through leaky condenser tubes, the condenser should be tested for leakage once every two weeks. The test should always be conducted on a condenser that has not been in use for the preceding 12 hours. Slowly open the vent valves on the water side, one at a time, and insert the exploring tube of a leak detector. If this test indicates that R-12 gas is present, the exact location of the leak may be detected by the following method:

1. Remove the water heads and listen at each section for the hissing sound that indicates gas leakage. If the leak cannot be definitely located, all the, tubes must be checked. However, if the probable location of the leaky tubes is found, treat that section as follows:

2. Wash the tube heads, and with a cloth or ball of cotton clean all tubes (while wet) until the inner walls are dry and shining. Then hold the exploring tube in one end of each condenser tube for about 10 seconds. As soon as fresh air is drawn into the tube, drive a cork into each end of the tube. If necessary, repeat this procedure with all the tubes in the condenser. Before proceeding further, allow the condenser to remain in this condition for 48 hours.

3. After the tubes have been corked up for 48 hours, put three men on the job, one to remove corks at one end, another to remove corks at the other end and handle the exploring tube, and the third man to watch the color of the flame in the lamp. Start with the top row of tubes in the section being inspected, remove the corks simultaneously at each end of the tube, and insert the exploring tube for 5 seconds.

4. Mark any leaky tubes for later identification.

5. Leakage of any of the tube joints is indicated by the presence of oil at the joint, after the 48-hour period.

To date, this procedure has been found to be the only method which gives conclusive evidence; in most cases, this method has given satisfactory results.

E. Retubing Condensers

The general procedure for retubing condensers has been outlined in chapter 6 of this training course. One specific illustration of retubing a refrigerant condenser is as follows:

1. Drill into both ends of the faulty tube or tubes, with a 19/32-inch drill, to a depth of 1/16 inch less than the actual thickness of the tube sheet.

2. Insert the condenser knockout bar. Then insert, in the other end of the tube, a bar 1/2 inch x 6 inches.

3. Proceed to the other end of the condenser and drive out the faulty tube by using the knockout bar.

4. Follow the above procedure for any further tube removal.

5. Cut the new tube 1/8 inch longer than the overall length of the condenser (heads removed).

6. Both ends of the tubes must be square and all inside and outside burrs removed.

7. Insert the new tube in the condenser, leaving 1/16 of an inch protruding from each end.

8. Secure the spacing bar over one end of the tube.

9. Oil the rolling tool, insert it in the tube, and roll the tube into serrations.

10. Remove the spacing bar and roll that end of the tube by the above method.

11. Insert the belling tool and keep rotating while belling. Do not strike too hard on the belling tool.

12. After belling both ends of the tube, grind off the ends flush with the tube sheet.

13. Open the discharge line valve into the condenser, and open any other valves necessary to get gas from the compressor into the condenser.

14. Using the pressure thus obtained, test the condenser for leaks, with the halide torch.

15. If any small leaks exist, reroll the leaking tube. (Spacers are used on the rolling tool to prevent the use of maximum rolling effect on a preliminary rolling operation. Additional rolling effect may be obtained by removing one of these spacers.)

16. Reassemble the condenser.

V. EXPANSION VALVES

In order to diagnose troubles in a refrigeration plant, it is essential that the mechanic ' have a thorough understanding of the principles and ope ration of expansion valves.

A. Thermostatic Expansion Valve

FUNCTION.– The thermostatic expansion valve controls the quantity of refrigerant admitted to the cooling coil and reduces the pressure of this refrigerant to that pressure maintained in the coil. The valve also operates to feed into the coil the amount of refrigerant necessary to keep the coil working at maximum effectiveness and in accordance with heat load variation, and to prevent the flooding back of liquid refrigerant to the compressor.

OPERATION. – It is apparent that, if the suction gas leaving the cooling coil is at the saturated vapor temperature of the refrigerant and the R-12 in the control bulb is also at this temperature, the control bulb pressure transmitted to the top of the valve diaphragm will be equal to the suction pressure transmitted to the lower side of the diaphragm through the equalizing line. The valve needle will be in the closed position, because of upward pressure exerted by the valve spring. The continued operation of the compressor maintains or lowers the cooling coil suction pressure, but since the valve is closed and no liquid refrigerant is supplied to the coil, the temperature of the coil rises because of the heat absorbed from the space being cooled. The R-12 in the control bulb is in turn heated; and its pressure increases to maintain a saturated pressure corresponding to the cooling coil suction gas temperature. The pressure on top of the power element diaphragm increases, overcomes the spring pressure, and causes the valve needle to open, thus permitting the flow of refrigerant liquid into the coil.

The liquid refrigerant is evaporated during its passage through the coil. Upon leaving the outlet end, the cold vapor cools the R-12 in the control bulb and decreases the upper diaphragm pressure, tending to close the valve. This reduction in valve opening reduces the quantity of refrigerant fed to the cooling coil and permits evaporation of all the liquid before the refrigerant reaches the outlet end where the control bulb is located. The refrigerant vapor becomes superheated during its passage through that part of the coil beyond the point where all liquid is evaporated.

The amount of superheat depends on the valve spring pressure exerted on the diaphragm. For a given spring setting, the valve maintains a relatively constant degree of superheat at the coil outlet, ensuring that all R-12 liquid is evaporated before it leaves the coil to return to the compressor.

EXTERNAL EQUALIZER. – The external equalizing connection is provided for relatively large cooling coil installations where a considerable pressure loss may be expected to occur because of the length of coil travel or the distribution method. This equalizing line is connected to the cooling coil at a convenient point where the desired operating pressures will be reflected. practically equal to that at the coil outlet where the control bulb is located; in such an installation the external equalizing line is unnecessary. Instead, the expansion valve is provided with an internal equalizing port, to adjust the pressure on the lower side of the diaphragm so that it will equal the pressure at the valve outlet.

For small installations the pressure drop through the coil is correspondingly small, and the refrigerant pressure at the valve outlet.

TESTING AND ADJUSTMENT. When the thermostatic expansion valve is operating properly, the temperature at the outlet side of the valve is much lower than that at the inlet side. If this temperature difference does not exist when the system is in operation, the valve seat is probably dirty and clogged with foreign matter.

Once a valve is properly adjusted, further adjustment should not be necessary. The major trouble encountered can usually be traced to moisture or dirt collecting at the valve seat and orifice.

By means of a gear and screw arrangement, the thermostatic expansion valve is adjusted to maintain a superheat ranging approximately from $4°$ F to $12°$ F at the cooling coil outlet. The proper superheat adjustment varies with the design and service operating conditions of the valve, and the design of the particular plant. Increased spring pressure increases the degree of superheat at the coil outlet and decreased pressure has the opposite effect. Many thermostatic expansion valves are initially adjusted by the manufacturer to maintain a predetermined degree of superheat, and no provision is made for further adjustments in service.

If expansion valves are adjusted to give a high degree of superheat at the coil outlet, or if the valve is stuck shut, the amount of refrigerant admitted to the cooling coil will be reduced. With an insufficient amount of refrigerant, the coil will be "starved" and will operate at a reduced capacity. Compressor lubricating oil carried with the refrigerant may tend to collect at the bottom of the cooling coils, thus robbing the compressor crankcase, and providing a condition whereby slugs of lubricating oil may be drawn back to the compressor. If the expansion valve is adjusted for too low a degree of superheat, or if the valve is stuck open, liquid refrigerant may flood from the cooling coils back to the compressor. Should the liquid collect at a low point in the suction line or coil, and be drawn back to the compressor intermittently in slugs, there

is danger of injury to the moving parts of the compressor.

In general, the expansion valves for air conditioning and water cooling plants (high temperature installations) must be adjusted for higher superheat than are the expansion valves for cold storage refrigeration and ship's service store equipment (low temperature installations).

If it is impossible to adjust expansion valves to the desired settings, or if it is suspected that the expansion valve assembly is defective and requires replacement, appropriate tests must be made. (First be sure that the liquid strainers are clean, that the solenoid valves are operative, and that the system is sufficiently charged with refrigerant.)

The major equipment required for expansion valve tests is as follows:

1. A service drum of R-12, or a supply of clean dry air at 70 to 100 psig. The service drum is used to supply gas under pressure. The gas used does not have to be the same as that employed in the thermal element of the valve being tested.

2. A high pressure and a low pressure gage. The low pressure gage should be accurate and in good condition so that the pointer does not have any appreciable lost motion. The high pressure gage, while not absolutely necessary, will be useful in showing the pressure on the inlet side of the valve. Refrigeration plants are provided with suitable spare and test pressure gages.

The procedure for testing is as follows:

1. Connect the valve inlet to the gas supply with the high pressure gage attached so as to indicate the gas pressure to the valve, and with the low pressure gage loosely connected to the expansion valve outlet. The low pressure gage is connected up loosely so as to provide a small amount of leakage through the connection.

2. Insert the expansion valve thermal element in a bath of crushed ice. Do not attempt to perform this test with a container full of water in which a small amount of crushed ice is floating.

3. Open the valve on the service drum or in the air supply line. Make certain that the gas supply is sufficient to build up the pressure to at least 70 psi on the high pressure gage connected in the line to the valve inlet.

4. The expansion valve can now be adjusted. If it is desired to adjust for 10° F superheat, the pressure on the outlet gage should be 22.5 psig. This is equivalent to an R-12 evaporating temperature of 22° F, and since the ice maintains the bulb at 32° F, the valve adjustment is for 10 superheat (difference between 32 and 22). For a 5 superheat adjustment, the valve should be adjusted to give a pressure of approximately 26.1 psig. There must be a small .amount of leakage through the low pressure gage connection while this adjustment is being made.

5. To determine if the valve operates smoothly, tap the valve body lightly with a small weight. The low pressure gage needle should not jump more than 1 psi.

6. Now tighten the low pressure gage connection so as to stop the leakage at the joint, and determine if the expansion valve seats tightly. With the valve in good condition, the pressure will increase a few pounds and then either stop or build up very slowly. With a leaking valve, the pressure will build up rapidly until it equals the inlet pressure.

7. Again loosen the gage so as to permit leakage at the gage connection; remove the thermal element, or control bulb, from the crushed ice, and warm it with the hand or place it in water that is at room temperature. When this is done, the pressure should increase rapidly, showing that the power element has not lost its charge. If there is no increase in pressure, the power element is dead.

8. With high pressure showing on both gages as outlined above, the valve can be tested to determine if the body joints or the bellows leak. This can be done by using a halide leak detector. When performing this test, it is important that the body of the valve have a fairly high pressure applied to it. In addition, the gages and other fittings should be made up tightly at the joints so as to eliminate leakage at these points.

REPLACEMENT OF VALVE. — If it is evident that the expansion valve is defective, it must be replaced. Often it is possible to replace a faulty power element or other part of the valve without having to replace the entire assembly. When replacement of an expansion valve is necessary, it is important to replace the unit with a valve of the same capacity and type, designed for R-12 systems.

B. Automatic Expansion Valve

Automatic expansion valves are generally similar in construction to thermostatic valves except that the thermostatic element is omitted. The refrigerant pressure in the cooling coil operates on the lower side of the diaphragm and atmospheric pressure operates on the upper side. The amount of valve opening depends upon the pressure existing in the coil. As the operation of the compressor lowers the coil pressure, there is a corresponding decrease in pressure on the lower side of the diaphragm; when this pressure becomes less than the atmospheric pressure on the upper side, the diaphragm is depressed and the valve opens. The pressure at which the valve will open can be predetermined by an adjustment of the valve. As the compressor continues to operate, the needle valve remains open enough to maintain the refrigerant evaporating pressure. When the compressor stops, the coil pressure increases and the valve automatically closes. Thermostatic expansion valves have proved to be more satisfactory than automatic expansion valves for refrigeration plant applications.

C. Hand Expansion Valve

A bypass line equipped with a manually operated expansion valve is installed around the strainer and the cooling coil liquid control valve assembly to permit repair or cleaning. The hand expansion valve is generally similar in design to the other refrigerant stop valves installed in refrigeration systems, except that the valve disk is sometimes specially shaped to permit accurate adjustment of flow. Hand expansion valves should be used only for emergency purposes, since there is the possibility of flooding liquid refrigerant back to the compressor.

D. Switches

In order to trouble-shoot or diagnose switch troubles, it is essential that you have a good understanding of pressurestats and thermostats. A pressurestat is an electric switch actuated by pressure from an outside source. The thermostat is actuated by temperature or heat on a specially prepared thermo-bulb, filled with a substance that expands and contracts with any change in temperature.

A switch that cuts out when there is an increase in pressure or temperature is known as a direct acting switch. When the pressure or temperature is decreased, the switch cuts in. The high pressure switch is a direct acting switch. A reverse acting switch is one that cuts in on an increase of pressure or temperature and cuts out on a decrease of pressure or temperature. The low pressure cutout, thermostat, and water-failure switches are reverse acting switches.

E. Evacuating and Dehydrating the System

Where moisture accumulation must be corrected, the system should first be cleared of refrigerant and air. The time required for these processes will depend upon the size of the system and the amount of moisture present. It is good engineering practice to circulate heated air through a large dehydrator and system for several hours, or as long as the dehydrator drying agent remains effective, before proceeding with the evacuation process. If possible, the dehydrated air should be heated to about 240° F.

Large dehydrators, suitable for preliminary dehydration of R-12 systems, are usually available at naval shipyards, and aboard tenders and repair ships.

After the preliminary dehydration, remaining moisture is evacuated by means of a two-stage high-efficiency vacuum pump having a vacuum indicator. (These vacuum pumps are available aboard tenders and repair ships.)

The vacuum indicator shown in figure 10-1 consists of an insulated test tube containing a wet bulb thermometer with its wick immersed in distilled water. The indicator is connected in the vacuum pump suction line. The suction line from the vacuum pump is connected to the charging connection in the refrigeration system. The refrigerant circuit should be closed to the atmosphere and the charging connection opened to the vacuum pump.

A two-stage pump is started for operation in parallel so that maximum displacement may be secured during the initial pump-downstages. When the indicator shows a temperature of about 55° F (0.43 inch Hg, absolute), the pumps are placed in series operation (wherein the discharge from the first step enters the suction of the second step pump). The dehydration process will be reflected in the temperature drop of the vacuum indicator, as shown in figure 10-2. Readings will initially reflect ambient temperatures, then show rapidly falling temperatures until the water in the system starts to boil.

When most of the evaporated moisture has been evacuated from the system, the indicator will show a decrease in temperature. When the temperature reaches 35° F (0.2 inch Hg, absolute), open the system at a point farthest from the pump; at this point, air should be drawn into the system through a chemical dehydrator, and meanwhile the pump should be operated to permit dilution of moisture present in the system. Close off the opening and re-evacuate until the indicator again shows a temperature of 35° F. At this point the dehydration process is complete; close the charging valve and then stop the pump.

Sometimes it will be impossible to obtain a temperature as low as 35° F in the vacuum indicator; the probable reasons for such a failure, and the corrective procedures to take, are as follows:

1. Presence of excess moisture in the system. The dehydration procedure should be conducted for longer periods.

2. Presence of absorbed refrigerant in the lubricating oil contained in the compressor crankcase. Remove the lubricating oil from the crankcase before proceeding with the dehydration process.

3. Leakage of air into the system. The leak must be found and stopped. It will be necessary to repeat the procedure required for detecting leaks in the system.

4. Inefficient vacuum pump or defective vacuum indicator. The defective unit(s) should be repaired or replaced.

F. Reactivating the Drying System

Immediately after each period of use, or after the system has been opened for repairs, the drying agent in the dehydrator should be replaced. If a replacement cartridge is not available, the drying agent can be reactivated and used until a replacement is available.

Reactivation is accomplished by removing the drying agent and heating it, for 12 hours, to a temperature of 300° F to bake out the moisture. The drying agent may be placed in an oven, or a stream of hot air may be circulated through the cartridge. These methods are satisfactory for reactivating commonly used dehydrating agents such as activated alumina and silica gel. Where special drying agents are employed, they should be reactivated in accordance with specific instructions furnished by the manufacturer.

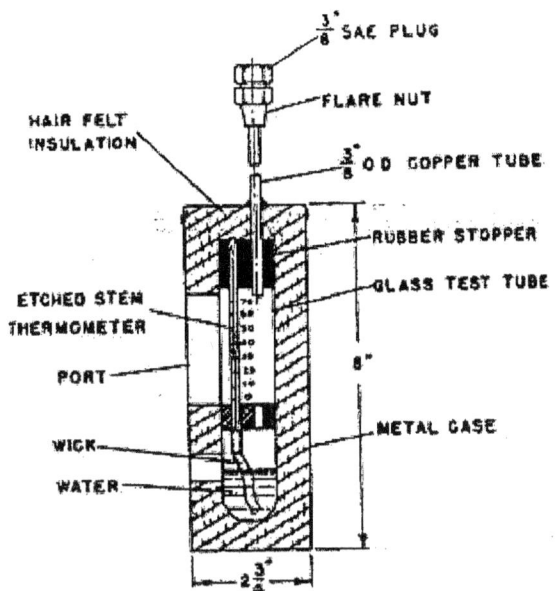

CONVERSION TEMPERATURE °F TO
ABSOLUTE PRESSURE INCHES MERCURY

TEMP. °F	ABS. PRESSURE INCHES MERCURY
60	0.521
55	0.436
50	0.362
45	0.300
40	0.248
35	0.204
32	0.181

Figure 1.—Dehydrator vacuum indicator.

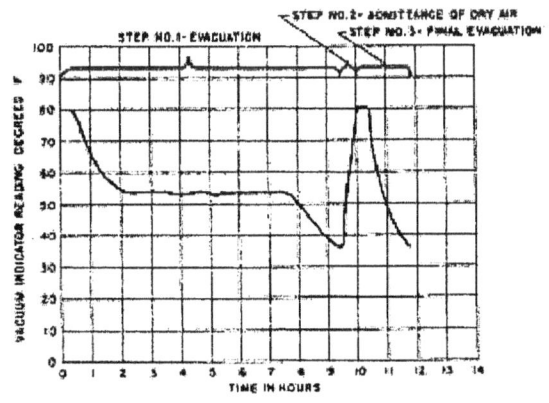

Figure 2.—Vacuum indicator readings plotted during dehydration.

After reactivation, the drying agent should be replaced in the dehydrator shell and sealed as quickly as possible, in order to prevent absorption of atmospheric moisture. When the drying agent becomes fouled or saturated with lubricating oil, it must be replaced by a fresh spare charge, or dehydrator cartridge, taken from a sealed container.

Remember that the dehydrators permanently installed in R-12 systems for naval ships are designed to remove only the minute quantities of moisture unavoidably introduced into the system. Extreme care must be taken to prevent moisture, or moisture-laden air, from entering the system.

G. Cleaning The System

Systems may accumulate dirt and scale as a result of improper techniques used during repair or installation. If such dirt is excessive and a tank-type cleaner is available, connect the cleaner to the compressor suction strainer. Where such a cleaner is not available, a hard wool felt filter, about 5/16 inch thick, should be inserted in the suction strainer screen. The plant should be operated with an operator in attendance, for at least 36 hours or until cleaned, depending upon the size and condition of the plant.

IV. DETECTING AND CORRECTING TROUBLES

Faulty operation of the refrigerating plant is indicated by various definite symptoms. These symptoms may indicate the presence of one or more conditions in the plant. Each condition must be eliminated by specific corrective measures. Space does not permit a detailed discussion here of abnormal plant conditions, but you can find complete information in the manufacturer's technical manual furnished with each refrigeration plant.

The following chart, listing symptoms, their causes, and the corrective measures to be taken, will assist you in correcting faulty operation quickly and efficiently.

A. Trouble-Diagnosis Chart		
Symptom or difficulty	Condition may be due to	Correction
High suction pressure	Overfeeding of expansion valve Leaky suction valves Improper functioning of low-pressure control switch Discharge valves leak slightly	Regulate expansion valve, check thermal element attachment. Examine valve disks, or piston rings; replace if defective. Readjust or replace switch. Examine valves. If leaking, replace if necessary.
Low suction pressure	Restricted liquid line, expansion valve, or suction strainers Insufficient refrigerant in system Too much oil circulating in system Improper adjustment of expansion valves Coils in refrigerators clogged with frost Thermal bulb of expansion valve has lost charge Forced air cooler airflow restricted or fan inoperative One or more solenoid valves closed Compressor capacity in excess of existing compartment heat load	Remove, examine, and clean strainers. Check for refrigerant shortage. Check for too much oil in circulation. Remove oil. (See "Oil leaves crank-case.") Adjust valve to give more flow. Defrost coils. Detach thermal bulb from suction line and hold in the palm of one hand, with the other hand gripping the suction line; if flooding through is observed, bulb has not lost its charge. If no flooding through is noticed, test and replace expansion valve if necessary. Check for air obstruction, dirty filters, or faulty electrical operation. Check electrical solenoid circuit for failure, and repair. Reduce speed of compressor or adjust compressor capacity reduction where provided.
Low suction line temperature	Excessive liquid refrigerant circulating in system	Check expansion valve adjustment and regulate.
High suction line temperature	Shortage of refrigerant in system	Check, test for leaks and add refrigerant as required.

Trouble-Diagnosis Chart — Continued		
Symptom or difficulty	Condition may be due to	Correction
High discharge pressure	Air or noncondensable gas in system Inlet water warm No water or insufficient quantity of water flowing through condenser Condenser tubes clogged Too much refrigerant in system (condenser tubes submerged in liquid refrigerant) Condenser improperly vented Air-cooled condenser dirty or receiving insufficient air	Purge air from condenser. Increase quantity by adjusting water-regulating valve. Adjust water-regulating valve, open manual valves, or start pump. Clean condenser tubes and water boxes. Draw off excess refrigerant into service drum. Vent condenser water boxes. Clean or remove obstructions. Check space ventilation for adequate supply of cool air and correct.
Low discharge pressure	Too much water flowing through condenser Water too cold or unthrottled Liquid refrigerant flooding back from cooling coils Leaky discharge valve	Regulate water valve. Reduce quantity of water. Change expansion valve adjustment, examine fastening thermal element. Examine. If leaking, replace.
High discharge temperature	Air or noncondensable gas in system	Purge air from condenser.

Trouble-Diagnosis Chart — Continued		
Symptom or difficulty	Condition may be due to	Correction
Low discharge temperature	Excessive liquid refrigerant in system	Check expansion valve setting and adjust.
Low oil pressure	Dirt in oil pump or strainer	Stop compressor. Check oil gage for accuracy. Clean, repair, or replace oil strainer and pump.
Excessive oil pressure	Clogged oil distribution lines	Stop compressor. Check oil gage for accuracy. Pump down, clean oil lines.
Oil leaves crankcase	Refrigerant flooding back to compressor Leaking piston rings or worn cylinder Expansion valves leaking Overcharge of oil	Adjust expansion valve and check for proper mounting of thermal elements. Replace rings, cylinder sleeves, or compressor. Rebore and refit. Valve seats and stem may be corroded from passage of refrigerant vapor. Check and replace if required. Check oil sight glass and remove excess. Check for continuing return and repeat process until oil level is constant.
Oil does not return to crankcase	Expansion valve not supplying cooling coil with sufficient refrigerant Valve in oil return line closed or stuck shut Oil trap or pocket in cooling coil or suction line piping	Check operation of expansion valve and adjust, if required. Open. Locate, open, and drain.
Oil sight glass shows presence of oil foaming	Excessive liquid refrigerant returning to compressor	Check expansion valve adjustment or leaking hand expansion valves. Adjust, repair, or replace.
Crankcase and cylinder temperature relatively warm with low suction pressure	Shortage of refrigerant	Test for shortage, add refrigerant if required, test for leaks.
Crankcase temperature relatively cooler than suction line with low pressure suction	Excessive oil is circulating in system	See "Oil leaves crankcase."
Crankcase and cylinder temperature relatively cold, sweating, or frosting	Liquid refrigerant being returned to compressor	Check expansion valve setting, adjust. Check for proper mounting of thermal element.
Compressor noisy	Vibration because the compressor is not rigidly	Bolt down rigidly.

Trouble-Diagnosis Chart — Continued		
Symptom or difficulty	Condition may be due to	Correction
Compressor noisy— (Continued)	bolted to foundation Too much oil in circulation causing hydraulic knock Slugging due to flooding back of refrigerant Wear of parts such as piston pins, bearings, etc.	Check oil level. Expansion valve open too wide; adjust. Thermo-bulb incorrectly placed or loose; check and relocate or fasten. Determine location of cause. Repair compressor.
Water supply pressure too low	Water pump suction line restricted Pressure-reducing valve in fire flushing line improperly adjusted	Check for closed valves, check strainer and clean. Check and readjust.
Water supply pressure too high	Pressure-reducing valve improperly adjusted Water valves open too wide.	Check and adjust. Check and close to proper pressure.
Water overboard temperature too low	Excessive water flow through condenser	Correlate with discharge pressure and check water regulating valve operation, adjust if necessary. (See "Water supply pressure too high.")
Water overboard temperature too high	Restricted water flow through condenser	Correlate with discharge pressure. Check water-regulating valve and adjust, if necessary. (See "Water supply pressure too low.")
Liquid line refrigerant temperature too warm	High condensing temperature	Check condenser for water quantity.
Liquid line refrigerant temperature too cold	Shortage of refrigerant Excessive oil in circulation	Test for shortage, charge with refrigerant, test for R-12 leakage. See "Oil leaves crankcase."
Sight flow indicator shows bubbles in refrigerant	Shortage of refrigerant	Test for shortage, charge with refrigerant, test for R-12 leakage.
Ice-making tank temperature too high	Automatic controls not functioning Brine solution too weak and freezing	Check electrical circuit for open switches, blown fuses, burnt solenoid coil, and repair or replace. Check adjustment of control switch. Check salinity of brine for proper density. Add stronger solution.

Trouble-Diagnosis Chart Continued		
Symptom or difficulty	Condition may be due to	Correction
Ice-making tank temperature too high (Continued)	Expansion valve not feeding sufficient refrigerant	Check for improper adjustment, or moisture at valve orifice. Adjust or clean. Put dehydrator in operation if moisture is in evidence.
Ice-making tank temperature too low	Automatic controls not functioning Hand expansion valve leaking	Check solenoid valve switch setting and adjust if necessary. Check position of valve for tight closing. Check for dirt or corrosion at seat and pin. Clean, repair, or replace.
Compartment temperature too high	Automatic controls not functioning Excessive frost on cooling coils Expansion valve not feeding sufficient refrigerant Airflow restricted on forced air coolers Excessive infiltration of uncooled air	Check solenoid valve switch or thermostat setting, electrical circuit, fuses, and solenoid coil. Repair or replace. If there is a forced air cooler, check to see that fan is operating. Defrost. Check for improper adjustment, or moisture at valve orifice. Adjust or clean. Put dehydrator in operation if moisture is present. Check filters, duct work obstructions, and fan operation. Clean and repair as required. Check unwarranted traffic in and out of compartment. Take steps to limit traffic as to personnel and entrance periods. Check compartment openings and door gaskets. Repair or replace.
	Introduction of warm and/ or moist product	Temporary. If within the capacity of equipment, temperature will eventually return to normal. Start an additional compressor if system is arranged for isolating loads carried by more than one unit in operation.

Compartment temperature too low	Automatic controls not functioning Hand expansion valve leaking	Check solenoid valve switch or thermostat setting, electrical circuit, fuses, and solenoid coils. Repair or replace. Check position of valve for tight closing. Check for dirt, or corrosion at seat and pin. Clean, repair, or replace.
Liquid refrigerant cycling through the cooling coil with wide variation in superheat at thermal element location	Excessive oil circulating through system Moisture or ice at thermal element contact with	Check other symptoms for a like condition. (See "Oil leaves crankcase" and "Oil does not return to crankcase.") Remove, dry, and properly insulate.

Trouble-Diagnosis Chart Continued

Symptom or difficulty	Condition may be due to	Correction
Liquid refrigerant cycling through the cooling coil with wide variation in superheat at thermal element location (Continued)	suction line affecting true operation Expansion valve defective Thermal element located in such a position as to be affected by airflow Expansion valve too large or has improper thermo-static charge Moisture in expansion valve port or working parts	Check thermal element for response. Repair or replace. Remove and relocate; insulate. See technical manual furnished with equipment for selected size and type. Install proper valve. Check heat valve body slowly taking care not to damage power element and gaskets. Heat will temporarily free valve parts and resume automatic operation. If moisture is present disassemble valve, clean and replace. Put dehy-drator into service.
Liquid refrigerant carrying through the coil and far beyond the thermal element location with little superheat at this point	Expansion valve open too wide Thermal element making poor contact with suction piping Thermal element improperly located or insulated. Expansion valve leaking	Adjust to close. Remove, clean both surfaces, and insulate. Remove, locate properly, and insulate. When compressor shuts down, check by listening at valve for a hissing sound. Check for dirt or corrosion of seat. Clean, repair, or replace.
Liquid refrigerant carrying partially through the coil with considerable superheat at thermal element location	Moisture in expansion valve port or working parts Liquid line strainer clogged or dirty Expansion valve improperly adjusted Shortage of refrigerant Expansion valve thermal element improperly located Expansion valve too small Refrigerant gas in liquid line	See same condition and correction as above. Remove, clean, and replace. Check superheat and adjust. Check storage, test for leaks and charge. Check and relocate. See technical manual furnished with equipment, and install proper size and type. Check for excessive pressure loss in liquid line. Open valves or restrictions affecting loss. Check subcooler, if installed, for proper operation.

Trouble-Diagnosis Chart Continued

Symptom or difficulty	Condition may be due to	Correction
Liquid refrigerant carrying partially through the coil with considerable superheat at thermal element location- (Continued)	Pressure drop through cooling coils excessive Expansion valve power element has lost charge of refrigerant Expansion valve equalizer line closed or restricted Expansion valve thermal element being affected by refrigerant from another cooling coil circuit	Check for restrictions, oil traps or valves partially closed. Drain oil or open restrictions as applicable. Remove thermal element and hand-warm to body temperature. If not responsive, replace power assembly or valve. Check, and open or replace. Check location of thermal element. Remove and properly locate.
Compressor will not start	Overload tripped, fuses blown Switch out No charge of gas in system operated by low-pressure control switch Solenoid valves closed No flow of circulating water through condenser to actuate water-failure switch	Reset overload, replace fuses, and examine for cause of condition. Throw in switch. With no gas in system there is insufficient pressure to throw in low-pressure control. Recharge system with refrigerant; check and repair leaks. Examine coil, switch, etc.; if defective or out of adjustment, replace or adjust. Provide condenser circulating water.
Compressor runs continuously	Shortage of refrigerant Discharge or suction valves leak badly Head gasket blown between cylinders Improper functioning of low-pressure control switch Overloaded compressor Stuck-open or leaky relief valve	Test for shortage of refrigerant; if insufficient, add proper amount. Test system for leaks. Test valves; if leaking, repair or replace. Replace gasket. Adjust or replace switch. Start an additional compressor if system is arranged for isolating loads carried by more than one unit in operation. Overhaul relief valve.
Compressor short cycles on high pressure cutout	High pressure cutout incorrectly set.	Check setting of high pressure cutout; switch should throw out at about 150 pounds head pressure.

Trouble-Diagnosis Chart Continued

Symptom or difficulty	Condition may be due to	Correction
Compressor short cycles on low-pressure control switch	Low-pressure control incorrectly set. (See "Low suction pressure.")	Check setting and adjust.
Water valve chatters	Water pressure too high	Reduce water pressure by adjusting water pressure-reducing valve or throttling stop valve.
Water runs continuously when compressor *is* shut off	Water-regulating valve open too wide Dirt under seat of water-regulating valve Valve mechanism stuck Pump motor controller contact stuck shut	Readjust valve to give correct head pressures corresponding to water inlet temperature and condensing pressure. Remove valve from lines, disassemble, and examine; replace defective parts, clean and reassemble. If valve then does not function properly, replace. Remove and disassemble. Clean valve seats and valve pins, lubricate, adjust packing, etc. Adjust
Head gasket leaks	Head bolts stretched, or washers crushed Oil or refrigerant slugging	Examine gaskets; replace if necessary. Tighten head bolts. Replace washers. Check operating conditions for flooding of refrigerant back to compressor. Correct.
Oil seepage at shaft seal connection is excessive	Failure of shaft seal	Test, repair, or replace crankshaft seal.
Oil seepage at refrigerant system piping and compressor connections	Leakage of refrigerant	Test; remake connections or provide replacement gaskets, as required.

REFRIGERATION AND AIR CONDITIONING TERMINOLOGY AND TROUBLESHOOTING

TABLE OF CONTENTS

		Page
A.	TERMINOLOGY	
	Absolute Pressure ... Bimetallic Element	1
	Boiling Point ... Conduction	2
	Conductor (Heat or Thermal) ... Equalizer	3
	Evaporation ... Humidistat	4
	Humidity ... Saturated Liquid	5
	Saturated Vapor ... Wet-Bulb Depression	6
B.	TROUBLESHOOTING	7

REFRIGERATION AND AIR CONDITIONING

TERMINOLOGY AND TROUBLESHOOTING

A. TERMINOLOGY

Many of the terms used in connection with refrigeration and air conditioning have quite definite and specialized meanings. In order to understand any written material in the field of refrigeration and air conditioning, it is essential to have a thorough knowledge of correct terminology. Some important terms used in connection with refrigeration and air conditioning are defined in the following list.

ABSOLUTE PRESSURE.—Pressure measured from absolute zero rather than from normal atmospheric pressure; the sum of atmospheric pressure plus gage pressure.

ABSOLUTE TEMPERATURE.—Temperature measured from absolute zero (-459.67° F, or -273.15°'C).

ABSORBENT.—A material that has the ability to extract certain substances from a liquid or a gas with which it is in contact, causing physical changes, chemical changes, or both during the absorption process.

ACCUMULATOR.—A shell placed in a suction line for separating liquid refrigerant entrained in suction gas; serves as a storage chamber for low side liquid refrigerant; also known as a surge drum or surge header.

ADIABATIC PROCESS.—Any thermodynamic process that is accomplished without the transfer of heat to or from the system while the process is occurring.

ADSORBENT.—A material that has the ability to cause molecules of gases, liquids, and solids to adhere to its internal surfaces without causing any chemical or physical change.

AIR CONDITIONING.—The process of treating air to simultaneously control its temperature, humidity, cleanliness, and distribution to meet the requirements of the conditioned space.

AIR CONDITIONING UNIT.—An assembly of equipment for the control of (at least) the temperature, humidity, and cleanliness of the air within a conditioned space.

AIR DIFFUSER.—A device arranged to promote the mixing of the air leaving the duct with the room air.

AMBIENT AIR TEMPERATURE.—The temperature of the air surrounding an object; in a system using an air-cooled condenser, the temperature of the air entering the condenser.

ANEMOMETER.—An instrument for measuring the velocity of air flow.

ATMOSPHERIC PRESSURE.—Pressure exerted by the weight of the atmosphere; standard atmospheric pressure is 14.696 psia or 29.921 inches of mercury at sea level.

BACK PRESSURE.—Same as suction pressure.

BAFFLE.—A partition to direct the flow of a fluid.

BAROMETER.—An instrument for measuring atmospheric pressure.

BAROMETRIC PRESSURE.—The actual atmospheric pressure existing at any given moment; at certain times, barometric pressure is not identical with standard atmospheric pressure.

BIMETALLIC ELEMENT.—A device formed from two different metals having different

TERMINOLOGY AND TROUBLESHOOTING

coefficients of thermal expansion; used in temperature indicating and controlling instruments.

BOILING POINT.—Temperature at which a liquid boils at a given pressure.

BORE.—Inside diameter of a cylinder.

BRINE.—Any liquid cooled by the refrigerant and used for the transmission of heat without change of state.

BRITISH THERMAL UNIT.—The amount of heat required to produce a temperature rise of 1° F in 1 pound of water. Abbreviated Btu.

CENTIGRADE.—A thermometric system in which the freezing point of water is 0° C and the boiling point of water is 100° C, at standard atmospheric pressure.

CENTRAL FAN SYSTEM.—A mechanical, indirect system of air conditioning in which the air is treated by equipment outside the area served and is conveyed to and from the area by means of a fan and a distributing duct system.

CENTRIFUGAL MACHINE.—A compressor employing centrifugal force for compression.

CHANGE OF AIR.—The introduction of new, cleansed, or recirculated air to conditioned spaces, measured in the number of complete air changes in a specified time.

CHANGE OF STATE.—The change from one phase (solid, liquid, or gas) to another.

CHARGE.—The amount of refrigerant in a system; also the act of putting refrigerant into a system.

CHILL.—To refrigerate meats, water, etc., moderately, without freezing.

COEFFICIENT OF EXPANSION.—The change in length per unit length per degree of change in temperature of a material; or the change in volume per unit volume per degree of change in temperature of a material.

COEFFICIENT OF PERFORMANCE.—The ratio of the refrigeration produced to the work supplied, with refrigeration and work being expressed in the same units.

COIL.—Any cooling or heating element made of pipe or tubing.

COMFORT CHART.—A chart showing effective temperature, with dry-bulb temperature and humidity, by which the effects of various conditions on human comfort may be determined.

COMFORT COOLING.—Refrigeration for comfort, as opposed to refrigeration for manufacture or storage.

COMFORT ZONE.—The range of effective temperatures over which the majority of adults feel comfortable.

COMPRESSION, MULTI-STAGE. — Compression in two or more stages, as when the discharge of one compressor is connected to the suction of another.

COMPRESOR, HERMETIC.—A compressor in which the electric motor and the compressor are enclosed within a sealed housing.

COMPRESSOR, "V" AND "W".—High speed, single-acting, multi-cylinder compressor with straight-line piston movement in the various cylinders; the cylinders are in the "V" position or the "W" position with respect to the shaft axis.

CONDENSATE.—The liquid formed by the condensation of a vapor. In steam heating, water condensed from steam; in air conditioning, water removed from air by condensation on the cooling coil of a refrigeration system.

CONDENSATION.—The process by which a vapor changes to a liquid when heat is removed from the vapor.

CONDENSER.—A vessel or an arrangement of pipe or tubing in which the compressed refrigerant vapor is liquefied by the removal of heat.

CONDENSING UNIT.—A specific refrigerating machine combination for a given refrigerant; the unit consists of one or more power-driven compressors, condensers, liquid receivers (when required), and the necessary accessories.

CONDUCTION.—The method of heat transfer by which heat is transferred from molecule to

REFRIGERATION AND AIR CONDITIONING

molecule within a homogeneous substance or between two substances that are in physical contact with each other.

CONDUCTOR (HEAT OR THERMAL).—A material that readily transmits heat by conduction; the opposite of an insulator.

CONTROL.—Any device for the regulation of a machine in normal operation. May be manual or automatic; if automatic, it is responsive to changes in temperature, pressure, liquid level, time, or other variables.

CONVECTION.—The movement of a mass of fluid (liquid or gas) caused by differences in density in different parts of the fluid; the differences in density are caused by differences in temperature. As the fluid moves, it carries with it its contained heat energy, which is then transferred from one part of the fluid to another and from the fluid to the surroundings.

COOLER, OIL.—A heat exchanger used for cooling oil in a lubrication system.

COOLING TOWER.—A device for lowering the temperature of water by evaporative cooling, as the water is showered through a space in which outside air is circulated.

COOLING WATER.—Water used in a condenser to cool and condense a refrigerant.

COPPER PLATING.—The depositing of a film of copper on the surface of another metal (such as iron or steel) by electrochemical action; in refrigeration, copper plating usually occurs on compressor walls, pistons, discharge valves, shafts, and seals.

COUNTERFLOW.—In a heat exchanger, opposite direction of flow of the cooling liquid and the cooled liquid (or of the heating liquid and the heated liquid).

CRYOGENICS.—The branch of physics that relates to the production and the effects of very low temperatures.

CYCLE.—The complete course of operation of a refrigerant, from starting point back to starting point, in a closed refrigeration system; also, a general term for any repeated process in any system.

DEGREE.—Unit of temperature.

DEGREE OF SUPERHEAT.—The amount by which the temperature of a superheated vapor exceeds the temperature of the saturated vapor at the same pressure.

DEHUMIDIFIER.—An air cooler or washer used for lowering the moisture content of the air passing through it.

DEHUMIDIFY.—To reduce, by any process, the quantity of water vapor within a given space.

DEHYDRATE.—To remove water (in any form) from some other substance.

DENSITY.—Mass per unit volume or weight per unit volume.

DESICCANT.—Any absorbent or adsorbent, liquid or solid, that removes water or water vapor from a material. In a refrigeration circuit, the desiccant should be insoluble in the refrigerant and refrigerant oils.

DEWPOINT.—The temperature at which water vapor begins to condense in any given sample of air; dewpoint depends upon humidity, temperature, and pressure.

DISTRIBUTOR.—A device for guiding the flow of liquid into parallel paths in an evaporator.

DRIER.—A device containing a desiccant placed in a refrigerant circuit for the purpose of collecting and holding within the desiccant all water in the system above the amount that can be tolerated in the circulating refrigerant.

ELECTROLYSIS.—Chemical decomposition caused by action of an electric current in a solution.

ENTHALPY.—A term used to mean TOTAL HEAT or HEAT CONTENT.

EQUALIZER.—Piping arrangement on an enclosed compressor to equalize refrigerant gas pressure in the crankcase and suction; device for dividing the liquid refrigerant between parallel low-side coils; a piping arrangement to divide the lubricating oil between the crankcases of compressors operating in parallel; the method by which refrigerant pressure is

TERMINOLOGY AND TROUBLESHOOTING

transmitted to the diaphragm or bellows of a thermostatic expansion valve.

EVAPORATION.—The change of state from the liquid phase to the vapor phase.

EVAPORATOR.—The unit in a refrigeration system in which the refrigerant is vaporized to produce refrigeration.

EXFILTRATION.—The flow of air outward from a space through walls, leaks, etc.

EXPANSION VALVE SUPERHEAT.—The difference between the temperature of the thermal bulb and the temperature corresponding to the pressure at the coil outlet or at the equalizer connection (where provided).

FAHRENHEIT.—Thermometric scale in which 32° F denotes the freezing point of water and 212° F denotes the boiling temperature of water under standard atmospheric pressure at sea level.

FIN.—An extended surface used on tubes in some heat exchangers to increase the heat transfer area.

FLASH CHAMBER. — A separation tank placed between the expansion valve and the evaporator in a refrigeration system to separate and bypass any flash gas formed in the expansion valve.

FLASH GAS.—The gas resulting from the instantaneous evaporation of refrigerant in a pressure-reducing device, to cool the refrigerant to the evaporating temperature corresponding to the reduced pressure.

FLUID.—The general term that includes liquids and gases (or vapors).

FOAMING.—The formation of a foam or froth on an oil-refrigerant mixture; caused by a reduction in pressure with consequent rapid boiling out of the refrigerant.

FREEZING.—The change of state from the liquid phase to the solid phase.

GAGE PRESSURE.—Absolute pressure minus atmospheric pressure.

GAS.—A substance in the gaseous state; a highly superheated vapor that satisfies the perfect gas laws, within acceptable limits of accuracy. See VAPOR.

GAS, INERT.—A gas that does not readily enter into or cause chemical reactions.

GAS, NONCONDENSABLE.—A gas in a refrigeration system which does not condense at the temperature and partial pressure existing in the condenser, thereby exerting a higher head pressure on the system.

GRILLE.—A lattice or grating for an intake opening or a delivery opening.

HEAD PRESSURE.—The operating pressure measured in the discharge line at the compressor outlet.

HEAT.—A basic form of energy, which is transferred by virtue of a temperature difference.

HEAT OF CONDENSATION.—The latent heat given up by a substance as it changes from a gas to a liquid.

HEAT OF FUSION.—The latent heat absorbed when a substance changes from a solid state to a liquid state.

HEAT OF VAPORIZATION.—The latent heat absorbed by a substance as it changes from a liquid to a vapor.

HEAT PUMP.—Refrigeration equipment; used for year-round air conditioning. In summer used to cool and condition the air in a space; in winter used to warm and condition the air.

HOT-GAS DEFROSTING.—The use of high pressure or condenser gas in the low side or condenser gas in the evaporator to effect the removal of frost.

HUMIDIFY.—To increase the percentage of water vapor within a given space.

HUMIDISTAT.—A control instrument or device, actuated by changes in humidity within the conditioned areas, which automatically regulates the relative humidity of the area.

REFRIGERATION AND AIR CONDITIONING

HUMIDITY.—The water vapor within a given space.

HUMIDITY, SPECIFIC.—The weight of water vapor mixed with 1 pound of dry air, expressed as the number of grains of moisture per pound of dry air.

HYDROLYSIS.—The splitting up of compounds by reaction with water. For example, the reaction of R-12 with water which results in the formation of acid materials.

INDUSTRIAL AIR CONDITIONING.—Air conditioning used for purposes other than comfort.

JACKET WATER.—The water used to cool the cylinder head and cylinder walls of a water-cooled compressor.

LATENT HEAT.—Heat transfer that is NOT reflected in a temperature change but IS reflected in a changing physical state of the substance involved.

LIQUEFACTION.—The change of state from a gas to a liquid. (The term liquefaction is usually used instead of condensation when referring to substances which are in a gaseous state at ordinary pressures and temperatures.)

LIQUID LINE.—The tube or pipe through which liquid refrigerant is carried from the condenser or receiver to the pressure-reducing device.

LIQUID RECEIVER.—A vessel permanently connected to the high side of a system for the storage of liquefied refrigerant.

LOAD.—The amount of heat imposed upon a refrigeration system in any specified period of time, or the required rate of heat removal; usually expressed in Btu per hour.

LOW SIDE.—The parts of the refrigeration system that are at or below the evaporating temperature.

MANOMETER.—A U-tube, or a single tube and reservoir arrangement, used with a suitable fluid to measure pressure differences.

MELTING.—The change of state from a solid to a liquid.

OZONE.—Triatomic oxygen (O_3). Sometimes used in cold storage or air conditioning installations as an odor eliminator. Can be toxic in certain concentrations.

PLENUM CHAMBER.—An air compartment maintained under pressure for receiving air before distribution to the conditioned spaces.

PNEUMATIC.—Operated by air pressure.

PREHEATING.—In air conditioning, to heat the air in advance of other processes.

PRESSURE.—Force per unit area.

PRESSURE DROP.—Loss of pressure, as from one end of a refrigerant line to the other, because of friction.

PRESSURE EQUALIZING.—Allowing the high side and the low side of the refrigeration system to become equal or nearly equal in pressure during idle periods, to prevent excessive starting loads on the compressor.

PRESSURE REGULATOR, SUCTION.—An automatic valve designed to limit the suction pressure to prevent motor overload.

PSYCHROMETER.—An instrument for measuring relative humidities by means of wet-bulb and dry-bulb temperatures.

PSYCHROMETRIC CHART.—A graphical representation of the properties of water vapor and air mixtures.

PURGING.—The act of blowing out gas from a refrigeration system, usually for the purpose of removing air or other noncondensable gases.

REFRIGERATION TON.—The removal of heat at a rate of 288,000 Btu in 24 hours or 12,000 Btu in 1 hour.

RETURN AIR.—The air returned from a space being conditioned.

SATURATED LIQUID.—A liquid which is at saturation pressure and saturation temperature; in other words, a liquid which is at its boiling point for any given pressure.

TERMINOLOGY AND TROUBLESHOOTING

SATURATED VAPOR.—A vapor which is at saturation pressure and saturation temperature. A saturated vapor cannot be superheated as long as it is in contact with the liquid from which it is being generated.

SATURATION PRESSURE and SATURATION TEMPERATURE.—The pressure and temperature at which a liquid and the vapor it is generating can exist in equilibrium contact with each other. The boiling point of any liquid depends upon pressure and temperature; a liquid boils when it is at the saturation temperature for any particular saturation pressure.

SELF-CONTAINED UNIT.—A refrigeration unit that can be removed from the premises without disconnecting any refrigerant-containing part.

SENSIBLE HEAT.—Heat transfer that is reflected in a change of temperature.

SILICA GEL.—A form of silicon dioxide which absorbs moisture readily; used as a drying agent.

SPECIFIC GRAVITY.—The density of a substance compared to the density of a standard material such as water.

SPECIFIC VOLUME.—The space occupied by unit amount of a substance at a specified pressure and temperature; often measured in cubic feet per pound.

SUBCOOLED LIQUID.—A liquid that is at a temperature below its boiling point for any given pressure.

SUBCOOLING.—The process of cooling a liquid to a temperature below its saturation temperature for any given saturation pressure.

SUPERHEATING.—The process of adding heat to a vapor in order to raise its temperature above saturation temperature. It is impossible to superheat a saturated vapor as long as it is in contact with the liquid from which it is being generated; hence the vapor must be led away from the liquid before it can be superheated.

TEMPERATURE.—A measure of the concentration of heat (thermal energy) in a body or substance.

THERMODYNAMICS.—The branch of physics that deals with heat and its transformations to and from other forms of energy.

THERMOSTAT.—A temperature-sensing automatic control device.

TOXIC.—Having temporary or permanent poisonous effects.

TUBE, CAPILLARY.—In refrigeration, a tube of small internal diameter used as a liquid refrigerant flow control or expansion device between the high side and the low side of the refrigeration system.

UNLOADER.—A device in or on the compressor for equalizing high-side and low-side pressures for a brief time during starting and for controlling compressor capacity by rendering one or more cylinders ineffective.

VACUUM.—Pressure that is less than atmospheric pressure.

VALVE, KING.—A stop valve between the receiver and the expansion valve, normally close to the receiver.

VAPOR.—A gaseous substance, particularly one that is at or near saturation temperature and pressure.

VENTILATION.—The process of supplying or removing air by natural or mechanical means, to or from a space; such air may or may not have been conditioned.

VITAL HEAT.—The heat generated by fruits and vegetables in storage; caused by ripening.

VOLATILE LIQUID.—A liquid that evaporates (vaporizes) readily at atmospheric pressure and room temperature.

WATER (OR BRINE) COOLER.—A factory-made assembly or elements in which the water or brine and the refrigerant are in heat transfer relationship causing the refrigerant to evaporate and absorb heat from the water or brine.

WATER VAPOR.—In air conditioning, the water in the atmosphere.

WET-BULB DEPRESSION.—The difference between the dry-bulb temperature and the wet-bulb temperature.

REFRIGERATION AND AIR CONDITIONING

B. TROUBLESHOOTING

The two trouble charts that follow may be used as a guide for locating and correcting malfunctions in refrigeration systems. The first chart deals with troubles that may be encountered in vapor compression systems. The second chart deals with troubles that may be encountered in absorption-type (lithium bromide) systems. If the points and procedures outlined in these charts are closely adhered to, a great deal of time can be saved in troubleshooting.

To use these charts, the first thing to do is to isolate the trouble. Then check all possible causes. And finally, make the indicated corrections. In general, the correction of a malfunction is a process of elimination. The easiest corrections should be made first; then, if necessary, the more difficult corrections should be made.

TERMINOLOGY AND TROUBLESHOOTING

Trouble	Possible Cause	Corrective Measure
High condensing pressure.	Air on non-condensable gas in system.	Purge air from condenser.
	Inlet water warm.	Increase quantity of condensing water.
	Insufficient water flowing through condenser.	Increase quantity of water.
	Condenser tubes clogged or scaled.	Clean condenser water tubes.
	Too much liquid in receiver, condenser tubes submerged in liquid refrigerant.	Draw off liquid into service cylinder.
Low condensing pressure.	Too much water flowing through condenser.	Reduce quantity of water.
	Water too cold.	Reduce quantity of water.
	Liquid refrigerant flooding back from evaporator.	Change expansion valve adjustment, examine fastening of thermal bulb.
	Leaky discharge valve.	Remove head, examine valves. Replace any found defective.
High suction pressure.	Overfeeding of expansion valve.	Regulate expansion valve, check bulb attachment.
	Leaky suction valve.	Remove head, examine valve and replace if worn.
Low suction pressure.	Restricted liquid line and expansion valve or suction screens.	Pump down, remove, examine and clean screens.
	Insufficient refrigerant in system.	Check for refrigerant storage.
	Too much oil circulating in system.	Check for too much oil in circulation. Remove oil.
	Improper adjustment of expansion valves.	Adjust valve to give more flow.
	Expansion valve power element dead or weak.	Replace expansion valve power element.

Trouble Chart for Vapor Compression Refrigeration Systems.

REFRIGERATION AND AIR CONDITIONING

Trouble	Possible Cause	Corrective Measure
Compressor short cycles on low pressure control.	Low refrigerant charge.	Locate and repair leaks. Charge refrigerant.
	Thermal expansion valve not feeding properly.	Adjust, repair or replace thermal expansion valve.
	(a) Dirty strainers.	(a) Clean strainers.
	(b) Moisture frozen in orifice or orifice plugged with dirt.	(b) Remove moisture or dirt (Use system dehydrator).
	(c) Power element dead or weak.	(c) Replace power element.
	Water flow through evaporators restricted or stopped. Evaporator coils plugged, dirty, or clogged with frost.	Remove restriction. Check water flow. Clean coils or tubes.
	Defective low pressure control switch.	Repair or replace low pressure control switch.
Compressor runs continuously.	Shortage of refrigerant.	Repair leak and recharge system.
	Leaking discharge valves.	Replace discharge valves.
Compressor short cycles on high pressure control switch.	Insufficient water flowing through condenser, clogged condenser.	Determine if water has been turned off. Check for scaled or fouled condenser.
	Defective high pressure control switch.	Repair or replace high pressure control switch.
Compressor will not run.	Seized compressor.	Repair or replace compressor.
	Cut-in point of low pressure control switch too high.	Set L.P. control switch to cut-in at correct pressure.
	High pressure control switch does not cut-in.	Check discharge pressure and reset H.P. control switch.
	1. Defective switch.	1. Repair or replace switch.
	2. Electric power cut off.	2. Check power supply.
	3. Service or disconnect switch open.	3. Close switches.

Trouble Chart for Vapor Compression Refrigeration Systems—Continued.

TERMINOLOGY AND TROUBLESHOOTING

Trouble	Possible Cause	Corrective Measure
Compressor will not run. (Cont'd)	4. Fuses blown.	4. Test fuses and renew if necessary.
	5. Over-load relays tripped.	5. Re-set relays and find cause of overload.
	6. Low voltage.	6. Check voltage (should be within 10 percent of nameplate rating).
	7. Electrical motor in trouble.	7. Repair or replace motor.
	8. Trouble in starting switch or control circuit.	8. Close switch manually to test power supply. If OK check control circuit including temperature and pressure controls.
	9. Compressor motor stopped by oil pressure differential switch.	9. Check oil level in crankcase. Check oil pump pressure.
Sudden loss of oil from crankcase.	Liquid refrigerant slugging back to compressor crank case.	Adjust or replace expansion valve.
Capacity reduction system fails to unload cylinders.	Hand operating stem of capacity control valve not turned to automatic position.	Set hand operating stem to automatic position.
Compressor continues to operate at full or partial load.	Pressure regulating valve not opening.	Adjust or repair pressure regulating valve.
Capacity reduction system fails to load cylinders.	Broken or leaking oil tube between pump and power element.	Repair leak.
Compressor continues to operate unloaded.	Pressure regulating valve not closing.	Adjust or repair pressure regulating valve.

Trouble Chart for Vapor Compression Refrigeration Systems—Continued.

REFRIGERATION AND AIR CONDITIONING

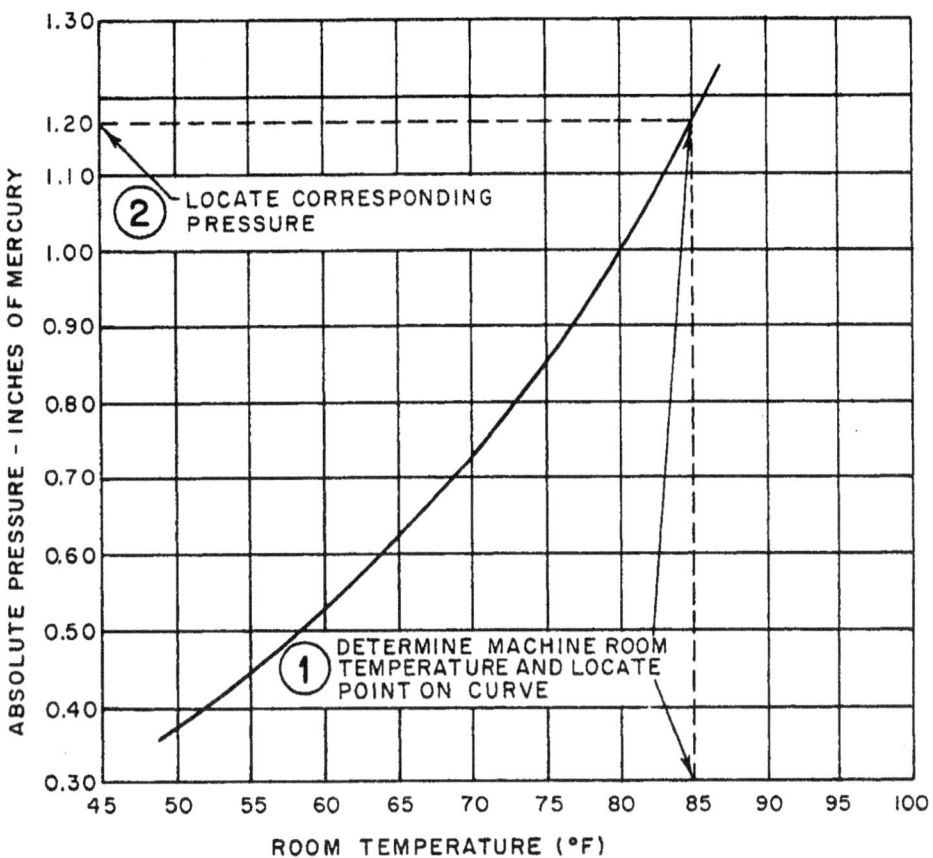

Figure 1. — Pressure temperature curve for lithium-bromide machine.

TROUBLE CHART FOR ABSORPTION TYPE (LITHIUM-BROMIDE) REFRIGERATION SYSTEM

TROUBLE: SOLUTION SOLIDIFIED AT START-UP

	CAUSE	CHECK	CORRECTION
1.	Dilution cycle too short.	- dilution cycle time delay relay.	-Reset time delay relay to 10 minutes.
2.	Steam valve did not close during dilution cycle.	- operation of steam valve and steam EP relay.	-Repair faulty operation. Steam EP relay should close when stop button is pushed and control air pressure at steam valve should go to 0 PSIG.
3.	Cooling load lost during dilution cycle.	- Shut down procedure.	Make certain that the cooling load remains on during the dilution cycle.

TERMINOLOGY AND TROUBLESHOOTING

TROUBLE CHART FOR ABSORPTION TYPE (LITHIUM-BROMIDE) REFRIGERATION SYSTEM—Continued.

TROUBLE: SOLUTION SOLIDIFIED AT START-UP—Continued

CAUSE	CHECK	CORRECTION
4. Condenser sea water too cold.	- 3 way mixing valve and sea water thermostat.	-Maintain a constant inlet sea water temperature of 85°F.
5. Air in machine.	- absolute pressure indicator before starting.	-Turn "Not Purged-Purged" switch to "Not Purged" until machine vacuum corresponds to that given in Fig. 12-1. Find reason for air entering machine.
6. Machine shut down on safety.	-All safety switches and settings. The following safeties will do this: 1. Low temp. cutout. 2. High temp. cutout. 3. Chilled water pump overload. 4. Absorber - generator pump overload. 5. Refrigerant pump overload. 6. Chilled water failure switch.	-Correct reason for safety cutout or reason for pump overload. -Correct reason for loss of chilled water flow.

TROUBLE: OVER CONCENTRATION OF SOLUTION IN ABSORBER

CAUSE	CHECK	CORRECTION
1. High solution temperature in absorber	- solution temperature at generator pump and condensing water temperature leaving absorber. If difference is greater than 10°F, poor heat transfer is indicated.	Add octyl alcohol. If this does not correct the trouble, clean the absorber tubes and check condensing water flow through the absorber.
2. Plugged spray nozzles in absorber	- discharge pressure of the absorber pump. This should be approximately 11" Hg. Vac.	Inspect and clean spray header and nozzles.

REFRIGERATION AND AIR CONDITIONING

TROUBLE CHART FOR ABSORPTION TYPE (LITHIUM-BROMIDE) REFRIGERATION SYSTEM—Continued.

TROUBLE: OVER CONCENTRATION OF SOLUTION IN ABSORBER—Continued

CAUSE	CHECK	CORRECTION
3. Low condensing sea water flow	- condensing water rise across absorber. At full load this should be 10°F or lower.	Clean inlet sea water strainer. Reset condenser bypass valve.
4. Air in machine	- refrigerant vapor pressure to absorber vapor pressure. Measure temperature at discharge of refrigerant pump and read corresponding vapor pressure on equilibrium diagram. Should be 2° or 3°F.	Reset purge pressure stat to allow more purge operation.
5. Insufficient purging	- purge cycle. With purge pump in operation the purge pump cycle should be about 1 - 1/2 hours. - specific gravity and temperature of purge solution.	Adjust drip tube. Purge valve not opening. This should be about 70° or less with a specific gravity of 1.57 or more to give a purge vapor pressure of less than .18" Hg.
	- pump impeller and jet evacuator for wear	If worn - replace
	- purge system for leaks	Turn off purge pump at the panel board. Blank off the carbon filter tube. Raise pressure in purge system to 25 PSIG and leak test. Correct any leaks

TROUBLE: POOR EVAPORATOR PERFORMANCE

CAUSE	CHECK	CORRECTION
1. Fouled heat transfer surface on chilled water coil	- at full load, check spread between evaporator temperature (at discharge of refrigerant pump) and	Clean tubes - chilled water side. Check division plate gasket in water box, if

TERMINOLOGY AND TROUBLESHOOTING

TROUBLE CHART FOR ABSORPTION TYPE (LITHIUM-BROMIDE) REFRIGERATION SYSTEM—Continued.

TROUBLE: Poor Evaporator Performance—Continued.

CAUSE	CHECK	CORRECTION
	leaving chilled water temperature. Spread should not be greater than 3°F.	out of position, reposition or replace.
2. Incorrect refrigerant pump discharge pressure	- pump pressure; should be approximately 4 PSIG.	Inspect evaporator spray nozzles. Clean if necessary.
	- Refrigerant charge.	Add refrigerant at full load until overflow temperature begins to drop.
	- refrigerant pump impeller.	If worn, replace.
	- pump rotation, should be counter-clockwise as viewed from the pump end.	If incorrect reverse motor rotation.

TROUBLE: WEAK SOLUTION IN ABSORBER, UNABLE TO CONCENTRATE WITH STEAM VALVE WIDE OPEN AT FULL LOAD. —Continued.

CAUSE	CHECK	CORRECTION
1. Vapor condensate above 110°F	- condensing water approach, leaving condenser water temperature to vapor condensate temperature should not be greater than 8°F.	Clean condenser tubes.
	- condensing sea water flow	Clean inlet sea water strainer - adjust condenser bypass valve.
	- refrigerant overflow temperature	If below 45°F, remove refrigerant until temperature begins to rise.
	- calibration of vapor condensate thermometer	recalibrate
2. Strong solution Temperature below 205°F.	- steam pressure	Raise steam pressure to 18 PSIG at generator inlet.
	- steam strainer	Clean strainer
	- steam traps	Open bypass valve, if any change is noted in solution temperature, repair traps.

REFRIGERATION AND AIR CONDITIONING

TROUBLE CHART FOR ABSORPTION TYPE (LITHIUM-BROMIDE) REFRIGERATION SYSTEM—Continued.

TROUBLE: SOLIDIFICATION DURING OPERATION—Continued

CAUSE	CHECK	CORRECTION
3. Low solution flow to generator	- calibration of strong solution thermometer - generator pump discharge pressure. Should be 4 PSIG, approximately.	Recalibrate Inspect valves for restrictions. Inspect generator spray nozzles. Clean or replace.

TROUBLE: SOLIDIFICATION DURING OPERATION

CAUSE	CHECK	CORRECTION
1. See over concentration of solution in absorber.		
2. See poor evaporator performance.		Desolidify machine
3. Sudden drop in entering condensing sea water temperature.	- 3-way pneumatic mixing valve (4) and condensing water temperature control.	Correct reason for malfunction of valve or control.
4. Sudden rise in steam pressure above 18 PSIG.	- control air pressure to steam control pilot and steam regulating valve bypass (12).	Reduce control air pressure to 15 PSIG and make certain valve is closed.

TROUBLE: LOST SOLUTION LEVEL IN ABSORBER

CAUSE	CHECK	CORRECTION
1. Heat exchanger strong solution valve restricted	- valve closed or collapsed diaphragm	Open valve. Replace diaphragm.

TROUBLE: PURGE WILL NOT OPERATE

CAUSE	CHECK	CORRECTION
1. Off on safety	- solution level in purge tank	Drain solution from tank. Clean probes.
2. Malfunction of purge pump.	- purge pump starter - purge level control - purge pressurestat - purge pump motor	Repair or replace if necessary.

TROUBLE: LOSS OF VACUUM DURING SHUT DOWN PERIOD

CAUSE	CHECK	CORRECTION
1. Valve open.	- all of these valves	Close valves and pull vacuum on machine.

TERMINOLOGY AND TROUBLESHOOTING

TROUBLE CHART FOR ABSORPTION TYPE (LITHIUM-BROMIDE) REFRIGERATION SYSTEM—Continued.

TROUBLE: LOSS OF VACUUM DURING SHUT-DOWN PERIOD. —Continued.

CAUSE	CHECK	CORRECTION
2. Pneumatic purge valve stuck open.	- purge valve operation air pressure to valve diaphragm	Repair if necessary. Open air bleed or correct reason for purge EP relay not closing and bleeding air.
3. Seal leak	- water level in seal water tank, should be above suction and connection of seal water pump.	Replace leaking seal
4. Check valve in seal water make up line did not seat	- ball check and check valve seat.	Replace ball check or repair valve seat.
5. Leak in machine proper	- leak test machine.	Repair all leaks

TROUBLE: LOSS OF VACUUM DURING OPERATION

CAUSE	CHECK	CORRECTION
1. Seal leak	- all pump seals	Replace faulty seal.
2. Malfunction of purge pump	- purge pump starter - purge pump motor	Repair if necessary Replace if burned out.

TROUBLE: REFRIGERANT OVERFLOW TEMPERATURE ALWAYS COLD MUST REMOVE REFRIGERANT PERIODICALLY

CAUSE	CHECK	CORRECTION
1. Tube leak.	- leak test across all tube bundles.	-Repair any leaks.
2. Purge cooling coil.	- level in purge tank for an extended period while purge pump is off.	-Repair leaky coil if level in tank rises during test.

TROUBLE: COPPER PLATING

CAUSE	CHECK	CORRECTION
1. Air leakage into machine.	- leak test.	-Repair any leaks.
2. Did not break vacuum with nitrogen and provide continuous bleed during repair work.	- procedure for breaking vacuum with nitrogen.	

REFRIGERATION AND AIR CONDITIONING

TROUBLE CHART FOR ABSORPTION TYPE (LITHIUM-BROMIDE) REFRIGERATION SYSTEM—Continued.

TROUBLE: MACHINE SHUT DOWN ON SAFETY

CAUSE	CHECK	CORRECTION
1. Power failure and control failure.	- fuses and power supply.	-Replace blown fuses and restore power.
2. Shutdown on low temperature cutout switch.	- switch setting.	-Set at 36°F.
	- chilled water temperature and steam valve.	-Recalibrate control and adjust steam valve.
3. Shutdown on chilled water failure switch.	- switch setting	-Set at 360 GPM minimum.
	- chilled water pump operation.	-Start pump.
	- chilled water flow.	-Open chilled water line valves.
4. Sea water pump, chilled water pump, refrigerant pump, or absorber-generator pump motor trips out on overload.	- heater elements.	-Install correct size.
	- amperage draw of motor.	-Find reason for overload if present.
	- power supply to all phases.	-Should be 440-3-60AC.
	- ambient temperature around starter too high.	-Provide air circulation or move starter.
	- pump head against pump curves.	-Correct reason for abnormal pump head.
	- binding due to impeller or bearing wear.	-Change impeller or bearings.
	- solidification in absorber-generator pump.	-Desolidify.

www.ingramcontent.com/pod-product-compliance
Lightning Source LLC
Chambersburg PA
CBHW081806300426
44116CB00014B/2256